# Make Your Own History

*This book is Number 2 in the Litwin Books Series on Gender and Sexuality in Information Studies. Emily Drabinski, series editor.*

# Make Your Own History

*Documenting Feminist and Queer Activism in the 21st Century*

*Co-edited by Lyz Bly and Kelly Wooten*

Litwin Books, LLC
Los Angeles, CA

Published in 2012 by Litwin Books, LLC

Litwin Books
PO Box 25322
Los Angeles, CA 90025

http://litwinbooks.com/

Cover art by Jenna Brager

Cover design by Alana Kumbier

Layout by Christopher Hagen

Indexed by Lynley Wheaton

Printed on acid-free and sustainably-sourced paper

Library of Congress Cataloging-in-Publication Data

Make your own history : documenting feminist and queer activism in the 21st century /
co-edited by Lyz Bly and Kelly Wooten.
    p. cm.
Includes bibliographical references and index.
ISBN 978-1-936117-13-0 (alk. paper)
    1. Feminism--History--Sources. 2. Feminism--Archival resources. 3. Feminism--Com-
puter network resources. 4. Gay rights--History--Sources. 5. Gay rights--Archival
resources. 6. Gay rights--Computer network resources. I. Bly, Lyz. II. Wooten, Kelly.
HQ1155.M346 2012
305.4209--dc23
                              2011050003

# Acknowledgements

We would like to thank the people who supported us during the process of producing this book.

Kelly would like to thank Dale Stearns, a supportive partner and reliable co-parent, Laura Micham, director of the Bingham Center and encouraging mentor; Erin O'Meara, Rachel Ingold, and Gene Springs for last-minute editing assistance, and all my friends and colleagues who said "that sounds cool!" (and meant it) when I mentioned that I was co-editing this book. Thanks especially to our wonderful contributors and to all the activists, writers, researchers, and archivists who have offered inspiration, whether they knew it or not. And of course Jenna Freedman, who told Emily Drabinski, the awesome editor of this series, to get in touch with me in the first place. And to Lyz for saying yes to being my co-editor.

Lyz is grateful to Kelly Wooten for giving her the chance to work with her on this book and will miss their regular telephone calls and emails (which — in the case of the phone conversations — often happened with the sounds of children and barking dogs in the background). She also thanks her partner, RA Washington for his support through the last few months of the project and for reviewing her introduction.

# Table of Contents

# Archives as Activism: a Preface

*Alison Piepmeier*

As Alexis Pauline Gumbs argues in this volume, documenting *is* activism. The process of producing a zine, a flier, or even an organization is momentary and can be ephemeral. When librarians and archivists collect these materials, the materials move beyond their momentary effects and become artifacts capable of longer-term importance. The scholars in this volume explain that it's a political decision to collect things that women, girls, and other underprivileged groups have produced. When the creators are on the margins, archivists are activists: when materials are archived, they achieve the status of something significant enough to be worth saving, and then those artifacts are available so that scholars, students, and other activists may continue engaging with them.

During the years when I was working on my book *Girl Zines: Making Media, Doing Feminism*, I visited the Sallie Bingham Center at Duke University's Special Collections Library multiple times to explore their zine collections. The first time I went, I remember a bit of anxiety: what should I expect from this archive? How am I supposed to act? Am I going to have to be fully professional, or can I squeal with delight at the zines I discover?

The staff was wonderful, and although I generally refrained from squealing, I vividly remember the excitement of having my own research table with large boxes filled with zines. Opening each box was like a holiday—I had no clear sense of what I'd find, and that uncertainty was great fun. As Angela L. DiVeglia notes in this collection, there are ways of rethinking the archive so that it's something that triggers reactions. She argues, "The concept of an 'archives of feeling' shifts the focus away from static, dusty records in a repository toward a dynamic model in which an archive can actively create change in its users and in society." While I feared that the zine archive would be a "static, dusty" place, I discovered it to be a place that triggered a spectrum of feelings in me, and also gave me a new perspective on my own creative productions as a child and teen. It created change in me by allowing me to recognize the importance of some of my own personal work and the work of girls.

Here's an example: in 1990, during my last semester of high school, my friends and I created a document that we saucily called *Naked*, a typed, hand-drawn, photocopied piece of work that we distributed to other friends and left at bookstores and music shops for other people to pick up for free. It wasn't until a few years later that I realized that *Naked* was a zine, part of a genre that was picking up momentum in the early 1990s, particularly where girls and women were concerned. In *Girl Zines*, I briefly discussed *Naked*, explaining that I, like many others, was inspired to create a document in which my own voice could be registered, a document that through its materiality, its visual elements, and its content articulated where I was at that moment in time. It's a material artifact that gives a glimpse at what it meant to be a girl in middle Tennessee in 1990, and part of what helped me to recognize the significance of *Naked* were my experiences as a scholar perusing the zine archives in the Sallie Bingham Center and in the Barnard Zine Library.

What the essays from *Make Your Own History* helped me to remember is that *Naked* wasn't my first zine. Years earlier, when I was only ten years old, my best friend and I created a neighborhood newspaper that we called *The North Dixien*. We took turns at the typewriter (not, please note, a computer) and shared the title "editor." We interviewed adults on our street and included articles critiquing new construction that was close enough that we could ride our bikes there. We discussed the animals our neighbors owned and our observations about traffic. I believe we even shared recipes. We were adorable.

Sarah Dyer, creator of *Action Girl Newsletter*, and Barbara Sjoholm, co-creator of Seal Press, share similar stories in this volume. It's likely, in fact, that other authors in this collection have the same experience of getting their girl voices out there into the world. My friend and I had things to say, and due to family support as well as a culture that wasn't horribly oppressive, we felt that our voices ought to be heard. Fortunately, our neighbors agreed; most adults were delighted (understandably so) with two ten-year-olds delivering their hand-made newspaper to all the houses on the street, and we got a great deal of praise. Like *Naked*, *The North Dixien* offers a glimpse of what it meant to be a girl—truly a lunchbox-toting, book-loving, bike-riding girl—in the world in 1982.

As I was assembling these thoughts, it occurred to me that the ten-year-old daughter of one of my friends also makes a newsletter, hers more focused on the household than the neighborhood, called *9½ News*. Like Sarah Dyer's, Barbara Sjoholm's, and mine, Nina's publication gives her a space to observe and assess the world she lives in (although she primarily uses a computer rather than a typewriter and her publication is adorned with clip art rather than the stickers we used in *The North Dixien*). She writes about family practices and even runs contests, like her recent "Who has the most embarrassing story?" contest.

What would we learn about girlhood if we had an archival collection of these sorts of documents? What would it mean to us as scholars and activists if we could go into the Sallie Bingham Center or the Barnard Zine Library and ask the staff to retrieve boxes and boxes filled with these sorts of publications created by young girls? How much more fully, and with how much more complexity, could we understand girlhood? Girls studies scholar Mary Celeste Kearney has offered compelling critiques of much early girls studies work which framed girls as consumers rather than producers of media. Zines, of course, are material that counters the girls-as-consumers model, but by and large when we discuss girls producing zines (as opposed to women), we're discussing people in their teens.

We have a limited amount of data created by actual girls. It makes my mouth water to think of getting to read through the intentional, voluntary publications of ten year old girls from the last thirty or forty years. As the scholars in this volume would observe, collecting this sort of work would be activism: it would draw our attention to this material that is often seen as disposable, "cute" at best and insignificant except for in a personal realm. I'm a feminist scholar, and yet even I had forgotten about my own girlhood cultural productions, and hadn't thought to examine *9½ News* as a significant document about the life of a girl. Archiving this material would allow scholars to develop a far more complex and interesting picture of girlhood, and to the extent that girls themselves had access to these archives, seeing this material esteemed as important would help validate their own acts of creative expression.

That's what this volume is about: drawing the attention of scholars and librarians to the political potentials of the work they do collect, as well as the work they can and should collect. *Make Your Own History* is a text that articulates the importance of archival activism. The essays address the theory as well as the pragmatics of documenting and archiving the past. Kate Eichhorn rightly notes the extent to which archives can shape a legacy, providing not only legitimacy but particular *kinds* of legitimacy (for instance, framing riot grrrl writing as having meaningful form as well as content). Authors identify the importance of having thorough collections so that activists don't have to continually reinvent the wheel, and they discuss the ways in which work should be made available so that various populations are safe and comfortable accessing the artifacts. They discuss logistics, from Jenna Freedman's negotiations of having zines as circulating documents vs. having them archivally stored, to Amy Benson and Kathryn Allamong Jacob's discussions of preserving blogs. Indeed, a number of authors in this collection examine the challenges and possibilities of paper alongside digital media. This volume draws much-needed attention to the broader political work archives do. It's a book that makes visible the various forms archives can take, and the activist importance these archives can have.

# Introduction
## Scholars, Archivists and Invisible Alliances

*Lyz Bly*

As a quintessential GenX feminist, I spent most of my twenties and early thirties critiquing pop cultural tropes on femininity and exploring what kind of feminist woman I wanted to be. Fanzines and riot grrrl music were central to these endeavors, as they established a broad community of feminist thinkers and activists who—like me—were passionate about taking apart gendered myths and celebrating feminism and grrrl/woman power. At the time it struck me that most of us were exploring some of the same issues—body image and beauty myths, the tenuous nature of language, double standards on sexuality, and the DIY (do-it-yourself) reclamation of "feminine" pursuits such as knitting, sewing, and cooking. However, when I began thinking about a dissertation topic in the spring of 2007 it did not occur to me to propose something so closely connected to my own experiences as a burgeoning feminist and to the observations I made during that phase of my life. It was not until my dissertation advisor and dear friend Renée Sentilles said, "Why are you not writing on riot grrrl or third wave feminism?" that the possibilities of writing a contemporary history that I was a part of came to life. From that moment on there was no turning back; I spent the next two and a half years [re]living and breathing the thoughts, theories, writings, and ideas of my third wave feminist sisters.

The research for my dissertation, which I ultimately titled *Generation X and the Invention of a Third Feminist Wave*, primarily took place at the Sallie Bingham Center for Women's History and Culture at Duke University and at the Sophia Smith Collection at Smith College. Like Alison Piepmeier, when I first sat down in the reading room of the Sallie Bingham Center amid boxes of hundreds of zines from the Sarah Dyer Collection, I felt elated—even giddy. Many of the themes that I recognized from my own zine collection were clearly evident in the Dyer collection, with the scope and breadth amplified by hundreds. The raw creativity of both the writing and artwork gave me candid insights into the minds and feelings of so many young women.

On that first day at the Bingham Center I could not imagine how much archivists' planning and expertise would shape my project. Nor did I yet know how much their work would inform my academic teaching. The sheer volume of zines at the Bingham Center provided more than ample primary evidence to support my most nuanced and broadest arguments. That there were few copy restrictions on the Dyer Zine Collection meant that I was free to copy as many zines as I wanted; it condensed time spent in the archive, as—armed with a change purse full of dimes—I spent many afternoons copying any and all zines that seemed even remotely related to my research. Months later, as the writing began to take shape, I perused my files and found new material to shore up my arguments. What came as a surprise was the other way that I used the copies from my research; images, flyers, quotes, and treatises that did not make their way into the dissertation showed up in lectures and presentations. My students benefit from my research; more pointedly, however, they come to a clearer understanding of women's history and experiences because of the range of materials collected by the archivists at the Bingham Center.

The archivists at the Sophia Smith Collection shaped *Generation X and the Invention of a Third Feminist Wave* in unexpected ways. I was awarded a research grant to travel to the Smith College archive, and the trip came after my work at Duke. The zine collections at the Sallie Bingham Center were fodder for the second half of my project and I had a very clear plan for the last two chapters. It was not until I was in the reading room of Sophia Smith that the first chapters began to take shape. As I studied hundreds of carefully filed and preserved newspaper and magazine clippings, comic strips, flyers, buttons, and ephemera from the Women's Liberation Collection, it became clear to me how much media images shaped my generation's image and understanding of the women's liberation movement of the 1970s. In the Foucaultian frame, seeing all of the materials together provided me with a window into the media as apparatus for creating knowledge on the women's liberation movement. Ultimately, the ways in which this collection was organized shaped chapter one of my project; the archivists—each of them who worked on the collection over the span of nearly 40 years—were my collaborators. I am extremely grateful for their foresight and expertise, as their work helped to shape my dissertation.

Given my own research experiences with the staff and materials of the Sallie Bingham and Sophia Smith Collections, co-editing *Make Your Own History* with Kelly Wooten has been an enlightening and humbling endeavor. I found affinities with the academic scholars who have shared their research projects and methods in our book, and learned a great deal from the archivists and librarians who see their work as a form of activism—as a vehicle for broadening the historic record to include the voices and experiences of riot grrrls, queers, community organizers, and everyday activists. Collaboratively, scholars, archivists, and librarians effect change by collecting, preserving, writing, and sharing stories that complicate historical metanarratives. Our alliances continue a course that began in the post-World War II decades and is connected to the grassroots activism of the era. We, however, use our privilege as members of prestigious institutions of higher learning and work to de-center elite white, patriarchal hegemony from the inside.

# Introduction
## Starting the Conversation


*Kelly Wooten*


Even if you don't follow the news through the lens of feminist bloggers and web-sites like Feministing.com, it's hard to avoid hearing about current events that are hot topics among feminist activists of today. Political sex scandals like former governor of California, Arnold Schwarzenegger's "affair" with one of his domestic staff, high profile rape cases like Dominique Strauss Kahn's alleged assault on a hotel worker and the New York City police officers who were accused of attacking a woman who had called for assistance, and the all-out attack on women's reproductive rights by conservatives at the state and national level are just a few examples of stories that have dominated the news airwaves in early 2011 when this book was being assembled. Feminist activists have responded to these national news stories with spontaneous protests coordinated by social media like Facebook and Twitter (in the cases of the Kahn and NY "rape cop" incidents), and blogging furiously and thoughtfully, pointing out the ways in which media coverage has (or, more rarely, has not) been sexist, perpetuating gender stereo-types and upholding a culture in which women are doomed to being sexual objects, among other actions.

One example of this is the "SlutWalk" protest march that started in Canada and ignited feminist activists' outrage and solidarity around the globe.[1] It began as a creative reaction to remarks given by an officer at a crime prevention forum at York University, who said that women could avoid sexual assault by not "dressing like sluts." Organizers Sonya Barnett and Heather Jarvis used the term "slut" in their reaction as a provocative way to draw attention to the victim-blaming and slut-shaming that makes it difficult for women to be in charge of their own sexuality and live without the expectation of violence. The initial march drew over 3000 people, and inspired women (and men) in over 100 cites in 15 countries to hold their own satellite SlutWalks. Organizing for these events is predominantly conducted online, through SlutWalk websites, Facebook, Twitter, and emails, or by texting or other mobile communications. There is ample media coverage and plenty of evidence of the events and discussion about them online, but there is no paper trail, and no one leader or central organization who could be the coordinator for documentation.

Most of the women (and men) at the forefront of activist movements are busy writing, speaking out, lobbying politicians, raising money, working hard to serve the underserved, working day jobs to make ends meet, volunteering time on weekends and

---

1  SlutWalk Toronto website: http://www.slutwalktoronto.com/

evenings, and taking care of themselves and their families. They don't have the time
to stop and ask, "Is anyone getting this down?" That's where the archivists come in.

As a librarian at the Bingham Center, one of my roles is collection development,
librarian-speak for working with people and organizations whose records may document
an aspect of women's history that we have decided to collect. When I first encountered
the Bingham Center in 2001, the archivists at the time had already begun documenting the third wave through zine collections and several small collections of individuals
and organizations. After I became a staff member in 2006, this area became one of
my responsibilities. Many third wave activists and writers are still early in their careers
and not quite ready to place their papers in an archive. It is still essential to identify
who these people are and talk to them about archives now, so they think twice before
recycling fliers or deleting files that have potential long-term value.

In order to inform my approach and to develop plans for documenting this active
movement in a meaningful way, I wanted to gather feedback from scholars, researchers,
and activists. Over the summer and early fall of 2008, I sent out an informal questionnaire to a handful of Bingham Center donors, researchers, and feminist email lists. I
wrote these questions to help identify key issues, ideas, individuals and organizations
that make up the third wave of feminism:

- How would you characterize or define third wave feminism?
- Do you consider yourself part of the third wave feminist movement?
- What do you see as the most important issues for today's feminist activists? On the flip
  side, are there issues or constituent groups that are left out of the third wave?
- Name a few individuals and organizations that you would consider to be key players in
  the third wave movement.
- What will be the most important things for us to save and collect in order to document
  third wave activism? What kinds of materials are you and the organizations you support generating that show evidence of the people, issues, culture, etc?

As my first question suggests, one challenge, of course, is defining third wave
feminism in the first place. Lisa Jervis famously rejected the term "third wave" in her
2004 *Ms. Magazine* article "The End of Feminism's Third Wave," saying point blank,
"We've reached the end of the wave terminology's usefulness."[2] She characterizes the
wave metaphor as shorthand that serves to place different generations of feminists in
opposition when really "we all want the same thing: To borrow bell hooks' phrase, we
want gender justice."

At the same time, there *are* differences between third and second wave feminism.
Alison Piepmeier calls "third wave" a highly contested term that loosely defines a
generational and political cohort born after the heyday of the second wave women's
movement. Third wave scholars explain that this cohort's "political activism on behalf

2    Lisa Jervis. "The End of Feminism's Third Wave: The cofounder of Bitch says goodbye." *Ms. Magazine*.
Winter 2004. *http://www.msmagazine.com/winter2004/thirdwave.asp* (accessed 8/14/11)

of women's rights is shaped by—and responds to—a world of global capitalism and information technology, postmodernism and postcolonialism, and environmental degradation. We no longer live in the world that feminists of the second wave faced." [3] For the purposes of the archives, we generally use a chronological definition more than anything, and acknowledge the difficulties of trying to define such a diverse movement.

Getting back to the question about how to document the movement, even just a few years ago, activists and archivists could not really conceive of just how challenging this would be. Even those who had an inkling knew that we didn't have the technological infrastructure in place to handle the growing amount of digital content and communications being generated by activist communities. We've got zines covered: the Bingham Center has about 5,000 zines; the Barnard Zine Library is another large and growing repository (curated by Jenna Freedman, a contributor to this volume); and many other archives have or are starting to follow suit. More ephemeral materials like show flyers and protest posters and handwritten correspondence (pre-email, of course), aren't as commonly archived, but some of this material has been captured tucked into zines, and may still be preserved in people's drawers and attics, where they might make it into the archives someday. Even the music associated with the third wave, including riot grrrl bands like Bikini Kill and Bratmobile, is becoming a greater challenge as tapes and CDs are superseded by electronic files, and music is often not collected along with other primary sources like zines.

Then we get into websites and blogs—possible to capture through services like Internet Archive if archivists take the time to identify what to preserve, but still grossly underdocumented. This comment from one of the respondents points to what is a last-ditch strategy in the face of no good technological solutions: "please print out a LOT of documentation from feminist websites. That's how we're getting our movement on." Unfortunately no one has the resources (time, paper, or ink) to print out every last feminist website. Archivists are starting to figure it out—perhaps a bit behind the curve of technology, but hopefully not lagging so far that the movement will be completely lost to history.

This book does not attempt to define the modern iteration of the feminist movement, and in collecting the essays for the topic of documenting feminist activism, it was hard to draw the line at any generational point due to the fluid nature of the movements. It was also hard to focus exclusively on the feminist movement, indeed one of the defining characteristics of this movement is intersectionality with other social movements for justice. Many of the issues of marginalization of voices and concerns about privacy come to bear when you start looking at how to document these activists' lives and the organizations and relationships formed in the process.

Our call for proposals suggested that this book would include the voices of activ-

---

3   Rory Dicker and Alison Piepmeier, "Introduction," in *Catching a Wave: Reclaiming Feminism for the 21st Century* (Boston: Northeastern University Press, 2003), 10.

ists, archivists, librarians, and scholars speaking to the practical material challenges of documenting and archiving contemporary activism; theoretical perspectives and conversations; online communities and communications; "third wave" feminism/youth and queer cultures/subcultures; digital archives; zines; and the work of activists who employ creative/artistic/cultural approaches to work for social justice. This was an ambitious premise and we hope this book succeeds in starting the conversation around these ideas, a conversation where archivists and activists and scholars find themselves as partners in making our own histories.

# Zines and Riot Grrrl

*Cut and Paste Your Own History*

# My Life In Zines

*Sarah Dyer*

## The Beginning

My personal involvement with self-publishing goes back about as far as I can remember. My parents were always involved in student groups and so on (my father was in college when I was young), and I remember seeing many newsletters, programs and such being copied when I was very little. I always thought that anyone could just type up something, copy it and hand it out. My first "DIY publication" was the Christmas card my dad made from one of my drawings when I was about 3 or 4, copied onto colored paper and sent out. (A pretty standard craft today, but back then it was a little out there!)

This was crucial moment number one: I always believed that you make your own printed objects – that it was no big deal! I was hardly alone in this, but in the pre-internet days, stepping across the production/consumption line was still pretty uncommon. There was no time in my memory that I felt like we "consumers" had to stay on the consumption side of things all the time.

My first independent venture into self-publishing was the "family newspaper" I wrote and illustrated (with a comic even!) at the age of about 10. All I remember from it was that the girl at the copy shop laughed when she read my comic—and that the circulation was probably about 5 or 6 copies. But it was a start! Just a handful of years later I started to see punk and alternative zines in a local used record store and thought it was a really cool idea.

This was crucial moment number two: seeing locally produced, xeroxed zines. The first zine I clearly remember looking through was a local punk zine called *No Worries,* which was published by Lois Sakany of the Mutley Chix. The clueless young me had no idea that a woman-authored zine was an anomaly, and that Lois was probably one of the very few women in the country publishing a zine! I just looked at the small assortment of zines, saw hers, and assumed that it was a totally co-ed field.

Not long after my first exposure to zines, I stepped up to help co-publish a handful of issues of a small local music zine called *The Silhouette.* This was a big educational experience as I learned first how to do basic page layout, xerox, collate and staple. Later I learned how to properly layout for print as we moved up to a cheap newsprint version. Not long after this, my zine experience actually helped land me a production job where I learned a lot more about printing, paste-up and layout – knowledge that would come in handy as I got more into doing zines!

A bit later I spent a few years co-publishing, co-writing, and co-editing the well-known zine *No Idea* for several issues. The *No Idea* projects also included putting on shows, releasing records as well as publishing zines. It was nearly a full-time occupation for me and my co-conspirator Var Thelin, one of the original founders of *No Idea* and the only one still involved at that point. While the zine wound down, Var kept going with the record label, which took on a life of its own and ended up becoming the important punk label that it remains to this day.

**My First Solo Flight**

As time went on and I became more and more active in everything we did with *No Idea*, I found myself becoming more and more frustrated as people we came in contact with continually dismissed my involvement because I was female. The peak of this was probably the show we put on with about 5 bands, during which members from every band continually thanked practically every male involved with the show, no matter how small the contribution, and my name was never mentioned. (However, I'd like to shout out to Ivy DuBois, the bass player for Sweet Baby at the time who noticed it happening and made a point of thanking me from the stage at the show they played the next night!) Eventually, I decided that it was time for me to start my own zine with no co-publisher if I wanted people to believe that I actually had anything to say.

And thus was born my first solo zine, *Mad Planet*. It was a music zine, with comics, recipes, and whatever else came into my head. It really was not a straight music zine, but straddled a line between music zine and personal zine (or girl zine, not that the genre existed yet). I had a lot of fun creating it, and had a small but national distribution, mainly through a large network of friends, bands, and record shops who would get a large stack of zines and hand them out for me. *Mad Planet* was almost always given away free.

Ironically, I often did not get the credit I assumed I would get as the sole publisher – male friends of mine who contributed would be credited with the entire zine in reviews.

**All Grrrls Together**

When I was publishing *Mad Planet*, there were very few women and girls involved in zine culture. The female voice was really lacking—on every front, not just on women's issues. I wanted to hear the female viewpoint as well as the male on all topics, and I began searching out that voice, tracking down every zine or mini-comic by a girl that I could find.

Unfortunately, there weren't many, and they were difficult to find. *Factsheet 5*, a major review zine, had shut down for a while, and virtually no-one was online yet in the early 1990s. I would just scour the classified ads and reviews in the well-known, established zines like *Maximum Rocknroll* and *Flipside*, looking for things that sounded like they might have female involvement. I was also reading plenty of zines by guys at the time, by the way—I just wanted to raise the percentage of female zines I read to something over 1%!

In the summer of 1992, I went on a trip to London and in a comic shop found Erica Smith's comic-oriented zine, *Girlfrenzy*, which had content exclusively by women—and in their review section I found several US-based zines that I'd never heard of before! I decided it was time to try and network all the girl zine and mini-comic creators I could find, and that fall I started the *Action Girl Newsletter*, my little *Factsheet 5*-style review sheet.

The first issue was just a handful of reviews and addresses—but that year saw the birth of the girl zine movement, fostered by both the riot grrrl movements and 3rd wave feminism, and a few months later, my mailbox was overflowing almost every day! Encouraged by what they were hearing about, whether it was in mainstream media or other zines, girls everywhere suddenly seemed inspired to start zines of all kinds, and I was reading and reviewing them as fast as I could!

Girls were starting zines for all sorts of reasons – some were in a supportive local scene where zines were being done already and were easily able to get started; some read about zines in a magazine like *Seventeen* or *Sassy* and got inspired to give it a try; and some tracked down my newsletter, ordered a lot of zines and decided to join in all the fun! I very often would get a girl's actual first attempt, sometimes with content that was handwritten or drawn! Another common thing was to get one of just a few copies of a zine with a very small run – presumably by girls who planned to make more if they got any orders.

As soon as I finished an issue of the newsletter, I'd send it back out to all the zines I'd reviewed along with whatever other recent issues I had laying around, enabling them to network with each other and trade copies between themselves. Some girls would just order their zines and pay for them, some girls didn't feel up to doing a zine but read them avidly, and some girls would send their zines out cold and hope to get another one in return. All these zines zipping back and forth across the country, reviewing each other and opening more and more doors – even though most of us, as creators, never got to meet any other zine creators, we had a real sense of community because of it. We knew each other, even though we'd never met.

**Winding Down**

After a few years, the girl zine genre was so well established (and I was, to be honest, personally so exhausted and burnt out from dedicating myself to it full-time), I began to focus more and more on my comic anthology, "Action Girl Comics." I still kept my hand in by doing reviews of minicomics and the occasional zine in the pages of AGC, but my personal involvement slowed down quite a bit.

I finally realized I was more or less retired from zine publishing myself, but I held on to every zine I'd ever received, as well as many older zines and women's comics that I'd bought over the years. I had enjoyed reading them all, and knowing how small the circulation of many of them had been, I realized that I might possess the only copies of publications that could completely disappear from people's memories. I had them all stored safely in actual magazine storage boxes and just thought I'd think of a use for them someday.

Then, after a move, we had a flood in our new house's basement. Thankfully, the zines were stored in an area that wasn't touched, but a lot of our other things were water-damaged and I decided that if I really wanted to see these zines preserved, I needed to find a safer home for them. I began searching for libraries that I thought might want them, and during one of my online searches found out about the Sallie Bingham Center.

Of all the libraries that I thought might be interested (there were no zine collections anywhere at the time − at least that I could find) I was the most attracted to the Sallie Bingham Center because of the collections they already had—there was an emphasis on ephemera and one of a kind items like diaries that made me feel like they would know what to do with my zines. So at the end of 1999, I sent off a blind "hey, do you think you might want this stuff I have" email and got a resounding YES back right away! After a few exchanges, I felt sure that my zines would be respected and well-treated there, and that my collection might really serve some useful purpose. So in 2000 I began shipping the archive box by box (a process that continues to this day as I continue to unearth more zines and comics!)

### The Present and Future

A decade later, the zine collection continues to grow, many other zine collections have also come to the Sallie Bingham Center to expand their holdings, and scholarship on girl zines has started to really flourish. I have been gratified beyond my imagination to see how much impact my decision has already had.

One thing that has worried me over the years is the discontinuity of history that so often happens when material is ephemeral or marginal − and zines are both! So much information and thinking is lost, and then so much information has to be rediscovered again and again, wasting time and energy that could be used to move forward. I have seen this happening in the modern (much smaller) zine world as well as the blogosphere. Many writers have no knowledge of the work that went before them within their own lifetimes, and I see much time spent on working through discussions that have taken place many times before. But now that zines are being preserved and studied, I hope that we can avoid a continuation of this − I hope that the work that went in to all these zines can be made more and more accessible.

And I hope that future writers will be able to build on the work of those that have gone before them instead of repeating it. I look forward to seeing just where they may take us!

# Self-Publication with Riot Grrrl Ideals:
## Zines ≠ Vanity Press Publications

*Jenna Freedman*

I have been questioning why I continue to type, cut, paste, and photocopy my words for others to read. I think that I do it to remain self aware and to document my process of living. It is a way to present my ideas to a wider audience than I normally would be able to, communicate and connect.[1] Eleanor Whitney, *Indulgence* zine

Zines are self-published, but the motivation behind their publication is different than that driving many vanity press and chapbook authors. Punk rock and riot grrrl community ethos are fundamental to zines, not just as the cultures that birthed them in their current incarnation, but also as what separates them from other self-publications. By collecting and preserving zines, the non-music primary sources of punk rock, librarians are documenting these movements in the participants' own voices—the voices of those too young, too politically radical, too crusty, and/or too bad mannered to appeal to the corporate media. It is important to note that zine producers are not only people who have been relegated to the margins but also people who have chosen to claim the margins. In contrast to most writers, many zine producers might choose to reject an offer from a corporate publishing house. Why let someone else control what you can say, when you can do it yourself?

Since the focus of this essay is on print publications, while I will discuss non-zine self-publications, for the most part, I am going to avoid print on demand and other online publishing outlets.

To set the stage for a discussion about self-publications, I quote from Chris Anderson's *The Long Tail*, what he identifies as "mental traps," or misconceptions people have about self-publishing ventures,

- Everyone wants to be a star
- Everyone's in it for the money
- If it isn't a hit, it's a miss
- The only success is mass success
- "Direct to video" = bad
- "Self-published" = bad
- "Independent" = "They couldn't get a deal"
- Amateur = amateurish

---

1   Eleanor Whitney, *Indulgence*, #5. Summer 2000: [2-3]

- Low-selling = low quality
- If it were good, it would be popular[2]

I assert that most of these assumptions are true of vanity press books, some are true of self-published works, and none are true of zines. I contrast the three publication types below in Table 1.

| Vanity Press | Self-Publications | Zines |
|---|---|---|
| Scorned | Tolerated | Invisible |
| Publisher does most of the work | Publisher does most of the work | Author does nearly all of the work |
| Author has minimal control over design or anything other than content | Author has more control | Author has total control |
| Publishing costs shouldered or shared by author | Publishing costs shouldered or shared by author | Author solely responsible for publishing costs |

*Table 1*

Vanity Press publications, almost universally scorned by serious writers, publishers, and libraries are ventures where the author provides some or all of the costs of publication, and the publisher in return edits for spelling and grammar, designs, prints, distributes, and to varying degrees publicizes the book, often by marketing to the author's friends and family members.[3] Some of this can also be true of self-publishing endeavors, the primary difference being who owns the book. Vanity publishers own the finished work, sometimes giving copies to the author as part of the initial contract, and/or selling the author copies at a reduced rate.

The vanity author also has less control over the finished product than his/her self-publishing counterpart. In the 1970s published poet Jose-Angel Figueroa chose a vanity press over small press or self-publication because he did not think a small press would be willing or able to take the risk of publishing his book in hard cover with high quality production and design, and because he did not have the resources himself for the latter method. However, when he dealt with Vantage Press, a major "subsidy book publisher," as they currently describe themselves,[4] and he wanted to hire his own designer, he had to have it written into his contract that Vantage could not reject the design.[5]

In addition to commanding a greater level of control and ownership, the self-

2   Chris Anderson, *The Long Tail: Why the Future of Business is Selling Less instead of More* (New York: Hyperion, 2006), 167.
3   Steven Zeitchik, "Don't Publish America?: Authors Allege Publisher Deception," *Publishers Weekly*, November 22, 2004, 13.
4   http://www.vantagepress.com
5   *Coda: Poets & Writers Newsletter*, "Vanity Press: Stigma or Sesame?" 4, no. 2 (November/December 1976): 7.

publisher may handle different parts of the editing, production, design, and distribution him/herself. Typically zine publishers handle every aspect of the process themselves, save for photocopying or printing. On the other hand, the word "typically" does not necessarily belong in the same sentence with the word "zine." While most zines are self-published, have a small self distributed print run, are low budget and outside the mainstream, and are motivated by a desire to share something with a subculture community, there are exceptions to each of these concepts. To illustrate what zines can be like, I will share a description of one zine I pulled off the Barnard zine shelf somewhat at random:

> Rainbow Flavoured Angst, #1 is a 20 page 4.25" x 5.5" zine by Hanh Nguyen. It includes a magic markered cover cartoon about racism, a two-page introduction, an essay on identity, a poem and essays about the war in Vietnam, a poem about a death penalty victim, an article about a husband getting advice from the author's aunt, a how-to article on writing a "letter to authority," a piece about a classmate's ignorance, guest pieces—on citizenship and a poem, a cartoon about American hypocrisy, a tribute to Matthew Shepard, some political quotes, and what is known in the trade as an "outro" (the opposite of an intro...duction). You also get the author's first name (her last name is included in an essay, so your discovery of it is incidental), email and postal addresses, the cost of the zine ($1 or two stamps or a zine trade). There is neither a date nor subscription information. The content is variably handwritten and word processed. There are drawings, photos, and clip art throughout. The back has a picture of the Simpsons, a quote from the Boondocks, and what look like two photocopied stickers.[6]

The desire to do it oneself and to retain a great deal of control is common to zinesters and many other self-publishers. What differentiates them is the punk rock/anarchist culture from which zines emerged and to which riot grrrl zines in particular evolved. To define punk rock ideals, I am going to quote from an article about how punk ideals affect food choices,

> "Being punk is a way of critiquing privileges and challenging social hierarchies. Contemporary punks are generally inspired by anarchism, which they understand to be a way of life in favor of egalitarianism and environmentalism and against sexism, racism, and corporate domination."[7]

To make this more specifically about riot grrrl, I want to share selected items from "Riot Grrrl Is" from the band Bikini Kill's zine:

> BECAUSE we must take over the means of production in order to create our own meanings. ...
> BECAUSE we don't wanna assimilate to someone else's (boy) standards of what is or isn't. ...
> ... the punk rock 'you can do anything' idea is crucial to the coming angry grrrl

---

6   Jenna Freedman, "AACR , Bendable but Not Flexible: Cataloging Zines at Barnard College," in *Radical Cataloging: Challenges and Possibilities*, K.R. Roberto, ed. 2008.
7   Dylan Clark, "The Raw and the Rotten: Punk Cuisine," *Ethnology* 43, no. 1. (Winter 2004): 19.

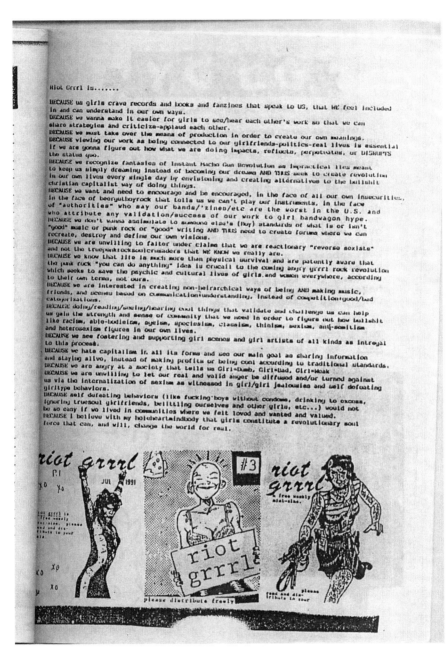

*Figure 1*

rock revolution which seeks to save the psychic and cultural lives of girls and women everywhere, according to their own terms, not ours. ...

BECAUSE we are interested in creating non-hierarchical ways of being AND making music, friends, and scenes based on communication + understanding, instead of competition + good/bad categorizations. ...

BECAUSE we hate capitalism in all its forms and see our main goal as sharing information and staying alive, instead of making profits or being cool according to traditional standards.[8] (Figure 1)[9]

Riot grrrl is angry, but it is also about love, support, and community, as evidenced in the following excerpt from Cindy Crabb's widely-distributed-for-a-zine *Doris* (Figure 2[10]):

Zine writers generally have not submitted manuscripts to mainstream publishers as many of their vanity and self-publishing counterparts have done unsuccessfully. The Do It Yourself (DIY) ethic that is so strong in punk rock, and mentioned in nearly every article I read on the subject, is not the only reason for this. In contrast to their traditional self-publishing counterparts, they do not *wish* to participate in corporate or mainstream publishing. They do not want their product to come out looking like a book from HarperCollins. Lailah, a sixteen-year-old riot grrrl interviewed in *Signs* puts it like this,

> It's important that you create your own culture that doesn't need the mainstream to exist, to go on. That allows people to grow, to learn as much as possible, to not make concessions. You need to take it away from the mainstream, build your own ballpark. It doesn't need to answer to anyone but yourself.[11]

In fact, riot grrrl not only rejected mainstream media, at one point participants put a freeze on giving interviews because the media were getting their message wrong and fetishizing the girls themselves while ignoring or misrepresenting the movement.[12]

Zines are more than self-expression. Zine communication, especially within riot grrrl, was supplemented substantially with letter writing and pen pal relationships. It wasn't enough to publish your work; you also had to respond to other writers with comments about their work.

Barnard's holdings include several women's self-defense guides, zines about racism in punk and activist communities such as *Evolution of a Race Riot*, and a potentially libelous comp (compilation) zine called *Baby I'm a Manarchist* about a man the authors regard as a sexual predator in the zine scene. I mention the libel issue to bring up the point that zines regularly flout rules and conventions their authors see as senseless or offensive or of which they are ignorant. Many zines come with anti-copyright state-

---

8   Bikini Kill, "Riot Grrrl Is..." written by Kathleen Hanna, *Girl Power*, no. 2: unpaginated. (Note, misspellings corrected.)
9   Ibid.
10   Cindy Ovenrack, "Secrets," *Doris* no. 17, "Reprints." Winter 2000: unpaginated.
11   Jessica Rothenberg and Gitana Garafalo, "Riot Grrrl: Revolutions from within," *Signs* 23, no. 3 (1998): 826.
12   Rothenberg, 828.

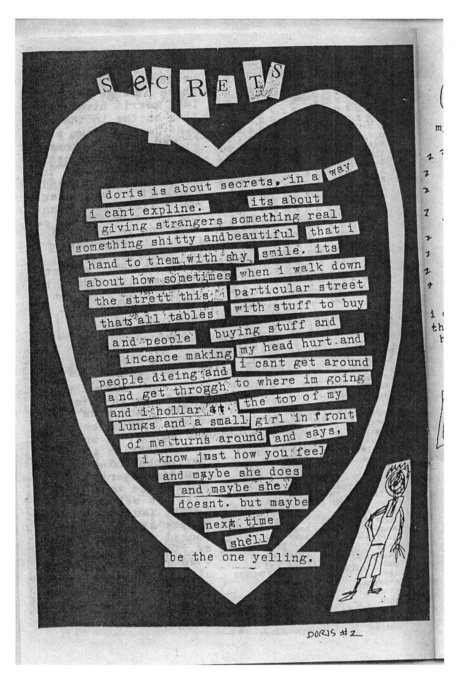

*Figure 2*

ments, my favorite being from a cookbook called *Please Don't Feed the Bears* that began its life as a zine,

> Everything in this book is anti-copyrighted. You can repress it and give your friends copies, take out things you don't like, smear tahini all over it, wear its designs in corporate magazines, claim recipes you like as your own, replace my musical suggestions with contemporary Christian rock, lick the pictures, or even take an image out of it, screen it on t-shirts, and sell them on E-Bay for $21 (not that that has ever happened or anything).
> Seriously, fuck copyrights. This books is yours now. Do with it as though wilt.[13]

Zines are also generous with other people's intellectual property, reprinting book, magazine, and other zine articles, private letters, and also for things few if any regular publishers would take responsibility, such as herbal abortion recipes or instructions on performing a DIY menstrual extraction. Their distribution is too small to attract the attention of most copyright holders, and they are likely not viewed as legitimate enough to cause much concern or warrant a lawsuit even if a wronged party were informed of the copyright infringement or personal abuse. Individuals that are attacked are free to respond in kind, in their own zines. And while we're on the topic of questionable practices in zine publishing, punk methodology also includes the tradition in zine publishing of liberating paper, supplies, and especially photocopies to produce the work for free (i.e. "scamming").

The majority of zines in Barnard's collection are personal and political zines with overt or inherent feminist themes.[14] Through donations from Asian-American and Latina zinesters (Yumi Lee, Lauren Jade Martin, and Celia Perez), we are comparatively strong in holdings by women of color in a movement often criticized for its white middle classness. Like many zinesters, we tend to eschew literary zines (fiction and poetry), which may have the most in common with vanity press publications in their quality and motives. We also have a few art zines, but like print on demand, they are a rich topic for another paper entirely.

Before I go further into Barnard's collection, largely excerpting an essay I wrote for *Radical Cataloging: Essays at the Front*, edited by K.R. Roberto, I would like to discuss more broadly libraries' role and responsibility to zines in particular and alternative press publications in general. The American Library Association has written into its Bill of Rights:

I.    Books and other library resources should be provided for the interest, informa-

---

13  Asbjorn Intonsus. *Please Don't Feed the Bears* (Portland, OR: Microcosm, 2006).
14  "Barnard's zines are written by women with an emphasis on zines by women of color. A woman's gender is self-defined. We also collect zines on feminism and femme identity by people of all genders. The zines are personal and political publications on activism, anarchism, body image, third wave feminism, gender, parenting, queer community, riot grrrl, sexual assault, and other topics." Collection policy from website, July 1, 2010. http://barnard.edu/library/zines/about.htm

# CFB 5

## Summer 2005.

Welcome to issue #5, nearly a year in the making. In case you don't know (part 34895): I'm April, I'm 26 years old, and I live and attend college in Atlanta, Georgia, known to many rap fans as "tha dirty south." You know how some people have hobbies like playing sports or painting or knitting? Well, this right here is my hobby, and it's one that I don't see myself growing out of any time in the near future.

I charge money for this to cover the costs of photocopies and postage, not because I think my writing merits some sort of a fee to be able to read it. It ain't even like that. I often charge tenses and use too many slang terms and cursewords, so overcharging for this would make me feel incredibly guilty.

The photograph on the cover was taken by someone else ¢ stolen by me from Morrissey's official website (please don't sue me. I don't have any money), however I myself screened the t-shirt he's wearing. Morrissey posing for a picture dressed in a garment I made myself is officially My Finest Moment In Life®. In the middle of this issue you will find a special 'Morrissey Tour Diary' section, detailing the nine shows I saw in October 2004 and explaining how he got

that awesome shirt. I'd like to think that even if you don't like Morrissey you'll find that section entertaining, but if I'm wrong feel free to send me all the hate mail you can afford postage for.

So, in the year since the last issue I saw Morrissey nine more times as I mentioned above, saw the Lucksmiths a couple more times in New York and Philadelphia did my very first tabling by selling my crafty wares at the Indie Craft Experience here in Atlanta, made it to my senior year of college and am now interning at a magazine. I'm looking forward to graduating in December and never writing another research paper again! WOO!

Thanks for getting this zine ¢ I hope it makes you chuckle at least a couple of times. (If you usually only read political zines, you're probably not going to like this one. Fair warning.) I'd love to hear from you, but be forewarned that if you send me some ridiculous hate mail (the kind that calls me an "ugly whore" - it's happened, folks) I will publish it on the internet and make fun of you relentlessly, especially if a lot of stuff is misspelled. Just letting you know.

*Figure 3[19] (Highlighting Added)*

tion, and enlightenment of all people of the community the library serves. Materials should not be excluded because of the origin, background, or views of those contributing to their creation.[15]

"Zines are usually written by people normally under- or not at all represented in library catalogs:

1. young people
2. poor people
3. people with ideas outside the mainstream
4. people who have bad spelling and grammar

These are some of the same people we are trying to serve and encourage to take better advantage of our collections. One way to do that is to make the collection better reflect the community it serves, by including materials published by its members."[17]

"As librarians know, sometimes self-censorship is more dangerous than the overt banning of particular items. In the case of zines, the self-censorship is carried out to such a degree that we do not even consider the materials that we are de facto rejecting. The number of public and academic libraries that I know to be actively acquiring zines for a discrete collection—either with or without the engagement of a degreed librarian—is around 20. With an estimated 122,573 libraries of all kinds in the United States,[18] I think we can do better."[19] [20]

Different types of libraries have different missions. Academic and research libraries have a responsibility not just to provide access to materials for current users, but to preserve items for future scholarship. The zine collection at Duke University is a perfect exemplar of this duty, and they're also hugely successful at integrating zines into coursework. Public libraries, when they emphasize popular use of a collection, especially when they circulate their zines, as a few of them do, necessarily select, process, and catalog their materials differently than an archival collection would. Many public library zine collections serve teen populations.

Take it from Loren, eighteen, of Lone Oak, Texas: "Young adults are at an awkward stage in life (I should know—I'm one!) and they need something that can relate to them. When I first read a zine, I was AMAZED at what these people were writing! I kept thinking, 'You'll never find this in a book!' Zines should never be kept secret." [21]

---

15    ALA Council, "Library Bill of Rights." American Library Association, as reaffirmed January 24, 1996, http://www.ala.org/work/freedom/lbr.html.
16    April Hornbuckle, "[Intro]," *Cartography for Beginners*, no. 5. Summer, 2005: unpaginated.
17    Freedman, *AACR, Bendable*.
18    American Library Association, "Fact Sheet 1." http://www.ala.org/ala/alalibrary/libraryfactsheet/alalibrary-factsheet1.htm.
19    Freedman, *AACR, Bendable*.
20    Figures updated per more recent factsheet http://www.ala.org/ala/professionalresources/libfactsheets/alalibraryfactsheet01.cfm
21    Sarah Hannah Gómez,"Teens and Zines," *Voice of Youth Advocates* 30, no. 1 (2007): 25.

Public librarians devise programs and workshops with their young adult patrons in mind, as do school librarians. The school library can serve as an excellent resource for housing zines made by punks, radical mamas, and DIY craft makers, but also for the creations of their own students.

At Barnard, through ignorance, audacity, and the advice of James Danky, formerly the Newspapers and Periodicals Librarian of the Wisconsin Historical Society, we became sort of a hybrid, attempting to preserve zines while also making them accessible to general users. We attempt to acquire two copies of each zine in our collection, the first for the climate controlled, acid free archive, from which zines must be paged. The second copy circulates from the open stacks. No matter what type of library, or how the librarian chooses to process the zines, it is vital that we use our expertise to collect and preserve these primary sources of punk. While many punk zine libraries and infoshops also collect zines, they should not be counted on as the sole repositories due to their lack of financial and physical stability.

> The research value of girl zines was lauded in *Youth & Society*:
> Using zines as a research tool provides a unique opportunity to hear girls speaking about their experiences outside of a clinical or research setting, because zines are examples of girls writing about their lives without an adult audience in mind.[22]

I recently taught a zines class to a group of high school students. They each read a zine from our collection and reported back on it. After each woman shared her experience of the zine, I asked her if the content or point of view presented in the zine was likely represented elsewhere in our library collection. At just over 200,000 volumes our collection isn't huge, but we do attempt to collect at a research level in women's studies. Yet, the answer to my question was inevitably "No" or "Not exactly." By shelving zines we are providing unmediated access to the mostly young writers' day-to-day lives as students, activists, workers, lovers, friends, survivors, defenders, mothers, musicians, builders, etc. We are letting them share their wisdom, anger, expertise, sadness, joy, community spirit and more with their contemporaries, as well as with generations that succeed them.

---

22   Kristen Schilt, "Zine Making As a Form of Resistance," *Youth & Society* 35, no. 1, (2003): 73.

# Archiving the Movement:
## The Riot Grrrl Collection at Fales Library and Special Collections

*Kate Eichhorn*

In the early 1990s, most people in North America, including most feminists, had never heard the term "riot grrrl." By early 1993, just a few months after an article on the movement was published in *Newsweek Magazine*, riot grrrl had become synonymous with a style and politic signifying a new feminism—a feminism for the "video-age generation…sexy, assertive and loud."[1] In many respects, the announcement of the Riot Grrrl Collection at Fales Library bore uncanny resemblance to the movement's initial "discovery" by the mainstream media. As Lisa Darms, Senior Archivist at Fales Library and Special Collections explains, news of the collection's development was never a secret, but its announcement was also not something that remained entirely in her control nor in the control of the collection's donors:

> We issued an internal newsletter, which is for the library. It's not private, but it's simply a print and pdf newsletter about acquisitions…They wanted to announce the acquisition of Kathleen Hanna's papers. It was amazing to watch how quickly—I think the next day—at the *L Magazine*, someone who was probably associated with NYU in some way, found it and scanned it in black and white and put it on their online magazine. From there, it went viral.[2]

However, neither Darms nor her donors, including Kathleen Hanna and Becca Albee who were preparing their papers at the time of the announcement, are strangers to the media's viral potential. In 1992, all three women were students at Evergreen College in Olympia, Washington, where they witnessed and to varying degrees were implicated by the initial media capture of riot grrrl. If anything, the conditions under which news of the collection's development went public were all too familiar.

While the *L Magazine*'s decision to scan and repost an article about the development of the Riot Grrrl Collection from an internal university newsletter and its subsequent impact is far less significant than the historical arrival of riot grrrl in the mainstream media, the similarities are worth considering.[3] Like riot grrrl in its early stages of development, which was both public and fiercely protective of its ability to control its

---

1 Chideya, Farai, Melissa Rossi and Dogen Hannah, "Revolution, Girl Style," *Newsweek*, November 23, 1992, 84-86.
2 Lisa Darms, interview, June 25, 2010.
3 Mark Asch, "NYU Libraries Acquire The Kathleen Hanna Papers for Their New 'Riot Grrrl Collection'," The L Magazine, January 7, 2010, http://www.thelmagazine.com/ TheMeasure/archives/2010/01/07/nyu-librar-ies-acquire-the-kathleen-hanna-papers-for-their-new-riot-grrrl-collection

representation and circulation, the development of the collection was by no means a
secret but from the onset, there was an attentiveness to maintaining control over how
the collection would be publicized.[4] As Darms explains, the desire to control the collection's representation was partly rooted in a commitment to ensuring it would not
be defined too narrowly: "I don't want it to be the 'Kathleen Hanna Collection.' She
feels the same way. It's a Riot Grrrl Collection, but most of the press was just about
Kathleen."[5] Darms was also concerned about mitigating the circulation of misinforma-
tion about who would be able to access the collection and under what circumstances.

In the days following the *L Magazine* post, news of Fales Library's Riot Grrrl Collection traveled quickly over multiple forms of media, proving especially viral in forms
of media that had not yet come into being when riot grrrl entered most people's consciousness in 1992 (e.g., blogs, Twitter and Facebook).[6] If many archivists and special
collections librarians spend years attempting to generate interest in their collections,
for Darms, this achievement was effortless. That news of an archival collection could
"go viral," however, reveals as much about riot grrrl as a cultural phenomenon as it
does about the significance of the Riot Grrrl Collection. The media interest in the collection points to what is potentially controversial about the collection's development. It
also points to the collection's status within a network of women, which includes women
old enough to have heard Bikini Kill play live in the early 1990s and young enough to
have been born after the *Newsweek* article, who identify with riot grrrl as an aesthetic,
cultural and political movement unique to their generation of feminists. My primary
concern, however, is neither with the controversy nor the affective attachments generated by the collection. As I explore throughout this article, preservation *is* a central
part of the Riot Grrrl Collection's mandate, but the collection holds the potential to do
much more than preserve riot grrrl as it has been understood to date. As the collection
develops, it also holds the potential to impact riot grrrl's legacy and more specifically,
the legacies of the women most closely identified with the movement.

Here, Pierre Bourdieu's theorizing on the field of cultural production offers a useful framework for beginning to understand how the creative products of a so-called
"subculture" might be transformed through their entry into the archive and more
specifically, how archivization might hold the potential to *retroactively* align previously

---

4    As an example, one might consider the "semi-publics" or "intimate publics" fostered by riot grrrl zinesters who primarily distributed their publications at concerts, meetings and by mail. This circulation strategy
enabled them to develop a readership while continuing to control their audience. For an extended discussion,
see Kate Eichhorn, "Sites Unseen: Ethnographic Research in a Textual Community," *International Journal of
Qualitative Studies in Education* 14, no.4 (2001), 565-578 and Alison Piepmeier, *Girl Zines: Making Media, Doing
Feminism* (New York: New York University Press, 2010).

5    Lisa Darms, interview, June 25, 2010.

6    Among other postings, see "Read all about it: Riot Grrrl Collection" on the blog *The Girls Are* (http://the-
girlsare.blogspot.com/2010/01/read-all-about-it-riot-grrrl-collection.html); "Feminist Sweepstakes" on *Jezebel*
(http://jezebel.com/5443605/feminist-sweepstakes); "Kathleen Hanna Bequeaths Papers to NYU..." on *The
Daily Swarm* (http://www.thedailyswarm.com/ headlines/kathleen-hanna-bequeaths-papers-nyu/); and "Kathleen
Hanna Helps Make the Library Cool Again" on *Fader* (http://www.thefader.com/2010/11/17/interview-kathleen-
hanna-on-the-raincoats-and-building-an-archive/).

unconsecrated cultural works with avant-garde movements. As Bourdieu maintains, every literary or artistic field is a *"field of forces"* and *"field of struggles,"* and the meaning of a work changes with "each change in the field within which it is situated for the spectator or reader."[7] What Bourdieu's theorizing aptly draws attention to is the extent to which literature and art are symbolic objects constituted by the institutions through which cultural products are endowed with value. While he lists many of the most obvious institutions engaged in such work, including museums, galleries and the academy, he does not list the archive. Since there is no doubt that the archive does belong in this list, the oversight is especially notable, but the archive is also uniquely situated in the field of cultural production. Unlike the gallery, art museum and even academy, which more often than not endow a literary or artistic work with value in the present, the archive's work is more often than not retroactive. In other words, it is uniquely located to the extent that it permits works to migrate across the field of cultural production at different points in history. In this respect, a work produced for a mass audience might become aligned with a work produced as "art for art's sake."[8] The archive, then, is not only an institution that Bourdieu overlooks in his theorizing on the field of cultural production but also the institution that arguably holds the greatest potential to disrupt the field as it is conceived in his work. Once more, as emphasized throughout this chapter, this is especially relevant to questions concerning the designation of an "avant-garde."

While Bourdieu's "field of cultural production" evidently privileges the spatial, his theorizing on the avant-garde is first and foremost temporal. If "conservatives" recognize their contemporaries in the past, the avant-garde has no contemporaries and "therefore no audience, except in the future." An avant-garde, according to Bourdieu, establishes itself not by recognizing their contemporaries in the past but conversely by pushing "back into the past the consecrated producers with whom they are compared."[9] If Bourdieu's theorizing on cultural production fails to account for the question of the archive, perhaps it is because the archive, more than any other institution, holds the potential to interrupt this supposed process by prying open opportunities for an avant-garde to be established retroactively. This is not surprising, however, since the archive is first and foremost a temporal apparatus—at once committed to the endless accumulation of time, as Foucault emphasizes in his theorizing on heterotopias[10] (of which the library and archive exist as one example among many)—but also to the reordering of time. In the archive, after all, materials are not necessarily aligned according to temporal logics. Players once estranged in the field of cultural production may become aligned. Contemporaries may be torn apart. Movements may be defined or redefined. In short, archival time challenges Bourdieu's assumption that avant-

7   Pierre Bourdieu, *The Field of Cultural Production*, ed. Randal Johnson (New York: Columbia University Press, 1993) 30-31.
8   Ibid. 49.
9   Ibid. 107
10   Michel Foucault. "Of Other Spaces," *Diacritics* 16 (Spring 1986), 22-27.

garde movements are necessarily established via a series of displacements—through the anachronization of one's predecessors. In the archive, an avant-garde conversely may be established via a series of strategic realignments that *make present* players who never had the opportunity to play in the same field but in many respects, comfortably occupy the same field nevertheless.

The archive, then, is an apparatus that can be effectively wielded in a reparative manner, and this is precisely the movement I chart here. Specifically, I examine how relocating the riot grrrl papers from haphazard personal storage situations across the United States to the Fales Library and Special Collections in New York City represents an attempt to redefine riot grrrl as a cultural movement as deeply marked by feminist politics and punk aesthetics as it is by legacies of avant-garde art, performance and literature. As this article demonstrates, the primary goal of the Riot Grrrl Collection is not simply to preserve and legitimize materials that may otherwise slip into historical oblivion but to authorize them as *cultural* rather than exclusively *subcultural* products and more significantly, as cultural products with a particular lineage in the artistic and literary avant-garde.

## Archive Viral

Historically, attempts to develop archival collections dedicated to women and the women's movements have met considerable resistance. By comparison, the development of the Riot Grrrl Collection solicited little criticism. Nevertheless, the first response to the announcement on the *L Magazine* website read, "At what point does this become ridiculous?"[11] Reactions to the provocation were uniformly critical of the writer's implied accusation that the riot grrrl papers do not merit archiving. As the first response asked, "Why look down your nose at this? It seems perfectly reasonable to me that this stuff would wind up in a library. You can't study feminism in 2010 (or 2005 or 1995, for that matter) and not talk about Hanna and the Riot Grrrl movement."[12] Subsequent responses on the *L Magazine* website and other blogs reiterated the fact that the collection is one of historical significance. For example, two weeks after the *L Magazine* announcement, the following blog post appeared on *Jukebox Heroines*:

> I have been trying to get copies of Kathleen Hanna's, as well as, other Riot Grrrls zines from eBay and such, with some success. I mean, since they were photocopied, you can make more, but after a while, the copies of copies of copies get rather hard to read. I am so happy that Riot Grrrl and the movement is getting some credit from the academic side. I mean they have for a bit, some texts have been written about it, but

---

11   Mike Lindgren, January 7, 2010 (4:09 p.m.), comment on Mark Asch, "NYU Libraries Acquire The Kathleen Hanna Papers for Their New 'Riot Grrrl Collection'," *The L Magazine,* January 7, 2010.
12   Mike Cocklin, January 7, 2010 (10:03 p.m.), comment on Mark Asch, "NYU Libraries Acquire The Kathleen Hanna Papers for Their New 'Riot Grrrl Collection'," *The L Magazine,* January 7, 2010.

preserving these documents ensures it will never be forgotten![13]

Like earlier responses on the *L Magazine* website, Emily's post emphasizes the historical significance of riot grrrl. Her post also suggests that despite the fact that a zine, for example, may continue to be copied and even sold on eBay for an indefinite period of time, there *is* an integrity to the original and that "originals" may be important, even in movements where appropriation and copying are integral and celebrated practices.

Defenses of the Riot Grrrl Collection's relevance were by no means limited to those rooted in making a case for the historical significance of the materials in their original form. In the days following the media leak, affective attachments to the papers being processed at Fales Library also came to the surface. Another participant in the spontaneous debate on the *L Magazine* website replied, "I applaud the NYU Library for taking the feminist movement and the *L Magazine* theory seriously, and am thrilled to see such a crucial part of *my* history, and countless others, illuminated by critical thought and inquiry. Not because we need the academy to validate who are...but because it's an historical moment in time worth knowing about" (emphasis my own).[14] Feelings of personal attachment are also expressed in Macy Halford's op-ed piece published as part of "The Book Bench" column in *The New Yorker*:

> I'm extremely happy that the papers of Kathleen Hanna—Riot Grrrl, Bikini Killer, Le Tigre—are going to the growing Riot Grrrl archive at N.Y.U.'s Fales Library. Happy because I live in New York and I might be able to think up a reason to gain access (I'm not in the academy, but would that stop any self-respecting grrrl?), and happier because it represents a major step toward overcoming the sticky formulation
>
> Girl = Dumb, Girl = Bad, Girl = Weak
>
> as Hanna and her sisters put it in the Riot Grrrl Manifesto, first published in 1991 in "Bikini Kill Zine 2." [15]

Notably, Halford assumes that the Riot Grrrl Collection will become a destination for researchers and fans and thus, serve as riot grrrl's equivalent to, let's say, Graceland. This assumption is shared by Alyx Vesey. In a post about the collection on *Feminist Music Geek*, Vesey enthused, "it's with great excitement that I report that Kathleen Hanna is donating her personal papers to NYU's Fales Library for their Riot Grrrl Collection (which I didn't know they had)...Looks like *this moi* has got some independent research to do. See you in the stacks."[16]

---

13    Emily, "Kathleen Hanna & Riot Grrrl Archives at NYU," *Jukebox Heroines* (blog), January 28, 2010, http://jukeboxheroines.wordpress.com/2010/01/28/kathleen-hanna-riot-grrrl-archives-at-nyu

14    Erin Fairchild, January 8, 2010 (1:18 p.m.), comment on Mark Asch, "NYU Libraries Acquire The Kathleen Hanna Papers for Their New 'Riot Grrrl Collection'," *The L Magazine*, January 7, 2010.

15    Mary Halford, "Quiet Riot," *The New Yorker*, January 12, 2010, accessed on January 8, 2011, http://www.newyorker.com/online/blogs/books/2010/01/quiet-riot.html

16    Alyx Vesey, "Kathleen Hanna, Archival Subject," *Feminist Music Geek* (blog), January 8, 2010, http://femi-

While these comments represent only a few of the hundreds of responses posted online in the wake of the Riot Grrrl Collection's announcement, they are representative of the public reaction to news of the collection's development. First, despite the critique expressed in the initial response to the *L Magazine* article, the collection solicited few questions about whose history and what types of history count. The absence of negative responses to the collection's development not only suggest that riot grrrl's legacy may already be well recognized (at least in some contexts) but also that both in and outside the academy, there is a growing recognition that histories of minorities, activist movements and subcultures are histories worth preserving. The initial response to the Riot Grrrl Collection also revealed that it is by no means a typical archival collection (despite its similarities to existing collections at Fales Library).[17] In contrast to most collections, for example, the papers and artifacts in question not only belong to living writers, performers and artists but to women writers, performers and artists who are, for all extensive purposes, still early in their careers.[18] In addition, it is significant that the excitement about the papers' arrival in the archive was not simply something shared by researchers but also fans and people with political affinities to riot grrrl. However, this is not to suggest that the researcher, fan and affinity group member are by any means mutually exclusive categories. In fact, both responses to news of the collection's development and the content of the collection, which provides further evidence of riot grrrl's intellectual roots, reveal how deeply entangled these categories can be and arguably always were in riot grrrl. Finally, the dialogue generated by news of the collection's development revealed the extent to which the collection, despite its location in an institutional setting, is part of the affective economy in which souvenirs, memorabilia and archival objects circulate. As Ann Cvetkovich reminds us, "memories can cohere around objects in unpredictable ways."[19] In other words, an object's meaning and value are invariably prone to drift, frequently becoming invested with attachments previously unimagined by the original producer or owner. Although these are the papers of individuals, news of the collection was received with enthusiasm because so many women feel that these papers represent and belong to an entire generation of feminists. It is precisely this identification that enabled the Riot Grrrl Collection to go viral before its contents were processed, but this identification or "over-identification" with riot grrrl and specifically, with its key figures may be what the collection's development ultimately quells.

Although it seems likely that news of the Riot Grrrl Collection traveled as quickly

---

nistmusicgeek.com/2010/01/08/kathleen-hanna-archival-subject

17    As Lisa Darms explained, "…a lot of the challenges or unusual things about the Riot Grrrl Collection, I've already dealt with in the Downtown, like the fact that I have living donors" (interview, June 25, 2010).

18    Kathleen Hanna was born in 1968 and the vast majority of the women whose papers are housed in the collection were born in the early 1970s. Moreover, while some of the women represented in the collection are no longer active as musicians, most of the donors continue to engage in some form of cultural production. Becca Albee, for example, was a member of Excuse 17 in the early to mid 1990s; she is now a New York City based visual artist and professor of art.

19    Ann Cvetkovich, *An Archive of Feelings: Trauma, Sexuality, and Lesbian Public Cultures* (Durham: Duke University Press, 2003), 242.

as it did because many women feel a personal attachment to the materials it does or will eventually house, the collection is defined by and asserts a much more narrowly defined understanding of riot grrrl than existing collections of riot grrrl materials. If existing collections, such as the zine collections at Duke University and Barnard College, have sought to promote an understanding of riot grrrl as a mass movement of girls and young women that originated in the 1990s, the Fales Library collection defines riot grrrl as a somewhat more temporally and geographically bound movement synonymous with the cultural contributions of a core group of women musicians, writers, performers and visual artists. Despite this mandate, which may strike some fans as being at odds with riot grrrl's ethos, it is important to recognize that the collection's existence is contingent on longstanding friendships and connections that date back to riot grrrl's inception in the early 1990s. As previously mentioned, Darms was a student at Evergreen College in the early 1990s. "I never went to a Riot Grrrl meeting," she explains, "But I was there and involved and doing the same things…I wasn't close friends with all the donors, but mostly, we were at least in the same places, at the same shows, at the same parties."[20] Perhaps more importantly, however, is Darms' *present* connection to the women she first met at Olympia in the early 1990s. As previously emphasized, the widespread interest in the collection has been due in part to the personal attachment so many women feel to the collection's materials. The collection arguably only exists, however, because the donors and archivists identify with and trust each other on the basis of their much less public history. According to Johanna Fateman, "It definitely helped that Lisa is a close friend, and that I trusted her to have a sensitivity to the issues surrounding the project."[21] Similarly, for Hanna, the decision to donate her papers to Fales Library appeared to be directly linked to Darms' position there as Senior Archivist. "I really don't think I would've been interested if someone else, besides Lisa Darms, had approached me," explained Hanna, "It just felt like the universe lined up and it was meant to be."[22]

Although many women who came of age in the 1990s and beyond feel a personal connection to the papers in the Riot Grrrl Collection, as suggested above, it is not necessarily *their* archive. That so many women have interpreted the collection as an archive of an entire generation of feminists rather than a collection that contains several individuals' personal papers, however, is not entirely surprising. Historically, documents and artifacts connected to traditionally marginalized groups are more likely to enter archives because they are representative of a demographic or cultural phenomenon than due to their connection to individuals. Many collections of women's archival materials, for example, are comprised of diaries and letters written by anonymous or unknown women writers rather than writers who gained notoriety for their work; the materials are valuable because they tell us something about the conditions

---

20    Lisa Darnms, interview, June 25, 2010.
21    Johanna Fateman, online interview, August 2010.
22    Kathleen Hanna, online interview, August 2010.

of women's everyday lives in a particular era and not because they tell us something about the individual writers. In many respects, both the zine collections at Barnard College and Duke University extend this tradition of collection development in women's archives. While both collections contain zines produced by or about the women whose papers are also housed at Riot Grrrl Collection, it is important to bear in mind that even the same zine, for example, represents something different in the collections at Barnard College or Duke University than it does in the collection at Fales Library. As Jenna Freedman, the founder and librarian responsible for the Barnard College Zine Library, emphasizes, her collection is one that belongs to and represents "every girl." A zine by or about Kathleen Hanna in the Barnard College collection is there as part of a larger and still growing collection of zines by girls and women and gender-queer subjects. By contrast, Darms emphasizes that her collection focuses on riot grrrl and more specifically, on the papers of the women most synonymous with the movement's development. In this context, a zine by or about Hanna is not representative of d.i.y. publishing or "girl power," as it might be elsewhere. At Fales Library, it is one document among many that tells us something about Hanna's development as an artist and performer and founding member of riot grrrl.

By creating a collection with a mandate "to collect unique materials that provide documentation of the creative process of *individuals* and the chronology of the movement overall" (emphasis my own), Darms is not only creating the first collection of riot grrrl *papers*, she is effectively relocating and redefining riot grrrl in ways that will profoundly impact how riot grrrl and specifically, particular riot grrrl figures will be written about in the future. In the remaining sections of this chapter, I examine how the collection's development, including the combined geographic and symbolic acts of relocation it entails, represents a realignment of riot grrrl that highlights the movement's intellectual and artistic lineages and by extension, highlights the archive's status as a historiographic technology.

### Institutionalization and Assimilation

Upon news of the Riot Grrrl Collection's development, many bloggers not only celebrated the development of an archival collection dedicated to riot grrrl but also the arrival of a new destination for fans. A response to a posting on *The Girls Are...* blog read: "How awesome! Yes, roadtrip!" *The Girls Are...* agreed: "Seriously, I think I [could] craft a roadtrip around this one activity!"[23] If the initial public response to the Riot Grrrl Collection was marked by preliminary plans for pilgrimages to Fales Library, as the conditions of the collection became more apparent, some fans responded with disap-

---

23    Indy Grrrl and The Girls Are, January 12, 2010 (2:25 and 10:26 p.m.), comments on "Read All About It: Riot Grrrl Collection," *The Girls Are* (blog), January 11, 2010, http://thegirlsare.blogspot.com/2010/01/read-all-about-it-riot-grrrl-collection.html

pointment. In November 2010, the following tongue-in-cheek article in the *Village Voice* appeared, both advertising the collection and clarifying the collection's access policy:

> ...the collection is only open to 'qualified researchers' (a/k/a academes) to view in the Fales' reading room. For the rest of us unqualified schlubs, Darms is also looking to sponsor symposiums and conferences centered around grrrl cultural/feminism/queer studies as well as possible exhibitions and screenings.[24]

While the *Village Voice* piece was presumably not intended as a critique, responses on their website and subsequent online debates suggest that at least some fans considered the collection's access policy at odds with riot grrrl's central tenets. On the *Village Voice* website, for example, Fran responded, presumably under the impression that Hanna had never agreed to the terms of the collection, with the following post: "i don't think that kathleen hanna would of donated this collection if she had of know that it was only accessible to the educated elite!"[25] Not surprisingly, Darms rejects suggestions that the decision to locate the riot grrrl papers in a special collections library at a private university is necessarily problematic. She explains, "Scholarly is something we interpret broadly, because many of our researchers are artists [but] I have made sure that the donations have happened with an understanding that the materials will be accessed for scholarly projects. This has been the motivation for the donors so far—a recognition that the materials will support research. They haven't donated their materials to make them more accessible to fans."[26]

Hanna and Fateman's support for the collection's development also emphasizes the importance of preservation. "I didn't want to give all my stuff to some collective that might close down in a month and throw my stuff in the trash," explained Hanna.[27] When asked about the collection's institutional location, Fateman also emphasized the desire to place her papers in an established archive: "There are DIY archives but are they committed to preservation? Likely not in the way an institutional collection is committed to presentation (should this be "preservation"?)."[28] In addition to emphasizing the importance of preservation and the fact that institutional archives, such as Fales Library, are typically better equipped to carry out preservation than collections located in community settings, which frequently lack proper storage facilities, Darms, Fateman and Hanna's shared response to critiques of the collection's location are consistent with at least two important tenets of riot grrrl.

---

24   "The Fales Library at NYU's Riot Grrl Collection," *The Village Voice*, November 3, 2010, http://www.villagevoice.com/bestof/2010/award/best-way-to-disseminate-feminist-punk-culture-through-a-public-institution-2167594/
25   Fran, November 3, 2010 (9:28 p.m.), comment on "The Fales Library at NYU's Riot Grrl Collection," *The Village Voice*, November 3, 2010.
26   Lisa Darms, interview, June 25, 2010.
27   Kathleen Hanna, online interview, August 2010.
28   Johanna Fateman, online interview, August 2010.

First, the collection, which will provide access to a wide range of academic and independent researchers but at the discretion of library staff, appears to reflect the riot grrrl movement's own commitment to open access *within limits*. On this account, it is by no means insignificant that in defense of the collection's institutional context, Hanna draws a parallel between the collection and zine production:

> It's like people who make paper fanzines in 2010 are making a specific choice to reach a smaller audience than maybe a blog could, it's an artistic decision. One that has to do with having a tactile object that exists in the real world and can be physically passed from person to person. Choosing an archive that has an intended audience and isn't for everyone is a similar choice to me...[29]

Darms also emphasizes the importance of understanding that this collection, unlike existing collections of riot grrrl related materials, contains personal papers and not simply zines, recordings or artwork. As a result, it requires more care and sensitivity and hence, a heightened degree of what some fans perceive as institutional gatekeeping:

> Much of the material is very personal and with the figures involved, it could be very divisive if certain information was freely circulated—we're collecting journals, letters, even legal documents. So I don't think that its material that really needs to be accessible to anyone. I feel strongly about that in terms of archival reading rooms, even if it's not a popular way to view library practice but in terms of the archive, this is really standard practice.[30]

This is not to suggest that Darms is not committed to supporting venues where riot grrrl materials are more readily accessible. In fact, she sees herself working in collaboration with other archivists and librarians building riot grrrl related collections: "...there are still going to be venues where people can go to look at zines and that's really important to me. That's what Jenna Freedman is doing up at Barnard. But people are also taking it upon themselves to scan zines and create online archives. Those online archives may not last very long but it does create a way to make the zines accessible now."[31]

In addition to extending riot grrrl's practice of facilitating access to information without entirely relinquishing control over its circulation, the Riot Grrrl Collection extends the movement's longstanding practice of tactically deploying the academic apparatus. As Hanna explains, "Universities have more money than most left political groups and personally I don't want lefty feminist groups spending their resources maintaining archives when they could be doing more important things."[32] In many respects, riot grrrl has always operated as a parasitic presence on the academy, never

---

29    Kathleen Hanna, online interview, August 2010.
30    Lisa Darms, interview, June 25, 2010.
31    Ibid.
32    Kathleen Hanna, online interview, August 2010.

colonizing its host but consistently deploying its resources (intellectual and material) to further its own agenda. Once again, in this respect, it is important to recognize that the movement emerged in and around a college campus. Known for its innovative curriculum and commitment to collaborative and self-designed programs of study,[33] Evergreen College not only served as an institutional base from which to initiate specific projects (e.g., a riot grrrl distribution network was started as an independent study course at the college),[34] at least indirectly, it supplied riot grrrl with the resources, material and intellectual, needed to start a movement.

However, in the early 1990s, riot grrrl was doing much more than leaching the academy of material resources. Referring to the early years of riot grrrl and her own college experience at Evergreen, Darms emphasizes that "...a lot of the materials people were reading were academic. It was a really smart movement, a well informed movement."[35] While academic feminist discourses by no means had been absent from an earlier generation's community newspapers and journals, the range of scholarly discourses in non-refereed second wave publications and forms of cultural production were limited. Outside the academy, and at times even inside the academy, it was *de rigueur* for second wave feminists to eschew theoretical discourses perceived as "elitist," "difficult" and "inaccessible." By the early 1990s, however, the divide between so-called "academic" and "grassroots" feminisms was already dissolving, and riot grrrl was what it was because it emerged at this particular theoretical and political moment.

On my first trip to access the Riot Grrrl Collection at Fales Library in February 2011, I spoke again to Darms, who I originally interviewed for this essay in June 2010 (before the collection was made available to researchers). After hearing about the form this essay was taking, she directed me to five file folders of photocopied articles in the still unprocessed papers of Kathleen Hanna. The dates of the articles suggest that they were likely collected over a long period of time, possibly beginning during Hanna's years at Evergreen College. The range of materials in the files not only points to the breadth of the artist's reading and influences, however, but also offers insight into the intellectual and political orientation of the riot grrrl movement. If we accept the fact that as one of the founders of riot grrrl, Hanna's personal reading inventory is by no means inconsequential to understanding the political and intellectual roots of the movement, the files are worth considering at length. First, there are several articles that point to the influence of deconstructionist, poststructuralist and postmodern theorizing (e.g.,

---

33    For example, Riot Grrrl Collection donor, Becca Albee (a visual artist and former member of the band Excuse 17) attended Evergreen College in the early 1990s. While there, she enrolled in a course on women's health. According to Albee, as part of the course, students were required to purchase a speculum and perform self-examinations on several occasions throughout the semester. Notably, the self-examinations took place *in* the classroom on class time. Albee's personal recollection offers insight into Evergreen's pedagogy and politics when riot grrrl was taking shape in Olympia in the early 1990s. (Becca Albee, discussion, January 2010).
34    Kathleen Eichhorn, "Cyborg Grrrls: New Technologies, Identities and Community in the Production of 'Zines" (master's thesis, Simon Fraser University, 1996), 156n78.
35    Lisa Darms, interview, June 25, 2010.

the reviews of books by and about Derrida, the excerpt from Butler's *Bodies that Matter*, the copied articles by and about French feminist theorists, and a chapter of Terry Eagleton's *Illusions of Postmodernism*). Second, there is substantial evidence that Hanna, like many of her peers at the time, was still grappling with second wave feminist debates (e.g., Laura Kipnis's article on reading *Hustler* and Hazel V. Carby's discussion on the "politics of difference"). At the same time, the inventory points to the strong influence of queer theory (e.g., writings by Gregg Bordowitz, Chris Straayer and Ann Cvetkovich). Notably, these scholarly articles intermingle with news clippings (e.g., the article about the massacre of fourteen women in a classroom at École Polytechnique in Montréal on December 6, 1989) and features from the radical press (e.g., the articles copied from the *Whole Earth Review* and *Z Magazine*). Finally, there are references to a particular lineage of avant-garde writers and artists (e.g., the references to William Burroughs, Yoko Ono, Hilton Als, and Kathy Acker).

While Hanna's papers at the Riot Grrrl Collection paint a deeply complex picture of riot grrrl's relationship to hardcore, punk, feminism, popular culture, critical theory, and avant-garde literature and art, to date, few scholars of riot grrrl have accounted for this complexity. In a scholarly study on riot grrrl published in the mid 1990s, Joanne Gottlieb and Gayle Wald conclude, "From its inception, Riot Grrrl emerges as a bona fide subculture."[36] Wald extends this position in her 1998 *Signs* article, "Just a Girl?: Rock Music, Feminism, and the Cultural Construction of Female Youth," referring to riot grrrl as a "female youth subculture" and "musical subculture."[37] In many respects, it was by no means misleading to construct riot grrrl as a subculture. However, as Fateman emphasizes, "Many academics viewed RG rather romantically and wishfully...there was a desire to see it as a spontaneous radical feminist teen movement that had a kind of 'street cred,' rather than something that was connected to campus women's centers, take back the night marches, feminist scholarship, and avant-garde literature."[38] The problem of bringing a subcultural studies model to bear on riot grrrl, then, may have less to do with what such a model imposed on the movement and more to do with what the model effectively obscured about the movement's origins, influences and long-term impacts. As Fateman further observes, "The 'girl gang' image was cultivated by some within the movement, and it was 'real' in terms of certain guerilla tactics and punk antics, but riot grrrl was also an aesthetic thing (rhetorical, theorized)."[39] She adds, "Its status as a political movement and social phenomenon still seems to overshadow its status as an artistic movement. Its products still aren't discussed much *as art*."[40] The

---

36    Joanne Gottlieb and Gayle Wald, "Smells Like Teen Spirit: Riot Grrrl, Revolution and Women in Independent Rock" in *Microphone Fiends*: Youth Music & Youth Culture, eds. Andrew Ross and Tricia Rose (New York: Routledge, 1994), 263
37    Wald, Gayle. "Just a Girl?: Rock Music, Feminism, and the Cultural Construction of Female Youth." *Signs: Journal of Women in Culture and Society* 23.3 (Spring 1998), 588 and 593.
38    Johanna Fateman, online interview, August 2010.
39    Ibid.
40    Ibid.

Riot Grrrl Collection at Fales Library, then, does not represent a form of institutional-ization nor assimilation but rather foregrounds something that was always already part of the riot grrrl movement—its link to the academic apparatus and to the theoretical and aesthetic movements the academy cultivates.

## Avant-garde Heritage

The idea that a radical movement might have an "avant-garde heritage" is, ad-mittedly, at least somewhat contradictory. If we understand the avant-garde along Bourdieu's lines, avant-garde movements are by definition *without* a "heritage" or "lin-eage" to which they can truly lay claim, since "'young' writers, i.e., those less advanced in the process of consecration…will refuse everything their 'elders'…are and do, and in particular all their indices of *social ageing*, starting with the signs of consecration, internal (academies, etc.) or external (success)…"[41] But this, evidently, is a perspective that is either no longer relevant to theorizing on how avant-gardes are formed, or one in which riot grrrl stands as a notable exception.

As Fateman emphasizes, "Some riot grrrls (especially after the *Newsweek*, *USA Today*, *Sassy* articles) were quite young and knew nothing about Kathy Acker, Karen Finley, Diamanda Galas, Barbara Kruger, etc., but those in the most notorious Riot Grrrl bands most certainly did."[42] Among the articles and newspaper clippings Hanna chose to keep and include in her donation to the Riot Grrrl Collection are dozens of articles by and about Acker. The influence of the writer and performer on Hanna is also evident in personal correspondence housed in the collection. A letter from Hanna to Fateman written shortly after Acker's death in 1997 begins, "Your letter came at the perfect time. I had just been thinking about you…also thanks for the Kathy memorial service thing. I was really sad, still am…After all one of the best writers in the world is gone. Anyways, I'm super flattered that you remembered how much she means to me."[43] However, the Hanna-Acker connection is also an exception. In contrast to other connections between established innovative writers and artists and the riot grrrl movement, this connection has already been recognized as part of riot grrrl history. In a 2002 article in the *Village Voice*, in which Acker is described as "a riot grrrl ahead of her time,"[44] Hanna discusses a fated weekend workshop with Acker in Seattle in 1990. As the legend goes, Acker told Hanna, "If you want to be heard, why are you doing spoken word? You should be in a band."[45] As we all know, Hanna went home and started a band, and Acker was right—bands get more airplay than poetry. Whether or

---

41    Bourdieu, *The Field of Cultural Production*, 59.
42    Johanna Fateman, online interview, August 2010.
43    Letter from Kathleen Hanna to Johanna Fateman, undated, Kathleen Hanna Collection (unprocessed at the time of access), Riot Grrrl Collection, Fales Library and Special Collections, NYU, New York City, NY.
44    C. Carr, "Theoretical Girl: The Legacy of Kathy Acker," *The Village Voice*, November 5, 2002, 49.
45    Ibid.

not Acker would have embraced the idea that she was a "riot grrrl ahead of her time" is unclear. After all, Acker was very much an individual, not a movement. Nevertheless, as a tough, sexually complicated, outspoken, punk writer and performer who had found a way to play with the boys and espouse feminist politics without being co-opted by either camp, Acker was an ideal role model for Hanna and her peers. She exemplified what it might mean to be both punk and feminist, political and theoretically engaged, a public figure but by no means an object of media manipulation.

Although the Acker influence on Hanna was the result of a direct encounter, for other riot grrrls, the influence of Acker and other avant-garde women writers and performers, such as Eileen Myles and Karen Finley, may not have been as direct nor as readily discussed, but it is apparent in the work nevertheless. In *Girls to the Front*, Sara Marcus makes a point of foregrounding these connections and to her credit, she carefully avoids implying that they were merely about young women searching for feisty feminist role models in the late years of the second wave feminist movement. As Marcus emphasizes, connections, such as the one between Hanna and Acker, were first and foremost intellectual and aesthetic. She writes:

> In *Blood and Guts in High School*, the 1978 novel that got Kathleen hooked, a young girl begs her father for sex, joins a gang, has two abortions, and goes to a Contortions concert—all in the first forty-three pages. The story is told in a fragmented, deadpan way, through shifting points of view and collage: fairy tales, scripts, poems, line drawings of men's and women's genitals, pages from a Persian-language workbook. *Blood and Guts* suggested that the realities of women's lives, especially with regard to sexuality and abuse, were too complicated to be told through typical narrative. Only contradictions, ruptures and refusals stood a chance of conveying the truth.[46]

Directly or indirectly, with few exceptions, early riot grrrl writing, such as the writing found in many of the zines published between 1990 and 1994, reflects this recognition that women's lives, especially women's experiences of sexuality and abuse, are too complicated to be expressed in linear narrative prose. Without diverging from the primary focus of this article, it is important to emphasize that many early riot grrrl writers (and notably, I am choosing to refer to them as *writers* rather than *zinesters* here) were, like Acker and her contemporaries in the avant-garde writing scenes in New York City and San Francisco, committed to creating a textual space where competing tendencies, narratives, truths, styles and aesthetics could co-exist—this, however, is something that has been largely ignored by researchers of riot grrrl. The question that remains is *why* critics have generally assumed that riot grrrls were doing what they were doing (on the page and the stage) more or less naively, without a sense of the innovative literary and art movements that preceded them?

One could easily conclude that the relative neglect of riot grrrl cultural production

---

46   Marcus, *Girls to the Front: The True Story of the Riot Grrrl Revolution* (New York: HarperPerennial, 2010)., 32.

as literature and art reflects the general status of women writers and artists, especially those affiliated with so-called avant-garde movements. Yet, in the case of riot grrrl, the problem is not necessarily one of recognition but *how* the movement has been recognized, and on this account, gender alone cannot account for the oversight in question. Returning once again to the question of riot grrrl writing, it is important to recognize that with few exceptions, researchers have tended to ignore the specificity of riot grrrl writing by classifying this writing within the broader category of girl zine writing. Read through this lens, what is most apparent are the common issues riot grrrl and other girl zines address (e.g., abuse, eating disorders, sexuality etc.) rather than the mode of address or procedures at work in the texts. In other words, content is invariably privileged over form, pushing aesthetic questions to the margins. This is evident in Alison Piepmeier's *Girl Zines: Making Media, Doing Feminism*. Notably absent from Piepmeier's study is any extended discussion of zine writing in relation to pastiche, détournement, appropriation or questions of authorship. While this is by no means a reason to overlook Piepmeier's important study on girl zines, it reminds us again—as Darms evidently hopes to foreground through the development of the Riot Grrrl Collection—that context matters and more specifically, context holds the potential to deeply inform the critical perspectives that amass around a given cultural product to determine its status as a symbolic object in the field of cultural production.

Far from preserving the history of riot grrrl as it has been preserved to date, then, the Riot Grrrl Collection represents a possible interruption of the field of cultural production. While the possibilities are, as of yet, mostly unexplored, as the collection is used by researchers, its possibilities will become increasingly apparent. As emphasized throughout this essay, without necessarily pushing riot grrrl's status as a subculture or sub-movement of punk entirely into the background, the collection's location at Fales Library and Special Collections relocates riot grrrl in relation to some of the "rarefied" and "consecrated" cultural products of earlier and concurrent avant-garde literary, art and performance movements, hence drawing attention to the fact that the "grrrls" were engaged in forms of cultural and knowledge production that can and should be taken seriously as art, literature and theory and not simply youthful rebellion. Once more, the collection's development, which is the result of the longstanding relationship between the collection's archivist and the cultural producers in question, reveals the extent to which the producers recognized the archive as the space and apparatus most capable of executing such a radical position-taking in the present.

# Outreach and Instruction at the Sallie Bingham Center

*Kelly Wooten*

## Introduction

Archives use public programs and exhibits to raise awareness about collections and their potential for research, as well as to draw attention to the relevance of historical documents and how they can inform understanding of the past and present. Events can draw together archivists, activists, scholars, donors, and community members and spark conversation about important issues. By creating opportunities to foster these points of connection between various populations and in relation to archival collections, an archives makes a statement about its value to its community of constituents and potential donors. This essay explores the potential for outreach by describing public programming, instruction, community outreach, and the use of social media by the Sallie Bingham Center for Women's History and Culture at Duke University, and illustrates why these things matter in relation to documenting feminist history now and in the future.

## Public Programming

The Bingham Center distinguishes itself through innovative public programming. Former director Cristina Favretto started a tradition of programs featuring dramatic readings thematically selected from letters, diaries, books, and other print sources including "Memoirs and Manifestoes" and "Cocktails, Casseroles and Contraceptives." Under the leadership of current director Laura Micham, the Bingham Center launched a series of academic symposia that bring together not only scholars and researchers, but also archives creators and donors, activists, and community members.

The first symposium was held in 2003 to mark the Center's 15th anniversary, as well as the 30th anniversary of Roe v. Wade, the landmark U.S. Supreme Court decision protecting women's right to abortion. "Abortion: Research, Ethics and Activism" created awareness of the importance of primary source materials to scholarship and activism on this topic and explored the ways in which the history of abortion affects its future.[1] This program challenged the notion of the archives as a static repository that receives manuscripts and print materials and then passively serves them up to researchers. Speakers covered the range of political opinions on the controversial topic, and participants included Duke faculty, students, and staff as well as activists,

---

1   Abortion symposium website: http://library.duke.edu/rubenstein/bingham/abortion-symposium/

health care providers, and creators of collections held by the Bingham Center. The symposium sessions addressed the relationship of feminism and abortion rights, the evolution of medical ethics, international perspectives on access to abortion, and other topics. By hosting this program in the library, the Bingham Center was able to position itself as a locus for critical conversations across disciplines, to show the relevance of historical events and documents to current events, and to demonstrate its commitment to engaging researchers, donors, the campus, local community, and activists with the materials placed in its care.

Since that time, the Bingham Center has held symposia on the topics of generational feminisms, women and artistic expression, and women and education. In addition to these large scale programs, the Bingham Center hosts readings by authors (usually writers whose papers are at Duke or who have used our facilities for research), lectures by visiting scholars (frequently, recipients of Mary Lily Research Grants for travel funded by the Center), programs featuring artists and activists, and more dramatic readings.[2] Bingham Center librarians also curate exhibits related to symposia or with their own associated programming, such as the 2010 "Book + Art" exhibit highlighting recent acquisitions to the collection of artists' books by women.[3] Managing all of these events does take a great deal of planning, staff time and energy, and financial resources, but there is no better way to engage our community with our unique historical materials and impart their value to an audience beyond the library's stone walls.

### Instruction

Another important element of the Center's outreach is active participation in the library's instruction program for courses taught at Duke and other local institutions. Each semester, librarians comb the course catalogs for potential matches, not just in the women's studies and history departments, but visual arts, literature, religious studies, and more. We work with instructors to select appropriate materials, schedule a visit to the library, and, ideally, help them integrate primary sources into their assignments. During a typical library instruction session, students have the opportunity to interact with materials such as flyers from the Robin Morgan Papers that offer a behind the scenes glimpse into organizing the 1968 Miss America pageant protest, the event which launched the women's liberation movement into the public consciousness and incidentally gave rise to the myth of bra burning.[4] Students love having the chance to handle historical documents and discuss how they relate to their class readings and their own personal experiences.

Working directly with primary sources can be a transformative experience for

---

2    More examples of past events: http://library.duke.edu/rubenstein/bingham/news/past.html
3    Book + Art exhibit website: http://exhibits.library.duke.edu/exhibits/show/bookart
4    Documents from the Miss America Protests, 1968-69: http://library.duke.edu/digitalcollections/missamerica/

students. A couple of examples of this can be drawn from our work over the past few years with "Women as Leaders," a Public Policy course with which the Center has an on-going relationship. During one class period where the students looked at a variety of women's liberation movement documents from the 1960s and 70s, one woman spent time reading and responding to an essay called "Why I want a wife" by Judy Syfers.[5] This student was amazed at how much that essay resonated with her perceptions of her own mother's experience in their household over twenty years after the piece was written. Seeing a student respond so personally to a document and spontaneously in-corporate a feminist analysis based on her other course readings and class discussions is the most rewarding thing that can come out of a class session like this.

During another semester, the Women as Leaders instruction session focused pri-marily on zines, which intrigued the students so much that they were inspired to create a zine about the campus climate for women as their final group project. I was invited back for a follow-up session, but this time I took paper, scissors, and markers (and an intern) to their classroom for a hands-on zine workshop. During this class, we went into more detail about how to make a zine, including typical components like intros, interviews, cut-and-paste collages, drawings, rants, and lists. I was thrilled to see the final product, "Duke Life: A Closer Look at Hookup Culture," which incorporated many of these elements, including my favorite, a quiz.[6]

**Community Outreach Through Girls Rock NC**

Though this zine workshop was the first one I conducted with Duke students, I already had the supplies on hand from leading zine workshops for Girls Rock NC's annual summer camp in Durham and Chapel Hill.[7] This form of outreach is one of the more unusual (and fun) ways to get outside of the archives and engage with young women and girls about the importance of their own lives in the course of history.

Our curriculum has evolved since our first Girls Rock zine workshop in 2006, but we usually talk a little bit about the Sallie Bingham Center, give an overview of U.S. feminist history, and introduce zines. Then each girl makes her own zine page that will be compiled into a group zine, copied, and handed out at the end of camp. During the introduction to the Bingham Center, we discuss the differences between a special collections library and a public or school library, and highlight our girls literature col-lection, mentioning series like the *American Girl* books, with which many of the girls are familiar, as well as items like the diary of 14-year-old Alice Williamson who lived during the Civil War and recorded her everyday experiences.[8]

In the overview of U.S. feminist history, we break down the "waves" into the most

---

5   Online transcription of "Why I want a wife" http://www.cwluherstory.com/why-i-want-a-wife.html
6   Duke Life zine: http://www.duke.edu/web/hookup/
7   Girls Rock NC website: http://girlsrocknc.org/
8   Alice Williamson Diary: http://scriptorium.lib.duke.edu/williamson/

basic concepts: first wave bringing the right to vote, second wave raising awareness about the need for gender equality in education, the workplace, and household, and the third wave continuing to fight against sexism and for equality in many of those same areas. We even have the girls jump up and do "the wave" to try to avoid sitting for too long. I'm always amazed at how lively the conversation can get when you bring up the wage gap to eight- to ten-year olds who have a keen sense of justice. Though the majority of girls who attend rock camp arguably feel quite empowered and are being raised in a time when they receive the superficial message that "girls can do anything," they are also sharply aware of the gender norms for appropriate behavior and roles for girls and women.

With the mini-lecture out of the way, we get to the whole point of the workshop: zines. Most of the girls are repeat campers, so they already know about zines, or at least have seen the camp zine before. We do still spend a little bit of time talking about how women and girls in the 1990s (pre-internet, pre-email, and pre-Facebook) used zines as a way to make friends and share ideas about things they loved (and hated). We brainstorm about all the different things you can put in a zine: favorite bands and sing-ers, interviews with friends or famous people, collages, lists of things you like, recipes or how-to's, drawings, and comics. More recently we've tried to help them think about what they would want people to know about them from reading their zines, now and in the future. Finally, we're ready to get down to business. We hand out blank sheets of paper and give them instructions on how to make their pages: Only draw on one half of the page, use dark colors (no yellow or orange since they don't photocopy well), and try to keep a margin (they never do!). They can use markers, pens, cut out images from magazines, clip art, rubber stamps, and lots and lots of stickers. The best thing about zines is how easy and almost instinctual they are to make. Some girls hesitate and spend time thinking and planning their pages carefully, but most see what a zine looks like and get started right away.

One of my favorite parts is collecting all the pages and putting them together into the camp zine. It's gratifying to see the creativity and fun the girls are able to put on each page, and nostalgic to watch each colorful section transform into a black & white copy that could have been made by any group of friends from the past two decades. The Bingham Center keeps a copy of each camp zine and will become the repository for the organizational records of Girls Rock NC, so we have a tangible connection to the organization beyond the annual zine workshops. It's harder to trace the ripples that may flow out from the zine workshops: I like to think at least one girl has created her own zine, lying on her bedroom floor with scissors and tape like so many girls before her. Having that hour with a group of young girls to share the idea that their own everyday lives are important and have meaning, that the pages they make for their camp zine will be forever preserved in a library, is something I look forward to every summer.

## Publicity and Social Media

Our work with Girls Rock NC has impact beyond just reaching the girls during camp and raising awareness about the Bingham Center among volunteers and campers' families. The Bingham Center uses a variety of methods to share news about its wide range of activities including Girls Rock Camp, including our website, a print and online newsletter, email list, Facebook page, Flickr account, YouTube, and participation in "The Devil's Tale" blog. In addition to promoting events, we use our newsletter, website, and Facebook page to share recent acquisitions of print materials, personal papers, and organizational records, fun things found during processing or by researchers in the reading room, and notes about instruction sessions. Even when there isn't something "happening" we can highlight newly processed collections by sharing finding aids, links to relevant issues in the news, or draw attention to important dates in women's history. It takes almost the same amount of time and energy to maintain all these platforms as it does to do the programming itself, and posting fresh, relevant content in a variety of formats requires vigilance and commitment.

To continue using the example of Girls Rock Camp, we write Facebook posts leading up to the zine workshops, highlighting our zine collections and letting people know about the Girls Rock program. During the workshops we take pictures (with permission) and then post them on our Flickr site to show the great pages that they make and how much fun we have. We've also featured these activities in our print newsletter. Whenever there is a mention of Girls Rock Camp in the media, we have this content at the ready to add a post to Facebook and help promote Girls Rock programs in general as well as our own role with the local camp.

For most major events we use multiple platforms to engage our constituents both before and after the event itself. For the 2009 symposium, "What Does It Mean To Be An Educated Woman" we promoted the program through our website, email list, print newsletter, postcard mailing, and media contacts, including an interview on local public radio.[9] We had a photographer take pictures throughout the day, including traditional shots of speakers and candid shots of attendees, which were later posted on Flickr. We also video-recorded all of the programs, and then posted them on YouTube and embedded them on our website. A few months after the program we hosted a lunchtime series of viewings of the DVDs, mainly for library staff who weren't able to attend the symposium, but were also open to the public. Many of our stakeholders and supporters are not able to attend events in person, but by sharing pictures and videos of events, we can make content available to a wider audience as well as simply demonstrating our wide range of activities. Currently we are engaged in a project to publish the proceedings of the symposium as an e-book, which is a new venture for the Bingham Center as well as Duke University Libraries.

---

9    What Does It Mean To Be An Educated Woman symposium website: http://library.duke.edu/specialcollections/bingham/education-symposium/index.html

## Why All of This Matters

Through its diverse array of outreach programming, the Bingham Center created a public image as a vibrant hub of activity, buzzing with excitement around primary source materials and their potential for not just scholarly research, but personal connections, activism, and even entertainment. The relationships we have developed with faculty, donors, and researchers are often based on the connections we have made with these individuals through various forms of outreach. It doesn't matter how great your archivists are at processing and preserving materials, or how wonderful your reference librarians are in connecting researchers and collections; if you don't tell people about these activities, precious few will get the chance to learn that about you. More importantly, these are the things that matter to donors. They want to know that collections are being (or will be) used—by researchers, by students, in classrooms, and for exhibits. With social media like Facebook, the Bingham Center is placing itself out into the regular news stream of our audience and making it easier for others to share our stories with their friends.

It's not too big a stretch to call our outreach program a form of activism as it draws attention to the importance and relevance of women's history, as well as the fact that many of the individuals and organizations whose records we hold are still doing feminist work on a wide range of issues, from reproductive rights to advocating for women in ministry. This element of activism appeals to many of our current and potential donors, and will most likely continue to grow in importance, especially for younger feminist activists who are starting to see themselves in the spectrum of history.

The amount of time, financial resources and energy we expend on outreach is truly an investment in the future of the archives. The returns come in the form of engaged students and researchers, donors who understand the context in which their papers are being placed and feel confident that they will be actively used, and a growing audience of supporters who will help our collections expand and increase use of existing collections.

# Archiving the Underground


## Jenna Brager & Jami Sailor


*Archiving the Underground* emerges from our investment in the DIY, ethical, and utopian possibilities of zine production and culture and in the often frustrating framework of academic institutions. The zine, published in 2011, is comprised of interviews with Milo Miller of the Queer Zine Archive Project; Alison Piepmeier, the author of *Girl Zines: Making Media, Doing Feminism*; Teal Triggs, the author of *Fanzines*; Adela C. Licona, the author of the forthcoming *Zines In Third Space: Radical Cooperation and Borderlands Rhetoric*; Lisa Darms, senior archivist at New York University's Fales Library; as well as a reprint of the blog post "Zines are Not Blogs" by Jenna Freedman of the Barnard Zine Library.

This chapter includes the text from the introduction to these compiled interviews, followed by a reprinting of the interview with Milo Miller of the Queer Zine Archive Project (QZAP). The Queer Zine Archive Project, founded in 2003, was a clear choice to include in *Archiving the Underground* as a project of preserving queer zines that is independent and community-supported rather than through a University or other governing body. QZAP works to preserve queer zines and make them available to anyone interested, primarily through digital archiving. With an emphasis on access and encouraging "current and emerging zine publishers to continue to create," the Queer Zine Archive Project is a clear example of enmeshed participation and preservation of subcultural practice.

From the Introduction to *Archiving the Underground*:

> We seek to conceive of an intervention by underground cultural producers in the academic project of archiving and "academicizing" the subcultural practices in which we participate. This zine hopes to ask: How do we conceive of a relationship between cultural producers and academics towards a mutual benefit, one that acknowledges that we occupy multiple roles in these conversations, and that sits in the contradiction of the University both as regulatory institution and liberatory project?
>
> The decision to interview academics and archivists concerning their work with zines arose both out of curiosity about the people doing work on the subject of zines, and from a desire to understand how academics interact with zine culture and zine makers. In addition, by positioning ourselves (the zine creators) as researcher, and the surveyed professors as researched, *Archiving the Underground* deconstructs the role of expert, creating the possibility of conversation rather than edict (the ability to "talk back"). We also seek to acknowledge through our methods, as many participants in this project did, that many of these so-called "experts" are also participants in zine culture, that in fact "minority subcultures...tend to be documented by former or current members of the subculture rather than 'adult' experts...[the] archivist or theorist and the cultural worker may also coexist in the same friendship networks, and they may function as co-conspirators."[1]

---

1    Judith Jack Halberstam, *In A Queer Time and Place: Transgender Bodies, Subcultural Lives* (New York: New

One question that came up throughout this project was: What exactly does it mean to be underground? Is it even possible to be outside of the mainstream? While in many ways it is impossible (and perhaps undesirable) to remove oneself from conversation with the "mainstream" or to remove oneself from some reliance on capitalist forms of consumption, what is most interesting and holds the most radical possibility is the way in which zine-makers and other subcultural producers *imagine* themselves as outside of the mainstream--the *desire* to be underground even if the actual possibility is limited. Thinking about the idea of "underground" culture, and its constant assimilation by the mainstream, one might (if they are as huge a nerd as Jenna) think of Gandalf's message to Frodo when he gives him the ring; "Keep it secret, keep it safe." Rather than buying into the notion that in order to be successful, zines must professionalize (in the words of QZAP co-founder Christopher Wilde, "grow up"), become glossy, and have huge print runs, zines cease to be as such when they gain too large a constituency, too professional a publisher, too famous an author, because once zines cease to be a "secret," hidden from the unblinking eye of the market, they can be reduced to advertising.

This anxiety is illustrated by the publication of and pushback (primarily by perzine authors) against the book *Fanzines*, by design professor Teal Triggs. Much of the controversy around this book hinges on discussions of copyright and permissions, a discomfort which has focused on the fact that *Fanzines* is a for-profit book (retailing for the steep list price of $40.00), put out by an (albeit independent) publishing house, and distributed at Barnes and Noble and Urban Outfitters, among other places. Concerns have also been expressed, for example by librarian and *Zine World* editor Jerianne Thompson, about multiple errors in the book—although *Fanzines* is not an academic work per se, Thompson and others fear that once a factual mistake is entered into the published record, it will be perpetuated in future zine scholarship.[2] Within zine communities, we see instances like Microcosm's new distribution criteria, which states that Microcosm will only publish the "most popular of zines" and requires distributed zines to sell at least 40 copies per issue per year in order to remain in the catalog. The collective's 2011 financial statement reads, "*Microcosm strives to add credibility to zine writers and their ethics.*"[3] The idea of credibility attached to increased market visibility is both in direct opposition to the idea of "cred" and makes us wonder why an ethic that disavows expertise, celebrity, and capital gain needs added credibility and from whom? These and other instances such as the seeming oxymoron of "famous zinesters" such as Aaron Cometbus (*Cometbus*) and Cindy Crabb (*Doris*) and the shift of zines such as *Bust* to glossy status, both undermines the idea of a perfect democracy within zine culture and tackles the

York University Press, 2005).
2    Jerianne Thompson, "Why I'm Mad About the New Fanzines Book," *Zine World*, February 10, 2011, http:// www.undergroundpress.org/zine-news/why-im-mad-about-the-new-fanzines-book/.
3    Microcosm, "2010 Financial Statement" Microcosm Publishing, January 27, 2011, http://microcosmpublish-ing.com/blogifesto/2011/01/2010-financial-statement.

concept of "selling out" in underground production. Jami Sailor writes in a blog entry:

> "For me, zines are about giving voice to people who may not have other mediums
> to express themselves, to see their voices (or others like theirs) in print. Zines are about
> individual stories, untold stories, and different points of view. I come from a zine culture
> where, and I know this opinion is not shared by all, someone's first zine is as important
> as their hundred and first zine. The zine community that I want to be a part of has no
> experts. There are no special guests. In the community I want to be a part of, no one's
> voice is more important than anyone else's, regardless of how many zines they have
> put out, how well they draw, which distro they run, or whether or not they are a good
> writer."[4]

Perzines in particular have been described as something between a magazine and a diary—when you hold a zine, you are being given a gift, the chance to "hear" the innermost thoughts of the zine's creator, as if they were whispering them in your ear. Zines are conduits for friendships, connections across space and time. To quote Alison Piepmeier, "The paper, then, is a nexus, a technology that mediates the connections not just of 'people' but of bodies. Paper facilitates affection."[5] Like a whispered secret, the truths that zines contain may be ephemeral. They shift and change from issue to issue, like the identities, situations and addresses of their creators. The danger in archiving individual issues of zines is that it cements a particular whisper. And the danger of publishing a book about zines is that you are projecting that whisper, far beyond its original and perhaps intended audience. When a cultural producer puts their work into the world, it takes on a voice of its own, an existence independent of its creator. But zines are often not widely available—when an academic publishes a critical paper on zines or a collection of excerpts from zines, readers of that academic work may not have access to the zines referenced. They would certainly not have access in the same way one would to a piece of canonical literature that is critically written about, so it is especially imperative that archives of subcultural productions include the voices and input of producers.

Through this project, we seek to support research methods which foster mutual aid and respect, which acknowledge that we are the experts of our own lives, and scholarship that both positions the author within their work and includes the voices of (often marginalized) subcultural producers. Additionally, we support archival methods that privilege the everyday and ephemeral, and acknowledge felt value as historical value. "The archivist of queer culture must proceed like the fan or collector whose attachment to objects is often fetishistic, idiosyncratic, or obsessional."[6]

---

4    Jami Sailor, "current frustrations." *Your Secretary Is Out*, December 16, 2010, http://yoursecretaryisout.
wordpress.com/2010/12/16/current-frustrations/.
5    Alison Piepmeier, *Girl Zines: Making Media, Doing Feminism* (New York: New York University Press 2009),
63.
6    Ann Cvetkovich, "In the Archives of Lesbian Feelings: Documentary and Popular Culture," *Camera Obscura*
49 (2002): 116.

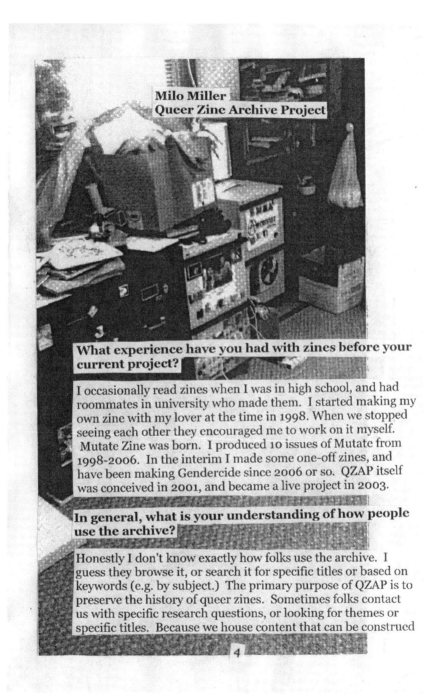

**Milo Miller
Queer Zine Archive Project**

**What experience have you had with zines before your current project?**

I occasionally read zines when I was in high school, and had roommates in university who made them. I started making my own zine with my lover at the time in 1998. When we stopped seeing each other they encouraged me to work on it myself. Mutate Zine was born. I produced 10 issues of Mutate from 1998-2006. In the interim I made some one-off zines, and have been making Gendercide since 2006 or so. QZAP itself was conceived in 2001, and became a live project in 2003.

**In general, what is your understanding of how people use the archive?**

Honestly I don't know exactly how folks use the archive. I guess they browse it, or search it for specific titles or based on keywords (e.g. by subject.) The primary purpose of QZAP is to preserve the history of queer zines. Sometimes folks contact us with specific research questions, or looking for themes or specific titles. Because we house content that can be construed as "dangerous" in many ways, we try not to look too hard at who is using the archive or for what purpose. Preserving anonymity of users has always been paramount to what we do.

**Can you speak more to the idea of "dangerous" materials and anonymity?**

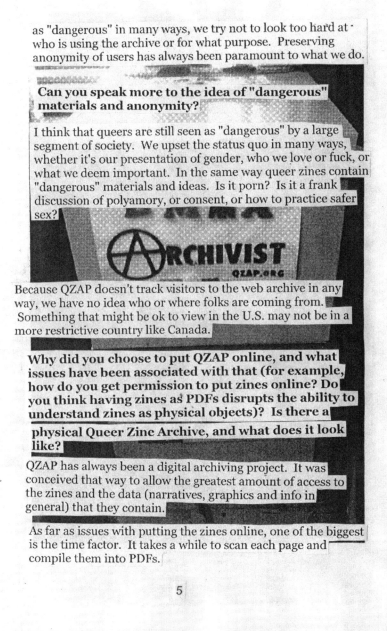

I think that queers are still seen as "dangerous" by a large segment of society. We upset the status quo in many ways, whether it's our presentation of gender, who we love or fuck, or what we deem important. In the same way queer zines contain "dangerous" materials and ideas. Is it porn? Is it a frank discussion of polyamory, or consent, or how to practice safer sex?

Because QZAP doesn't track visitors to the web archive in any way, we have no idea who or where folks are coming from. Something that might be ok to view in the U.S. may not be in a more restrictive country like Canada.

**Why did you choose to put QZAP online, and what issues have been associated with that (for example, how do you get permission to put zines online? Do you think having zines as PDFs disrupts the ability to understand zines as physical objects)? Is there a physical Queer Zine Archive, and what does it look like?**

QZAP has always been a digital archiving project. It was conceived that way to allow the greatest amount of access to the zines and the data (narratives, graphics and info in general) that they contain.

As far as issues with putting the zines online, one of the biggest is the time factor. It takes a while to scan each page and compile them into PDFs.

5

For permission, we do what we call "due diligence" in trying to contact zine makers to ask for permission to include their works in a digital form. Our Fair Use statement explains it best:

*"Because of the nature of zines, many of the materials are presented to the public as Anti-Copyright, Copy-Left, freely duplicatable, or more recently in the Creative Commons. Often zines are donated to us with the express purpose of digitization and reproduction. When we come across material that we believe fits into our archive we also perform due diligence as best we can in terms of contacting original authors and creators to ask permission to include their work in our archive. If you come across your work on the QZAP website and would like it to be removed, please contact us."*

I don't think that the PDF format is disruptive to understanding zines. I would feel very different if our archive were HTML, or a series of embedded images within a web page. That said all members of the QZAP collective continue to produce zines on paper, and we strongly encourage the practice.

**Do you think archiving zines creates a zine canon? If so, do you think this is a positive or negative process?**

I guess so. I think that said canon has existed for a long time, and archiving isn't the sole reason. Any documentation of an art or literary form does the same. With zines and self-publishing in general the canon can be anything. I think that's refreshing, and part of why zines are so cool. I see the archiving of zines, either as objects in a physical collection or in digital form as a positive process. Would you ask the same question of an art museum? :D

**After QZAP scans zines, what happens to them? Is there an organizational system for paper zines? Where do you keep them? Do you send them back to the author?**

It depends on the situation. Most zines are retained by QZAP. We try to keep them organized (both alpha by title, and alpha by title within a collection... more on that in a minute.) In some instances we've been leant zines to scan with the promise that we will send them back when we're finished.

6

As for keeping the zines themselves, currently the archive is in our dining room here in Milwaukee. A majority of them are in file folders stored in filing cabinets. The "general collection" as we refer to it contains zines given or sent to us by individuals, the initial collection of 350+ that we started QZAP with, and zines that we've picked up over the past 7.5 years. We've also got "named collections" (one more minute...) We've been working slowly but diligently toward having a physical space for QZAP that people could visit to read and make zines or do research.

**Do zines belong in archives? How do zines pose problems for archival standards such as provenance?**

Yes, I think zines belong in archives. They're a very important type of populist media and deserve preservation. Since I'm not a real librarian, I don't know what "provenance" means in this context.

**Jami Sailor on provenance: The question of provenance gets at the idea of ownership. In most archives collections are attributed to donors and reflect actual physical ownership of materials. Who do you see as the "owner" of the zines in QZAP? How does QZAPs collection transcend the idea of ownership by blending the physical/material with the digital? Are there special considerations surrounding the idea of ownership when dealing with zines (for example, the stink a few years ago concerning people reselling their collections on ebay)? How do you solicit donations and what does donor relations look like for QZAP?**

OK, so I'm going to start with "named collections." In several instances people have donated their whole zine collections to QZAP. In cases like this we ask the donor to name their collections, and we keep separate manifests and catalogs for them. Among our "named collections" we've got:

• The Emma Center collection from the old Emma Center infoshop in Minneapolis

7

• The Lane McKiernnen Collection donated by Lane who used to put out Quarter Inch Squares zine

• The Misty Minx Experience (I can't remember the name of the person who donated that, but that's what they asked the collection to be called)

• The Simon Strikeback collection (Simon is in Actor Slash Model and puts out Bound to Struggle zine)

In terms of "ownership" I guess QZAP or the QZAP Collective "owns" the physical media, and because of the way we approach Fair Use have felt that we're able to put zines online. We seek permission from the zine creators as best we can, but because of the ephemeral nature of zines we sometimes aren't able to always ask. In those cases we do the best we can, and honor requests to remove items from the digital archive. That doesn't happen very often, but we've had a few.

When scanning and preparing zines to go online we depaginate them so that they're harder to reproduce as original zines. We also provide access to them for free, so there's no question that we're taking someone else's work and making any money off of them.

Donor relations... basically we just ask people to give or send us their zines, or they'll contact us and ask how to donate. The expectation on bothe sides (zinester and QZAP) is that we have permission to add them to the digital archive unless otherwise noted. We send thank-you emails, and occasionally will pay for postage to help folks get zines to us. We'll also sometimes trade copies of *QZAP:meta* or send stickers and buttons to folks as a way of saying "thanks."

**Is there a zine hierarchy (particularly in terms of what zines get academic "credibility")?**

I personally don't think so. I think that it can be determined individually by the academic researcher or institution. IF they think that people in general have value in the world, then they

8

should also value the writing and creations of humans. If some people and their work is superequal or subequal then I imagine that the academy will use that as a determination of what work is credible.

**Many zinesters and other underground cultural producers operate under the assumption that academic "experts" will misrepresent, appropriate and commodify their work (Judith Halberstam writes about this in "What's that Smell? Queer Temporalities and Subcultural Lives"). Do you think this is a valid concern?**

I do think it's a concern, but shouldn't be an automatic assumption. I've had academics come to me and say "Zines are like newspapers, right?" Another case in point would be the current flap around Teal Triggs' book *Fanzines*, where the author used images from zines without seeking permission and miscrediting creators.

The flipside of that is where academics look at the medium, media being created, and creators and hit it dead on. I'm thinking of *Girl Zines: Making Media, Doing Feminism* by Alison Piepmeier and Andi Zeisler or Stephen Duncombe's *Notes from the Underground: Zines and the Politics of Alternative Culture.*
The commodification question is a bit trickier. I think that we as zinesters do that ourselves. We place value on these hand-crafted limited edition objects known as zines. We value them for lots of reasons, whether it's the stories and information contained within or the production values or aesthetic styles or our relationships with the people who create them. It follows that others who may not be within the "zine community" would also see zines as a commodity and recognize that there is value to them.

**How would you envision the relationship (real or ideal) between academics/archivists and underground artists and cultural producers?**

9

I think this question sets up a false dichotomy. Many folks
who are "cultural producers" are also academics and archivists
(this interview being a case in point.) I also think that at this
point in time, a lot of the research and archiving is happening
by folks who are already within the zine community. We've
decided that our work and our lives/experiences are valuable
and so we're making the effort to preserve and analyze them in
various ways. I think that this is happening both with and
outside of "the Academy" with lots of efforts being made by
unaffiliated or "indy" libraries and archives. QZAP is one
example of this, but there's also ZAPP in Seattle, the Denver
Zine Library, The Chicago Underground Library, Girl Zines A-
Go-Go and so on. Folks are also writing about their
experiences and research with zines *in* zines and on blogs and
in anthologies that get read by more and different folks than
would necessarily have access to a journal or institutional
press.

• • •

# LGBT Archives

*Queer Your Own History*

# Eternal Summer of the Black Feminist Mind:
## A Queer Ecological Approach to the Archive

*Alexis Pauline Gumbs*

"One thing we know as Black feminists is how important it is for us to recognize our own lives as herstory. Also as Black women, as Lesbians and feminists, there is no guarantee that our lives will *ever* be looked at with the kind of respect given to certain people from other races, sexes or classes. There is similarly no guarantee that we or our movement will survive long enough to become safely historical. We must document ourselves now." -Barbara and Beverly Smith
"I Am Not Meant to Be Alone and Without You Who Understand": Letters from Black Feminists 1972-1978 in *Conditions 4*

Survive long enough. One way to understand the impetus of the Black feminist independent publishing movement from the late 1970s to the early 1990s in the United States, Canada, and the United Kingdom is as a safeguard against the predicted failure of the archive to document the lives and political work of Black feminists. And while important community, public, and university-based archives prioritize diverse approaches to feminist history issues of funding, access and representation remain. Ultimately, documenting Black feminism *is* activism.

The Eternal Summer of the Black Feminist Mind is inspired by the mandate of late 20$^{th}$ century Black feminists to end the interlocking oppressions of capitalism, racism, sexism, heteropatriarchy and all related oppressions and to enact, respect and celebrate a meaning of life that teaches that all life is interdependent. [1] It is a "by every means necessary" educational approach, accountable to the community, that uses potlucks, partnerships with community organizations, social media networks, podcasts, buttons, t-shirts, videos, public access TV and sidewalk chalk to create spaces for conversations about how critical engagement with the legacy of Black feminism can inform a plethora of social movements and interested learners in the present and beyond.

Emphasizing "summer" as a queer time and space imagined as outside of the academic calendar and the strictures of "school," this article elaborates on the ecological approach that the Eternal Summer of the Black Feminist Mind takes to growing the presence, impact and collective memory of Black Feminism in the progressive and popular consciousness. The Eternal Summer of the Black Feminist Mind is invented and reinvented by people without formal training in library science (though we are excited that some participants are in library science school right now!). Therefore, this engagement, which is meant to converse with other community archivists and expand

---

1   Eternal Summer of the Black Feminist Mind website: http://blackfeministmind.wordpress.com/

the meaning of the activity of archiving by creating a record through letters to some of the living and deceased Black feminist activists whose work survives in the Eternal Summer, is a description of the Eternal Summer of the Black Feminist Mind as an educational project, and a treatise about our ecological approach.

### Dear Audre,[2]

The Summer of Our Lorde was an experiment borne of my initiation in the implications of your work, my critique of exclusively academic, and therefore canonized, conversations about knowledge production, and a desire to talk about the depth of your work with people who treasure your words for their own excessive, drastic and desirable reasons. For one summer, for three months, I set up potluck gatherings in partnership with three different organizations:

• UBUNTU-a women of color survivor led coalition to end gendered violence and create sustaining transformative love founded in Durham, NC, in the midst of the Duke Lacrosse Rape Case
• SpiritHouse- an arts based cultural activism organization organizing in Durham, NC to empower those most impacted by the prison industrial complex
• Southerners on New Ground a regional queer liberation organization rooted in working class communities and communities of color which was headquartered in Durham, NC, at the time and is now based in Atlanta, GA

People gathered to read three of your essays. Who knew that an integrated reading practice would encourage people to bring their best minds and their best food, to engage your words as if they could save their lives and transform their communities? Maybe you knew that already from your participation in the Black Feminist Retreats that the Combahee River Collective organized in the 1970s. The phrase from your 1983 essay "Black Women, Hatred and Anger" that "we can learn to mother ourselves" takes on a life of its own, showing up as a resource for a new approach to racial justice, food justice, economic justice, immigration rights, and queer liberation discussions in this city and everywhere that people read blogs. Maybe you could have predicted that, knowing how portable poetry is, how intimately and promiscuously it travels from our lips to where it needs to go.

And maybe it shouldn't have been a surprise that in a university/plantation town,

---

2   Audre Lorde, self-identified Black lesbian feminist poet warrior and mother was one of the most acclaimed poets of the late 20th century and an iconic figure in the second wave feminist movement and the Black lesbian feminist movement. She was also an educator trained in library science at Columbia University. Her analyses of difference and power laid the groundwork for third wave feminist critique and has inspired many queer people of color. The Audre Lorde Project, a queer and trans people of color organization in New York and the ALORDE collective, a Black lesbian health collective in Detroit, are two manifestations of her ongoing legacy. Audre Lorde died of cancer in 1992.

no one would want the summer to end. But they didn't. After August, people in the grocery store, in the street, and in the middle of a meeting about something else would ask, when is the next gathering? When? When? It became clear that summer was not over, and that you, "our Lorde," had a sacred role in the lives of our community. You became our Lorde of an awakened need and a renewed faith in the practice of gathering, breaking bread and turning over words in our open mouths and our outstretched hands. The Eternal Summer of the Black Feminist Mind potluck series was born from uplifting texts by Claudia Jones, the black communist feminist, from Octavia Butler, the black feminist prophet, from the very same Combahee River Collective.

I wonder what ideas you thought would emerge in your name. I wonder how you feel about all of this, if you had hints of it while you were living your life everyday and sharing it like a sacred text, and rewriting it like a palimpsest. People believe in you, you know. Your words register beyond the intellectual. Queer Black Sunday school, a place to study the sacred texts of your letters to Joseph Beam, and eventually the School of Our Lorde, a night school in your name, allows people who follow you as poets, teachers, activists and publishers to embrace a collaborative methodology, to learn from your victories and your mistakes.

When you used to write letters reflecting on the Black Feminist Retreats to Cheryl Clarke to redistribute you would enclose money for the postage and photocopies that you knew it took to keep the conversation going. I wonder what you would think now of our multimediated community of donors and participants, of the School of Our Lorde webinars and social-network facilitated satellite campuses. I wonder if you imagined that so many people would follow your example, sending small amounts of money towards a collective vision. In a now famous poem that you enclosed "for all of us" in one of your letters to the Black Feminist Retreat participants through Cheryl, you pointed out that "we were never meant to survive." I saw that letter in the Black Gay and Lesbian Archive in the Schomburg Library in New York where Cheryl Clarke, still active, has donated her papers. In this instant and this triumph. I wonder what you would say if you could see the specific ways that your work and the work of other Black feminist activists survives. This instant and this triumph. I ultimately believe that you are smirking and instigating this intimate manifestation everyday.

Love,

Lex

## I. Eternal Summer of the Black Feminist Mind

The Eternal Summer of the Black Feminist Mind is based in, accountable to, and in love with Durham, North Carolina, a post-industrial southern city in a state with a history of plantation slavery, a contemporary practice of exploiting and targeting migrant workers. Something is happening here that has been happening for too long. Something new is also happening here.

Durham, as a city, has a large Black working class population, a growing Latino population and also a history of Black wealth as defined in the destructive capitalist sense and also as defined in the subversive sense that Nikki Giovanni proposes when she says "Black love is Black wealth."[3] Durham is also a university city with a history of plantation slavery and migrant exploitation. Although the content of the labor required by the university is for the most part different in content from the labor of the plantations, with the most marked similarities being the domestic facilities and grounds-keeping labor performed by non-unionized workers, the similarities in form between the university and the plantation system as organizing structures, and the fact that local Durham residents refer to Duke University, the largest employer in the city as "the plantation" tells an important story about the reproduction of oppression in the New South iteration of Durham, North Carolina. The Eternal Summer of the Black Feminist Mind is accountable to these local conditions and seeks to fortify the loving and dynamic relationship between contemporary visionaries and the legacy of Black feminist activism, creativity and thought, specifically through the creation of ritual educational spaces that invite the participation of Black feminist ancestors.

The ground that nurtures the Eternal Summer of the Black Feminist Mind's perpetual growth and expression through media, educational interactions and interactive research is a transformative activist and organizing community, watered in particular by the women of color, sex workers, survivors of sexual violence, queer and gender queer people and allies who created UBUNTU, a coalition dedicated to ending all gendered violence through the intentional creation of a communal practice of sustaining transformative love.[4] It is also supported by a network of collectives, organizations, and projects committed to racial and economic justice, abolishing the prison industrial complex, growing community-raised healthy food, an intersectional approach to queer liberation, and the creation of a people's Durham led by working class women of color. The premise of the Eternal Summer of the Black Feminist Mind and its "by every means necessary" approach is the belief that Black feminist educators, community organizers, writers, and scholars are evidence of a spiritual reality, a revised meaning of life that not only challenges, but also implies an alternative to the deadliness of capitalism.

The Eternal Summer riffs on and points out global warming, peak oil, and the cumulative friction of a global capitalist machine that expends life for profit as evidence that a different meaning of life is necessary now. The good news, or gospel, of the Eternal Summer of the Black Feminist Mind is that BLACK FEMINISM LIVES as a spiritual practice, a political legacy and a critical intersectional possibility that people of all backgrounds and experiences have the opportunity to be transformed by when they get with it.

---

3   Nikki Giovanni, "Nikki-Rosa" from *Black Feeling, Black Talk, Black Judgment*, 1968.
4   UBUNTU is named for an African concept emphasizing the importance of relationships, essentially translated as "I am what I am because of who we all are."

The Eternal Summer of the Black Feminist Mind is revolutionary because it models what is possible in community as transformation. In much the way that the very existence of maroon communities where Africans who had escaped slavery in the Caribbean and Latin America was an alternative space of Black freedom that inspired enslaved Africans trapped on plantations to rise up and rebel, the Eternal Summer of the Black Feminist Mind provides loving transformative spaces and technologies sustained by the brilliance of the oppressed genius communities to which we are accountable. The *Eternal Summer* hopes to inspire those working for necessary change within the non-profit industrial complex to remember that we do not need to wait for or pander to foundation funding or a corporately validated organizational structure to create what we need. The most radical danger is here in the already existing genius of oppressed people, constrained by a system that devalues that genius.

We believe that all of that brilliance is available under the right circumstances. Or as Jamaican theorist Sylvia Wynter says "the ceremony must be found."[5] Therefore time is the most valued resource in the ecology of the Eternal Summer of the Black Feminist Mind. Ancestral time, time as community, intentional time, and time across space are what make the Eternal Summer of the Black Feminist Mind eternal. Our time together is sacred. "We were never meant to survive."[6]

*Ancestral Time:* This means both setting intentional time for ancestor attention *and* an understanding of time that acknowledges the presence of all the energy that ever has been. I wake up at five o'clock in the morning, when no one else is interested in speaking to me, specifically to listen for what long noticed or newly announced ancestors will demand, suggest or make known. Kifu Faruq, Eternal Summer of the Black Feminist Mind participant, sustainer and community food justice worker, calls this practice being present to the "dream download." These ancestors often bring specific instructions, exciting possibilities, and new details for how all of our dreams are possible. This practice provides a miraculous clarity to an eternal day.

*Time as Community:* This means creating sacred and regular times to gather as community and also that our connections and accountability to each other is what makes our brilliance influential and eternal. Along with the energy of our ancestors, the loving energy of the community, the way we bring our whole selves into the room with a spirit of play, and desired intimacy for transformation is another key resource of the Eternal Summer of the Black Feminist Mind. This is what makes it summer, the heat (sometimes literal) of our bodies in the space.

The Eternal Summer of the Black Feminist Mind is eternal because it is inter-generational. We are learning to create child-inclusive, parent-supportive spaces. We have consistent participation from elders and babies who remind us to improvise and be present.

---

5    'The *Ceremony* Must Be Found: After Humanism' Boundary II, 12:3 & 13:1, (Spring/Fall 1984): 19-70.
6    Audre Lorde, "A Litany for Survival" *The Black Unicorn*, 1978, 31.

The participants own and fund the projects in many ways. Participation itself is the most valuable contribution. Participants and supporters also donate food, shoe racks and coat racks, tea and childcare, reiki sessions, photocopies and art supplies, advice, money (literally enough to sustain the rent and utilities of the Inspiration Station where I already lived), documenting and spreading the word.[7] The ecology of the Eternal Summer of the Black Feminist Mind is ever evolving and folks self-identify their contributions. Many of the most important parts of our interactions are non-verbal. We breathe the presence of our ancestors. They join us in celebration and in warning.

The Eternal Summer process is an ongoing lesson in what is and is not sustainable. Tobacco, the plantation crop that was once the economic base of our city was replaced by gentrified post-tobacco processing plant lofts, and appropriated and commodified knowledge and culture for sale. Durham is a place where we trained ourselves to grow a plant that we cannot eat in order to transform each other into cancer and then built the premier cancer treatment center without functionally shifting the plantation economy of the region. There is much unlearning to do here. The Eternal Summer, a tiny grassroots educational project literally next to a huge university, is an experiment in what nourishment might feel like. We therefore find it important not to get carried away from our routes by trends in the funding world and we take care to make sure that our engagement with national and international contexts is grounded in our local timelines and processes. This is another way of staying present. I am often reminded of this in direct, cosmic, physical and spiritual ways.

*Time Across Space:* We understand our work here as intimately related to a transformation happening at the level of the planet. Our DIY multi-media work through podcasts, a nationally syndicated public access TV presence, online videos, the School of Our Lorde webinars and social networking sites are designed to be intimate, portable space, useful for *and transformed by* communities that are inspired by our work in Durham and accountable to their own local conditions. (And by DIY we mean for real do-it-yourself. There has been no purchase of software for media creation so far.)

In the tradition of Ida B. Wells, Kitchen Table Press, and radical women of color bloggers, we use every means necessary to make our love accessible to our wider community of comrades and kindred spirits. We are thrilled by the resonance and participation that folks around the United States and world have found in these projects that we created out of ancestral inspiration and our own local specific necessity. When we had the "Summer of Our Lorde" and read an essay by Audre Lorde and had discussion potlucks every month, like-minded people participated through the blog and had their own gatherings in the Bay Area, New York, Chicago and DC and some folks even continued with an Autumn of (Gloria) Anzaldúa. The School of Our Lorde (a night school in my living room in Durham) has satellite campuses in Tuscaloosa,

---

7    The Inspiration Station is a residential rental in the first intentionally integrated neighborhood in Durham, NC, around the corner from the childhood home of Black feminist Pauli Murray.

Chicago, New York, and Fayetteville, NC, and webinar participants as far away as the Rio Grande Valley and Cairo. Queer feminist organizers in Beruit, Lebanon (Meem); Nairobi, Kenya (Fahamu) and Chennai, India (the Shakti Center) are using the multimedia educational tools and versions of the practices to support their own amazing and specific work! Long distance lovers all over the world also donate to Eternal Summer, mobilize resources at their school, job, or organization to hire me to do a workshop, lecture or training, buy educational materials, donate proofreading, share connections, and give abundant advice, and love.

### Dear June,[8]

We just finished the first unit of the Juneteenth Freedom Academy on the methodology of Angry Letters and Protest Poems that you practiced so passionately, so brilliantly, sometimes so recklessly. I had more anger than I knew about, I was not fully prepared for how sharp anger can be, how intentional we have to be so that the anger is released instead of settling in our cells like cancer, how careful we have to be that our anger unleashed does not slice the opening throats of our comrades. The next unit is about Palestine, about your insistence on the liberation of Palestine, and your campaign to make the impact of U.S. support for Israeli imperialism against Palestine, Jordan and Lebanon visible. I am excited that so many people are ready to gather in your name. That your example can inspire people to think about solidarity with Palestinian women, and Arab women in general in this time of intense anti-Arab racism as a black feminist act, with a history, your specific legacy.

The June Jordan Saturday Survival School for families in Durham was like you, present, intense, sometimes unpredictable, but very, very clear. Queer families of color gathered to read all of your children's books and present about them to each other. They even drew a rotating mural that is still in the hallway of the Inspiration Station. This mural illustrates their visual interpretations of the theories about children's literature that you expressed in your talk at Berkeley about "The Creative Spirit" and children's literature, which I found at the Schlesinger archive, and your talk at the Howard Writer's Conference in 1971 called "Towards a Survival Literature for Afrikan Children," which Lucille Clifton saved. She was on the same panel, and it ended up in her boxes of papers that are housed at Emory University's Manuscript and Rare Book Library. And listen to how these relationships remake themselves across time: it turns out that in every family that participated in the June Jordan Saturday Survival School, at least one adult was a survivor of childhood sexual abuse. Lucille Clifton, who kept your essay, was a survivor of childhood sexual abuse too, and as you know, she wrote about

---

8    June Jordan was a self-identified bisexual Black feminist poet essayist and teacher. She was the author of several books for children, young people and adults and was the founder of the Poetry of the People curriculum at UC Berkeley. She was also a noted peace activist in solidarity with women in Palestine and Nicaragua.

it in her poetry, and like you, she wrote brave children's books, the Everett Anderson Series that spoke about the problems that children face and their solutions in a brave, nuanced and affirming way. I know you weren't into ALL of Lucille's children's books, because I've read your reviews in the *New York Times*, but the Everett Anderson books seem to really take on the "Survival Literature" model you proposed. And your idea of survival and your connection of that term to environmental accountability COMPLETELY informs the ecological approach of Eternal Summer of the Black Feminist Mind. And because you were brave enough to write about your experience of physical abuse in *Soldier*, and because Lucille Clifton was brave enough to write about surviving sexual abuse from her father we are now in the midst of the Lucille Clifton ShapeShifter Survival School, an intergenerational process informed by the work of organizations including Generation Five, INCITE! Women of Color Against Violence, and projects like the Atlanta Transformative Justice Collaborative where we are using poetry and storytelling to look at and hopefully end cycles of physical and sexual child abuse in our families and communities, and to end gendered violence period.

Look at what your bravery has made possible. Thank you for speaking your truth.

Love always,

Lex

## II. An Ecological Approach: A Treatise

In a time when the planet is preparing to stop tolerating our collectively destructive relationship to life resources and the future, the Eternal Summer of the Black Feminist Mind is a specific example of how to orchestrate an intimate, influential, profound and living feminist praxis. What the project itself exemplifies is an ecological approach based on the principles that: we have what we need (each other); everything is useful, everyone is priceless; we are part of a larger environment that we can relate to symbiotically or destructively; our ecology includes spiritual, physical, practical, social, emotional, technological and intellectual resources.

We offer an ecological approach as a necessary alternative to an economic approach to the planet that reifies capitalism as a resource model, and disrespects the vitality of other resources, especially spiritual and emotional resources and the wisdom of oppressed people. This approach is very much informed by an approach called organic pragmatism wherein participants co-design curriculum and programming, developed and practiced by SpiritHouse, a Durham-based social justice arts organization.[9]

*An ecological approach is beautiful.* It matters whether we face each other in a circle or stand shoulder to shoulder in a line. Spiritual leader, scholar and transnational feminist activist Jacqui Alexander teaches that the spirit responds to an aesthetic. Three-year old spiritual teacher and gender queer baby Jibs (an Eternal Summer participant), practices

---

9  For more about SpiritHouse see www.spirithouse-nc.org

this truth by ritually granting each person in our circle a hug and a kiss at transitional moments in our gatherings. We understand the way we organize ourselves as a creative process, with shapes, visuals, and rhythmic and sonic resonances. In other words, any structure is an expression of an aesthetic that may or may not serve our vision, invite our ancestors or allow energy to flow. An ecological approach means being artists with our lives, our relationships and our organizing such that energy and inspiration move through us. What this looks like, feels like, sounds like, will be different in particular areas of our shared environment and will evolve.

*An ecological approach is accountable.* Because we know that we need each other, and that everything is useful and everyone is priceless, an ecological approach must be accountable to communities and individuals in specific ways.

*Account (a story):* In order to be accountable, it is key to create safe, sacred, informal and regular spaces for the people we are accountable to share their stories or *give an account* of their experiences, visions and insights. People may give accounts through food preparation, song, text messages, body language, showing up or not showing up. The forms that we create and listen for participation must be as multiple as we are.

*Account (a reckoning of resources):* Accountability also means knowing that the people own the project. In an educational project it means remembering that all knowledge belongs to the people. In an activist project it means remembering that the power for transformation lives inside the people. In a practical sense it means the project is owned, supported, co-created by, and transparent with the community it nurtures and grows within. This is very different from giving an account (a.k.a. a grant report) to an outside funding source. The life source of a transformative community project is obviously that same transformative community, ancestors included. A funding source that sees itself as separate can disrupt our relationship to our life source. However when the viability of a project depends on the people activating resources, literally feeding each other, looking for ways to mobilize or siphon resources from their jobs, supporting the project with money that is in no way disposable, the project has to be accountable. We will not sustain a project that we do not see as nourishing in our everyday lives.

Accountability activates us.

*An ecological approach is reflective.* This means studying the herstories in which we are grounded, and by which we are inspired. And also means cultivating a loving practice of self-criticism that remembers that our relationship to the planet is in need of transformation. As poets Alixa and Naima of Climbing Poetree remind us, "raindrops let go, become the ocean."[10] We are mostly water, so is the planet. The world will only transform to the extent that we ourselves transform. This applies individually to each of us and also to what we create collectively. Our organizations, projects, and initia-

---

10    Climbing Poetree, *Hurricane Season: The Hidden Messages in Water*, National Tour 2006-11.

tives are only transformative if they transform. So we honor our vision of a radically different world when we let go of ego and organizational ownership and embrace our purpose in relationship to something much greater than ourselves. Transformation means letting go of who we thought we were, facing painful experiences and our own practices that harm each other. This will almost definitely involve tears.

*An ecological approach means staying rooted.* If we are accountable to and interdependent with our community as an environment, we must also acknowledge that we have the capability to disrupt or harm our eco-system with behaviors that forget or disrespect our interconnection. This means staying, even when it is hard, and transforming our relationships instead of pretending that we can sever them. We cannot live without each other; our connections persist even across death.

*An ecological approach is long-term.* The intentional practice of growing a vision for a lovingly transformational way of life in an economic system that seeks to make our lives and love unthinkable feels ambitious and risky. It is actually as simple as remembering who we are, what life is, and acting accordingly, for the rest of our lives…and with an intergenerationally accountable relationship to the future with us always. Revealing the world we need and deserve within the world we have is an everyday practice of unlearning what we think we know and becoming present to how the miraculous future is already evident here.

# Accessibility, Accountability, and Activism:
## Models for LGBT Archives

### Angela L. DiVeglia

"From my involvement in this work, I have been struck by the active interrelation-ships among lesbians and gay activists, archivists, and scholars. Each of these groups contributes to creating historical records, to finding materials that should be preserved, to placing them in an archival home, and to interpreting and telling the stories of our lives. Queer history is created by networks of people."
Brenda Marston, "Archivists, Activists, and Scholars"[1]

"History saves lives by validating lesbian, gay, and queer peoples' right to live a full and rich life free from oppression and censure."
Elise Chenier, "Preserving Lesbian Oral History in Canada"[2]

Responding to the growing scholarly interest in queer studies, as well as the grow-ing historical interest in LGBT history and culture, an increasing number of archives are documenting the LGBT community.[3] While outreach methods used with other potential donors—telephone calls and meetings, "show and tell" events, or institutional tours—are appropriate for some segments of the LGBT population, they can fail to address the unique concerns of many other potential LGBT donors. From increased privacy needs to an inherent distrust of large institutions, the desires and goals of mem-bers of the LGBT community who possess personal papers or organizational records may differ from other potential donors. This article, and the larger study from which it stems, begins a conversation within the archival community about questions that affect all repositories building collections of LGBT materials: Are these donors distinct from other donors, including those from other marginalized groups, and if so, how? What are the concerns of this population, and why are they choosing or refusing to deposit their materials in an archives? What models can community archives offer, and what

---

1   B. J. Marston, "Archivists, Activists, and Scholars: Creating a Queer History," in *Daring to Find our Names: The Search for Lesbigay Library History*, ed. J. V. Carmichael, Jr., (Westport, Conn.: Greenwood Press, 1998), 139.
2   E. Chenier, "Hidden from Historians: Preserving Lesbian Oral History in Canada," *Archivaria* 68, (2009): 265
3   LGBT is an acronym standing for Lesbian, Gay, Bisexual, and Transgendered. (Transgendered refers to individuals who identify with a gender other than that assigned to them at birth.) This acronym can appear in other forms, such as GLBT (Gay, Lesbian, Bisexual, and Transgendered), LGBTQ (Lesbian, Gay, Bisexual, Transgendered, and Queer/Questioning), or LGBTTQI (Lesbian, Gay, Bisexual, Transgendered, Transsexual, Queer, and Intersex). The term queer may also appear in this article; while once a derogatory term, many (especially younger) members of the LGBT community may use it positively to refer to people of sexualities or gender identities outside of the heterosexual, male/female norm. Queer is generally considered to be more inclusive—and also more politically charged—than the term LGBT. Although I hope to include anyone who identifies with this community, for the purposes of this article I will refer to the population as LGBT.

are the opportunities for cooperative relationships between formal and community archives? Focusing on the latter question, this article examines community archives as alternatives to formal archives, and also explores how community archives meet the needs of the LGBT population—and how formal archives can follow suit.

## The study

This article includes selections from a longer study on LGBT archival donors' motivations and concerns, and their implications for outreach. Research took the form of a case study of the Sallie Bingham Center for Women's History and Culture in the David M. Rubenstein Rare Book & Manuscript Library at Duke University. A series of flexible, in-depth interviews were conducted, focusing on topics such as privacy, trust, accountability, and activism within archives. Interviewees included Laura Micham, the Director of the Bingham Center; Mandy Carter, a civil rights and LGBT activist whose papers are housed at the Bingham Center; and four potential donors who are LGBT community activists living in the southeastern United States. Each potential donor has personal papers, organizational records, or other collections that fall within the parameters of the Bingham Center's collection policy. Each interviewee participated in one interview, conducted between February and June of 2010.

For purposes of privacy, potential donors are not identified by name in this article; instead, their comments are credited with alpha-numeric identifiers (PD1 – PD4).

## Archives and power

To understand the goals of community archives and the structures that some LGBT community members (and some archivists) aim to subvert, let us first discuss the relationship between archives and power.

While many library employees think of themselves as great supporters of freedom, and while the American Library Association focuses on the freedom to read and the privacy of library users, librarians and archivists still work within bureaucratic settings and act as cultural enforcers. The structures of these organizations ultimately restrict employees' actions, as "bureaucracies and institutions reward employees for not bringing attention to themselves, not asking embarrassing questions, and not articulating long-range implications of silence about the major issues of our time."[4]

On the most concrete level, archives can be construed as instruments of power inasmuch as they are frequently associated with universities or state/federal governments. Through this alignment with decision-making institutions, archives can be

---

4   J. Cooper "Librarians as Cultural Enforcers," in, *Daring to Find our Names: The Search for Lesbigay Library History*, ed. J. V. Carmichael, Jr. (Westport, Conn.: Greenwood Press, 1998), 114.

seen as enforcing the status quo in terms of representation, oppression, visibility, and access. Additionally, archivists themselves exercise significant power through the ability to determine significance (or lack thereof) by selection, description, interpretation, provision of access, reference services, public programming, exhibits, outreach efforts, and collection-building. The archivist, describing collections by determining access points such as subject headings in a catalog record, bears significant power over how and why materials will be used by researchers. For instance, a collection bearing the subject heading "Female friendship" will receive very different use than one bearing the subject heading "Lesbian relationships."

Within the brokered relationship between the researcher and the document, the archivist holds ultimate sway; aside from playing an integral role in the often-complex archival research process by identifying potentially useful collections and helping the user to navigate finding aids and other access tools, the archivist must also physically retrieve the document and deliver it to the researcher: the researcher must essentially ask for the archivist's permission to access documents. With a nod to Foucault's discussion of the panopticon,[5] Maynard notes that the physical layout of the archive itself further enforces this power, by ordering "individuals in space so as to create a generalized and constant surveillance."[6] Surveillance in archives can include physical observation by archives staff, video monitoring, and searching of researchers' belongings.

While all interviewees expressed that archives play an essential role in the documentation of LGBT history, many also expressed an awareness of or discomfort with the power imbued in the function of value creation, as well as in the role of steward or gatekeeper. PD2 (one of the potential donors, referred to as PD1 − PD4) explicitly discussed the physical space of archives, with the hierarchy of archivist over researcher reflected in the physical layout of the research room:

"First of all, you have to ask someone who's a professional, who's automatically an 'other,' unless you yourself are a librarian or an academic. So you have to ask permission, and you have to know what you're asking for... There's a desk. And there's a person on the other side who's the expert, and you're the layperson... that automatically creates hierarchy. That feels very different from going into a community space where everyone, hopefully, ... is on the same level."

Particularly for activists who are working to eliminate hierarchies within their own communities, non-hierarchical spaces can feel more comfortable.

A deep discomfort with needing to ask "permission" to view potentially sensitive materials will be especially acute if the archivist does not appear to be part of the LGBT community or seem visibly sympathetic. Huffine notes, "it is always uncomfortable to approach someone different from oneself in some sensitive fundamental way... for

---

5    See Foucault, Michel. "The punitive society," in *The essential works of Foucault, 1954-1984*.
6    S. Maynard, "Police/Archives," *Archivaria* 68, (2009): 168.

help, and this is especially true in libraries."[7] Even researchers who are not members of the LGBT community may feel discomfort requesting sexually explicit materials or materials that they believe the archivist may consider controversial.

Understanding that archives can be construed as an instrument of power, one begins to understand the complex and often uneasy relationship between archives and marginalized or oppressed communities. Additionally, as many members of marginalized communities (not unrealistically) conflate archives with universities and the state, their mistrust of the state as a tool of repression transfers to a general mistrust of all powerful institutions as extensions of the government.[8]

Members of the LGBT community often take one of two approaches to dealing with the uneven power dynamics inherent in the structure of archives: either they subvert the power structures in order to re-build and reclaim them, or they build their own, more democratic or non-hierarchical alternatives. Using LGBT models to disrupt power structures is a central element of queer theory, resulting in the use of "queer" as more than just a reclamation of a once-derogatory term, but also as a verb, meaning to disrupt, subvert, or consider in alternate ways. This subversion can be seen in instances ranging from the homosexualizing of authority figures in gay erotica[9] to the creation of extensive oral history projects where the interviewer strives to eradicate the typical researcher-research subject dichotomy.[10] Numerous articles refer to "queering archives" as a process of recreating the foundations of archival practice, such as Gentile's "Resisted Access?"[11] Others describe LGBT subversion of archival practice using more playful terms, such as Topher Campbell's comment that "There's always a bit of mischievousness in us. rukus! [a black, queer archive in the United Kingdom] is the finger up at the same time as the embrace and the kiss... We're not far away from the punk generation of the seventies, so there's a kind of shiftiness and abrasiveness about the way that we are."[12]

Interviewees offered examples of the subversion of existing power structures through the construction and maintenance of LGBT archives. PD3 noted that while archives can reinforce problematic historical power dynamics, "part of that process of truth and reconciliation is figuring out how to interrogate and break down that power and democratize its use." Laura Micham, director of the Sallie Bingham Center, described the potential subversiveness of documenting social movements at what may seem like a highly traditional institution of higher education. "Duke might appear to be a super-

---

7    R. L. Huffine, "Social Responsibility and Acceptable Prejudice," in *Daring to Find our Names: The Search for Lesbigay Library History*, ed. J. V. Carmichael, Jr. (Westport, Conn.: Greenwood Press, 1998), 213-214.

8    M. Barriault, "Hard to Dismiss: The Archival Value of Gay Male Erotica and Pornography," *Archivaria* 68, (2009): 219-246.

9    Ibid., 238.

10    Chenier, "Hidden from Historians: Preserving Lesbian Oral History in Canada," *Archivaria* 68, (2009): 251.

11    P. Gentile, "Resisted Access? National Security, the Access to Information Act, and Queer(ing) Archives." *Archivaria* 68, (2009): 141-158.

12    A. X, T. Campbell, & M. Stevens. "Love and Lubrication in the Archives, or Rukus!: A Black Queer Archive for the United Kingdom," *Archivaria* 68, (2009): 292-293.

traditional, white, heterosexual male place, but if you can fill it with boundary-crossers and people who transgress in positive ways, then you can use the substantial resources that might have caused the power inequity to begin with to remedy it."

Part of the interrogation of power mentioned by PD3 is the explicit acknowledgment of historical power relationships. PD1 mentioned the need for universities to openly and directly address power relationships with marginalized communities that they now wish to document.

> "I think there's a lot of distrust, and I think that it's justified... A lot of people understand their archival legacy to be a version of their life, and some people, because of their politics, wouldn't want to spend their lives affiliated to [a particular] organization, so the logic goes that they wouldn't want their legacy on paper to be there, either... I think that those institutions need to really think about that and address that."

With that in mind, however, she also pointed out that once we exit the theoretical realm, all people have some affiliation with institutions like nation-states, and that sometimes compromises are necessary to "allow some kind of version of survival" and visibility.

## Community (and) archives

Through the creation of extensive community archives, LGBT community members not only "queer" the practice of existing archives, but also subvert the entire notion that only professionals can adequately document history. Community archives are housed within the community that created them—this location is geographical, but also means that they are designed, run, and staffed by the same group whose history they document. Founded in response to the dearth of documentation representing non-mainstream lives within archives and libraries, community archives are essentially the formalization of personal, grassroots-level collecting.[13] LGBT community archives are widespread throughout North America, with some of the largest and most well-known including the Lesbian Herstory Archives in New York, the Canadian Gay and Lesbian Archive in Toronto, the Gerber/Hart Library in Chicago, and the ONE Institute and Archives in West Hollywood. Community archives play an important role in the larger LGBT community; not only do they provide an alternative to often exclusionary archives, but they also allow a greater focus on community- and identity-building through the reclamation and self-production of history.

History itself plays a very specific role within identity-building in oppressed communities, as a move to claim and occupy space. Bill Lukenbill remarks that "identities are developed through experience, and the community of identity is constituted through historical experience.... Gay and lesbian libraries and archives... are needed to help

---

13    B. B. Parris, "Creating, Reconstructing, and Protecting Historical Narratives: Archives and the LBGT Community," *Current Studies in Librarianship*, 29, no. 1/2 (2005): 5-25.

define and clarify historical experiences."[14] As part of a desire to build identity and create an activism of visibility, many LGBT groups have built community archives to counter the historical silencing and obscuring of LGBT histories.[15]

Additionally, community archives frequently serve as community spaces, with room for meetings and comfortable space for relaxing or browsing materials. This communal space allows people to come together and also to meet and connect with others who share their values or lifestyles. Rothbauer discusses the role of LGBT bookstores, where "investing in a vibrant local literary community was... a way to enact a public and shared understanding of what it meant to claim a lesbian or queer identity."[16] Rothbauer's study focuses specifically on the act of reading in creating LGBT identity in young women, but notes that her participants "recognized and valued the guidance and support of people who acted as role models and gatekeepers to gay and lesbian culture."[17] Archivists can, and often do, fulfill this same role in the community; while creating a sense of historicity through collection-development and cooperation through less-hierarchical archival repositories, they also serve as role models and active participants in the development of LGBT culture and community.

Since many LGBT community archives have open stacks or items on display in reading areas, visitors are surrounded by representations of LGBT culture and varied images of LGBT identity and lifestyle. Just as Pecoskie describes how lesbian women develop a sense of community and perform social exploration through reading, so do visitors to community archives develop a sense of a larger community through interaction with varied representations of LGBT culture (including documents from people outside of their immediate social circles) and perform social exploration through interaction with various representations of what it can mean to live as an LGBT individual.[18]

The role of social learning in developing a concept of a larger "imagined community" can be especially important for young people or people who are just joining the LGBT community.[19] Not only do new community members   rely on social learning

---

14    B. Lukenbill, "Modern Gay and Lesbian Libraries and Archives in North America: A Study in Community Identity and Affirmation," *Library Management* 23, no. 1/2 (2002): 95.

15    Parris, "Creating, Reconstructing, and Protecting Historical Narratives: Archives and the LBGT Community," 5-25.

16    P. Rothbauer, "'People Aren't Afraid Anymore, but it's Hard to Find Books': Reading Practices that Inform the Personal and Social Identities of Self-identified Lesbian and Queer Young Women," *The Canadian Journal of Information and Library Science* 28, no. 3 (2004): 66.

17    Ibid., 67.

18    J. L. Pecoskie, "The Intersection of 'Community' within the Reading Experience: Lesbian Women's Reflections on the Book as Text and Object," *The Canadian Journal of Information and Library Science* 29, no. 3 (2005): 335-349.

19    See Anderson, B. (2006). *Imagined communities: Reflections on the origin and spread of nationalism.* New York: Verso. Anderson uses the term "imagined community" in his discussion of nationalism, describing the ways that people develop a sense of affinity and belonging with large groups of people, most of whom they will never meet. Anderson partly credits this belief in imagined community to the development of "print-capitalism" and the rise of people reading materials printed in the vernacular. Similarly, printed materials and manuscripts housed in LGBT community archives allow new members of the LGBT community to understand the boundaries and characteristics of the LGBT community in which they are developing a sense of belonging. This issue is also discussed in Jill Johnston's *Lesbian nation: The feminist solution.*

as they develop their identities and learn to situate themselves within a larger LGBT community, but they also may find great comfort in physical spaces where they feel accepted and less isolated. In an article on outreach to LGBT youth, Hughes-Hassell discusses the need for safe spaces for youth who "usually come of age in communities where few gay adults are visible, attend schools with no openly gay staff, and interact with peers who use 'fag' and 'dyke' as the favored insult...."[20] By providing youth and other isolated members of the LGBT community with "access to virtual communities" through resources, space, or documents, people who work in LGBT community archives can provide essential support and a safe space for personal development.[21]

Part of the essential role of archives within community-building is the development of historical memory and shared memory, especially within marginalized groups whose history has been neglected or under-documented. Mary Stevens describes archives as "part of the process of fostering a shared memory that emerges only through dialogue" between members of a larger community.[22] Part of this dialogue surfaces through the process of witnessing events and lives that have been ignored by history and frequently forgotten (or never known) by the modern LGBT community. By documenting the stories of repression and hurt within the LGBT community, these archives can allow for a process of "witnessing and retelling."[23]

Bringing a painful past to light can be legitimizing in that it allows community members to recognize and mourn for ways in which their predecessors have been harmed, while producing accountability for governments and social forces that have persecuted LGBT people throughout history. The archival record can be especially important in terms of accountability for abuses, through police records or descriptions of experiences of persecution, allowing researchers to "shine the light of history on these dark corners of our past."[24] While forgetting painful events can be an essential part of a survival strategy, recalling those very events can help construct the past, allowing individual pain to be re-formed into collective memory and community history.[25] A connection to the pain of one's LGBT ancestors can be an important element of an LGBT identity; as Lynn Sipe, the former president of the One Institute and Archives' Board of Directors, states, "It is terribly important that gay people and those who are interested in gay life and history know that we do have a rich and varied history—much of it painful but much of it worth celebrating as well."[26]

---

20   S. Hughes-Hassell and A. Hinckley, "Reaching Out to Lesbian, Gay, Bisexual, and Transgender Youth," *Journal of Youth Services in Libraries* 15, no. 1 (2001): 39.
21   Ibid.
22   X, et al., "Love and Lubrication in the Archives, or Rukus!: A Black Queer Archive for the United Kingdom," 294.
23   Ibid., 276.
24   L. Dick, "The 1942 Same-sex Trials in Edmonton: On the State's Repression of Sexual Minorities, Archives, and Human Rights in Canada," *Archivaria* 68, (2009): 217.
25   Gentile, "Resisted Access? National Security, the Access to Information Act, and Queer(ing) Archives," 155-156.
26   J. Gallagher, "History Under One Roof: The One Institute and Archives is the Largest Gay and Lesbian

The development of collective memory also allows for intergenerational work, wherein members of the LGBT community actively build a legacy for young people. Topher Campbell describes the importance of passing on history to the next generation, even (and especially) within a geographically disparate LGBT community, where older community members have "seen their heritage pass before their eyes, so there is a personal stake in this... Our generation wants to see its experiences placed in the mainstream."[27] Isolated members of the LGBT population, whether isolated through geography, family background, race, or other elements, may feel a complete disconnect from the lives of others who have shared their experiences and lifestyles. Legacy work, like the creation of LGBT community archives, helps connect people to a larger narrative of the lives of LGBT people. "In the future when someone says, 'Black gay history, what is it? There isn't any,' or people from our own community say, 'We have no legacy,' we'll be able to point to the archive and say, 'This happened or that happened.' And share that with friends in our circle or family members who are twenty years younger or twenty years older."[28] Interaction with these LGBT archival legacies can be an intensely emotional experience, as a person engages with the community's past and reacts to the intersections of those experiences with his or her own life.[29]

Archival creation and historical production not only serve cathartic purposes, but can be construed as intensely politically-infused acts. Topher Campbell describes hearing LGBT people's stories about their experiences and beginning to "realize that the collected memory is not getting stored anywhere... Reclaiming that history is a political act."[30] Reclaiming history is a way of recognizing and claiming stories that have been denied to members of marginalized communities. Chenier roots this attitude in the social movements of the 1960s wherein "history was regarded as a tool for the liberation of the oppressed."[31] By challenging mainstream beliefs and attitudes, the documentation of LGBT history "was a way to write gay and lesbian experience into existence, to challenge heterosexism and traditional history, and to engender pride within a community long forced to live on the social, economic, and political margins of society."[32]

---

Collection in the World." *The Advocate*, June 2001, 53.
27   X, et al., "Love and Lubrication in the Archives, or Rukus!: A Black Queer Archive for the United Kingdom," 280.
28   Ibid., 281.
29   K. J. Rawson, "Accessing Transgender // Desiring Queer(er?) Archival Logics," *Archivaria* 68, (2009): 123-140.
30   X, et al., "Love and Lubrication in the Archives, or Rukus!: A Black Queer Archive for the United Kingdom," 279.
31   Chenier, "Hidden from Historians: Preserving Lesbian Oral History in Canada," 251.
32   Ibid., 252.

## Models for LGBT archives

While many aspects of community archives have developed in response to perceived lacks within current formal archival practice, an understanding of the motivations of these community archives and a careful examination of those elements of their operation that are deeply valued by the LGBT community can help archivists in formal settings develop models that meet the needs, desires, and expectations of LGBT donors and users. Additionally, this examination can open the door for mutually-productive partnerships or cooperative collection development. The following sections examine some elements of LGBT archival work, often displayed in community archives that can be integrated into formal archival work.

## Visibility

An essential element of LGBT archives is their ability to create visibility for a large and historically repressed population. By countering silencing (including what Dick deems "historiographical silence"), archives can create a newly-defined model of the LGBT community. This is especially essential for an "invisible" group like the LGBT community, where community members are not necessarily readily identifiable through visual cues or even personal acquaintance.[33]

Tapping into the common theme of "gay pride," archives can serve as a venue for a joyful visibility developed on the community's own terms. Community-defined visibility can be a form of self-expression and of legitimizing the LGBT community's place in greater society. Topher Campbell describes this process in the rukus! archive by saying that "rukus! is not about saying we're victims; we're very much about redefining and replacing ourselves publicly."[34] This redefinition of identity echoes some community members' reclamation of the term "queer" as a positive label describing the possibility of a re-imagined identity and society.

Nearly all interviewees in this study mentioned emotional moments of connection with historical documents and the pivotal role that this connection played in their personal development. Carter remembered her sense of isolation before discovering LGBT role models of color like poet and activist Audre Lord. "I remember when I was first coming out, there was no one, not one person that I was aware of that was a black gay or lesbian role model for me, no one," she said. "And to come out in a predominantly white movement, and you're looking around trying to get your own identity, that was very hard for me."

---

33    Dick, "The 1942 Same-sex Trials in Edmonton: On the State's Repression of Sexual Minorities, Archives, and Human Rights in Canada," 183-217.
34    X, et al., "Love and Lubrication in the Archives, or Rukus!: A Black Queer Archive for the United Kingdom," 278.

PD3 described his experience seeing photographs from the 1979 Spiritual Conference of Radical Faeries and "feeling like I was connected and my experiences were
connected, to this historical trajectory." PD1 likewise has been moved by stories of
people who have engaged in work similar to her own. "I know I've definitely had experiences in the archives where being able to identify with somebody in the past for lots of
reasons—I mean, because they were committed to love, because they were overworked
and overdriven, because of whatever—being able to identify with somebody living in
a different time has been actually really incredible to my spiritual practice, to feeling
like I have a spiritual legacy that I can participate in." PD4 likewise felt strongly about
seeing an enormous volume of materials at the Lesbian Herstory Archives. "Just the
fact that it exists is such a comforting circumstance, to me. And the way it has been
housed now... [in] a three-story brownstone... it's there just for that purpose" of documenting lesbian history.

### Self-determination

By retaining control over selection, description, and access of materials in community-based collections, members of the LGBT community maintain ownership of their
own histories rather than letting others determine how and by whom their materials will
be used. Recalling Annemaree Lloyd's concept of assigning significance to materials as
a political act, the desire for self-determination indicates a desire to act politically and to
assign significance to one's own life and the lives within one's community.[35] The founders of the Lesbian Herstory Archives address the concept of significance (and those who
have the power to assign it) when stating that "Our collection policy has been that the
community defines what is important to preserve about their lives."[36] This community
determination and definition also means that archives are filling a community-defined
need and desire for documentation, rather than meeting outsider interest.

Self-determined collecting helps members of the LGBT access their own histories,
which, through silencing, have historically been taken from them. As the Statement of
Purpose for the Lesbian Herstory Archives asserts, community collecting of histories
provides access to "our herstory denied to us previously by patriarchal historians in the
interests of the culture which they serve."[37] Parris defines this language as essentially
"self-protective," a response to historic wrongs perpetuated by systems of power, of
which the formal archives is perceived as an agent. Polly Thistlethwaite echoes this in
a 1995 Gay Community News article in which she states that members of the LGBT
community do not want to "turn over control of our history and memory to a system

---

35   A. Lloyd, "Guarding Against Collective Amnesia? Making Significance Problematic: An Exploration of Issues," Library Trends 56, no. 1 (2007): 53-65.
36   M. Wolfe, "The Lesbian Herstory Archives," S. A. Archives Journal 40, (1998): 20-21.
37   Parris, "Creating, Reconstructing, and Protecting Historical Narratives: Archives and the LBGT Community," 10.

still structured to work against us."[38] While this separatism may seem alarmist or counterproductive to some, James Carmichael points out that its focus on "integrity, safety, and collective will" is essential to many LGBT donors, and these concerns are ones that all archives, community and formal alike, would be wise to address.[39]

Interviewees had various suggestions about how self-determination can be integrated into formal archives, as well as varying opinions about the degree to which this integration is feasible. While PD1 believes that the true integration of self-determination in formal archives would "require a major structural shift," universities can still make great strides by demonstrating accountability to their donors. Additionally, while no employee remains at an organization indefinitely, "it's important to have people there who are, by affinity, accountable to communities they love and feel a part of and feel loyal to," despite the fact that the archivist must also be accountable to the institution and "might have to answer to somebody who will not always support their vision." PD4 stated that self-determination is largely dependent upon the archivist's desire and ability to fight university administration and reinvent the archival model.

Further along the spectrum, PD2 stated that any formal archives that are seriously working to build LGBT collections need to find ways to help the LGBT community maintain some control. She mentioned the possibility of a task force, as well as the archivist asking community members questions about responsibility and motivation. This balance of community control, she believes, can help counteract possible feelings of entitlement when archivists enter communities and take away their materials. Otherwise, she said, it can feel as if archivists are saying, "'Give us your documents. We're a library. Of course you want to give us your documents!'" Considering the need for donors to feel a sense of control over their own papers, PD3 said that self-determination could take the form of "revising the intake procedures and the consent forms and practices of consent around taking in archives." Specifically, he wishes donors could define access and design their own consent forms or donor agreements. He also envisioned community discussions. "If some university was going to open an LGBT archive, then they should have a series of public discussions that are advertised within the media and forums of that community, to say, 'Hey, we're creating this archive. What can we do to be accountable to the community that's being documented? What policies of access make the most sense? How can we be respectful of privacy and confidentiality concerns?'"

Micham's approach integrates several of these suggestions: "We get [community members] involved in the whole process, from how and when they document themselves to even how and when materials are used by researchers." Additionally, community members are welcome to—and often do—join in the Bingham Center's efforts through volunteer work.

---

38    Ibid., 19.
39    Ibid.

### Accessibility

Many members of the LGBT community donate materials to archives with the hopes of making them accessible for their immediate communities as well as the larger LGBT community, and especially to new or isolated community members for whom they can act as an important anchor and source of identification.

One important aspect of accessibility, described in detail by Rawson, is ensuring a comfortable archival experience for transgendered researchers. Rawson noting potential (and generally unintentional) exclusionary elements of many archives, such as single-sex bathrooms and archivists who do not use a patron's desired pronoun.[40] While an archivist may believe that he or she has very few transgender users, one must recall many donors' desire to create a body of materials for the use of their own communities, and thus the real need to create a space that can be accessed and used by all members of those communities.

As Maynard notes, denying or discouraging accessibility is "the ultimate police/archives tool."[41] For the LGBT user, bureaucratic registration processes, a fear of not receiving "permission" to view documents, or even a lack of visible representations of the LGBT community may create such discomfort that the user may feel unwelcome or unable to make use of the collection. Additionally, a lack of adequate descriptive tools may make it impossible for users to discover or access LGBT materials. While a lengthy discussion of descriptive tools for LGBT materials is beyond the scope of this paper, it is worth noting the many authors who point to the need for better description if such materials are to be used and accessed—and the integral role that creating accessibility plays in demonstrating a repository's positive attitudes toward the value of LGBT materials, refusing to obscure LGBT lives and stories.

Numerous authors indicate the importance of the terminology used within descriptive materials and its relationship to internally-defined vocabulary as well as more mainstream terms for different components of LGBT community and culture.[42] For an in-depth discussion of LGBT materials and subject access, see Grant Campbell's 2009 article entitled "Queer Theory and the Creation of Contextual Subject Access Tools for Gay and Lesbian Communities."

Interviewees expressed deep concern about the accessibility of collections to members of the LGBT community. Carter expressed a desire to house her materials in multiple repositories to increase accessibility: community spaces, black spaces, and LGBT spaces, taking into account the complexity of her identity. "I'm black, I'm a woman, I'm a lesbian, I'm a southerner, so why can't I... make that accessible to others in addition to always [having] to come" to the Bingham Center? In addition to

---

40    Rawson, "Accessing Transgender // Desiring Queer(er?) Archival Logics," 123-140.
41    Maynard, "Police/Archives," 168.
42    Chenier, "Hidden from Historians: Preserving Lesbian Oral History in Canada," 247-269. And, Rawson, "Accessing Transgender // Desiring Queer(er?) Archival Logics," 123-140.

housing materials in multiple physical locations, she mentioned a desire to increase accessibility through technology, especially through the Internet. Remembering her own isolation during her early coming-out experiences, she asks, "How do we make sure that people who are just looking around and wouldn't necessarily know where to look, how can they bump into [our history] or have easy access to it?" Carter believes that internet accessibility can be especially important for the privacy of researchers, lending them a sense of safety "if you don't want to be out and visible, particularly in communities of color."

Like Carter, PD1 expressed a desire to house her materials in as many places and in as many ways as possible. In her desire to maximize visibility, she said, "whatever type of impact I want to have on the world, whatever possibility I want to leave in my wake, can be done with a multiplicity of institutions, and outside of institutions, and with relationships to people, and with stories, and with memories, and with feelings." She feels that increasingly, digital access and interconnectedness make individual repositories' collections less important than LGBT history as a greater body of work.

PD3 felt strongly about the need to avoid restricting use to those with academic sponsorship or university affiliation. "I think that's one of the lines along which research and scholarship and storytelling gets restricted and condensed along class lines, and also along other lines of privilege versus marginalization. And I would be really excited to see universities make it clear in their policies that anybody who has an interest, whether scholarly or otherwise, in accessing archives should be able to do so." While many university archives are open to community use, members of the public often are not aware of this fact. For instance, PD3 is uncertain about his own ability to access his community's records as someone without a university affiliation. He also describes the registration process as a barrier, stating that "I'd have to fill out lots of forms, and deal with lots of straight bureaucrats," unlike in community archives where "I could just walk in off the street and... I knew that I could just talk to the friendly queer person who was staffing the desk and find out what I would need to do if I wanted to access [materials]."

### Privacy

One very concrete way to increase the comfort of donors, especially, is through a significant focus on personal privacy. While sexual and gender identity are important aspects of people's public lives, many of their papers revolve around personal relationships and deal with sex and sexuality. Additionally, the archivist cannot assume that everyone mentioned within a donor's papers is "out" in all aspects of his or her life; for instance, a person may openly claim his gay identity among friends, but may strive to keep this identity secret in professional contexts. "Outing" someone, or revealing his or her sexual identity against his or her will, can be viewed as a very serious violation of privacy. James Carmichael puts it well when he says that "outing anyone against their will is a perpetuation of the kind of emotional violence to which people of earlier generations were routinely subjected."[43] Respecting a person's desires regarding his or her sexuality shows sensitivity and respect for the donor's decisions.

Opinions about the need to respect people's closeted identities vary widely through-out the LGBT community. For instance, Dick believes in striving for as much openness as possible in regards to public records, noting that

> public archival documents bearing on the historical experience of minorities hold a collective importance extending beyond the privacy rights of individuals. Protecting individual privacy is essential, but this principle should not negate the equally valid principle that the common good must be served through appropriate access to records bearing on human rights and other important issues of public policy.[44]

From this vantage point an unnecessary focus on privacy can actually further issues of repression. Conversely, Chenier focuses on legitimizing the privacy needs of those documented in oral histories, stating that "understandably, these narrators have heightened concerns over privacy, and often feel the need to protect their own reputa-tion as well as their family's. In some cases, narrators have reason to be concerned that if placed in the wrong hands, their testimony could compromise their personal safety and security in the present day." [45] Others feel that only through openness and a loving acceptance of people's lives and identities can the LGBT community build visibility and pride and erase shame and oppression.

Mandy Carter noted that she did not have any privacy concerns upon donating her collection. The fact that she had been filing materials with an eye toward long-term preservation meant that her public and private papers were never intermixed in the first place. Similarly, PD4 said that if and when her materials are ready for donation, she already will have separated sensitive materials, donating more public materials to an archives while keeping private or personal records for her own family.

Other interviewees expressed little concern about sharing information that they have already made public. PD2, as someone who has written and spoken extensively as an LGBT activist and is comfortably out in both personal and professional settings, acknowledged that her own privacy is not a major concern. Likewise, PD1 identified herself as a very open person, and stated that she already documents her life heavily in public forums and on the Internet.

In terms of privacy, PD3 discussed ethics involving informed consent for partici-pants in his oral histories and other documentary projects. For him, following this set of ethics is essential for "folks who may feel like they have a lot at stake in revealing their histories, and since queer and trans folks have been marginalized legally and

---

43    J. V. Carmichael, Jr., "'They Sure got to Prove it on Me': Millennial Thoughts on Gay Archives, Gay Biogra-phy, and Gay Library History," *Libraries & Culture* 35, no. 1 (2000): 94.
44    Dick, "The 1942 Same-sex Trials in Edmonton: On the State's Repression of Sexual Minorities, Archives, and Human Rights in Canada," 216.
45    Chenier, "Hidden from Historians: Preserving Lesbian Oral History in Canada," 259.

socially and politically in so many ways, it definitely is an important thing to navigate confidentiality and privacy within those contexts." While he acknowledged that many of his participants may have deep privacy concerns, he said that those concerns have been addressed carefully during the act of creating oral histories, and need not be considered further upon donation.

Third-party privacy concerns among interviewees deviate somewhat from their general lack of concern about personal privacy, indicating that they are aware that some members of their community maintain a desire for confidentiality or are not as open as they are about issues regarding their sexualities. Micham said of her donors that "they're very concerned about third-party privacy rights, to a larger degree than some other living donors might be, because they're a targeted community." This reluctance is balanced, she maintained, by

> a greater sense of urgency about their desire to document themselves and other members of their community, because they realize that they're history makers, and they realize that it's only in the recent past that their history has been taken seriously enough by the academy such that people like me would exist to preserve it.

To respect these concerns, she and her staff maintain awareness of potentially sensitive materials during processing and use. Micham said, we "bring to their attention what we consider to be materials of potential sensitivity, specifically related to third-party privacy rights, and give the donor a chance to decide whether or not the material should be restricted." Additionally, Micham believes that with many LGBT collections, archivists must "process at a more granular level to make sure that we are taking into account the privacy needs of the members of the community."

Several potential donors were proactively prepared to address third-party privacy concerns with people mentioned in their collections prior to donating, rather than expecting the archivist to do most of this work. PD2 said that she "would feel most comfortable contacting folks that I worked together with and saying, 'Okay, Duke or whoever wants this stuff. What do we think about that?'" She recognizes that the transgender community has particularly significant privacy concerns; in order to respect the needs of her activist colleagues, "if I was submitting anything that had any identifying information of other transgendered folks, I would have to majorly get lots of okay[s] from them." PD1's concerns revolved around family issues: "There's a difference between me choosing to be public about my own life and putting my family members out," she stated. While she knows that third-party privacy can definitely be an issue for some people, she said, "I'm not super committed to the perpetuation of someone's closeting, even beyond their lifetime. Not to say that I'm insensitive to someone's wishes about their own publicity or privacy, but I don't feel a deep investment in protecting people from being known to have had whatever kind of diverse set of experiences they've had." While these statements do not make vigilance like Micham's unnecessary, they do show that privacy concerns vary across the spectrum of LGBT donors, and that ongoing conversations with donors may be necessary in order to understand and address their needs.

## Accountability

The image of archivists as advocates for—and as ultimately accountable to—marginalized populations is widespread within community archives, reflected explicitly in statements such as that of the Lesbian Herstory Archives that "we aim to be totally accountable to our community and to be a diverse, inclusive reflection of lesbians in the US and around the world."[46] While the notion of activist librarians is in direct opposition to the "neutral," objective librarian or archivist, it offers a model for those who wish to build strong LGBT collections with the support of the community.[47] As Carmichael notes, "Library historians and archivists are in a unique position to discover and publicize gay archives... they should be pioneers rather than followers in establishing acceptable historical standards... [and] addressing the professional antipathy to the sexual nature of biographical subjects."[48] Pateman furthers this call to activism by asking librarians to feel emotionally moved by historical mistreatment of marginalized groups and use this energy to work for inclusion and representation. "What we need, as a profession," he writes, "is a collective anger for the rights of the oppressed and the discriminated."[49]

Importantly, many community archives do not just emphasize their archivists' responsibility to the greater community, but also emphasize the community's role in maintaining the archives. Many community archives are staffed by volunteers, and community members play essential roles in decision-making. The ONE Institute and Archives, in a 2001 fundraising campaign, even emphasized this community responsibility in terms of financial investment, saying that "'It's the responsibility of the community to preserve its heritage.'"[50]

When asked what that responsibility looks like to them, most interviewees conveyed that responsibility to individuals involves good communication and ongoing relationships. Carter expressed that the archivist's primary responsibility to donors is "staying in touch, giving some sense of is anyone looking at this stuff... not being like, 'Okay, we got it, goodbye, never see you again,' but more of an ongoing relationship." PD3 did not disagree, but noted that responsibility depends on the donor's needs and expectations; some may require significant attention or expect an ongoing relationship,

---

46   Wolfe, "The Lesbian Herstory Archives," *S. A. Archives Journal* 40, (1998): 20-21.
47   Parris, "Creating, Reconstructing, and Protecting Historical Narratives: Archives and the LBGT Community," 5-25.
48   Carmichael, Jr., "'They Sure got to Prove it on Me': Millennial Thoughts on Gay Archives, Gay Biography, and Gay Library History," 99.
49   J. Pateman, "Reasons to be Wrathful," *Library Management* 23, no. 1/2, (2002): 18.
50   Gallagher, "History Under One Roof: The One Institute and Archives is the Largest Gay and Lesbian Collection in the World," 55.

while others may be content to donate materials and then essentially forget about them.

PD1 also expressed a need for clear communication, although she focused more on the archivist sharing relevant information about the institution. She said that responsibility requires

> really, clearly communicating with an individual about the structure and politics of that institution, like literally what happens with their stuff... who goes in the archive... revealing as much about itself institutionally as the person is revealing about themselves personally, with all these records of their lives.

In terms of responsibility to the greater LGBT community, Micham believes that her obligations are multifaceted. "I'm responsible for being as familiar with the community I'm documenting as possible," she said. This means cultural literacy to "know what's going on and what people are doing and where the organizations are going." She tries to keep up with the names of people in leadership roles within LGBT organizations and to understand the community's history, as well as the researcher interest in different aspects of that history. Striving to be a "responsible documentarian," she believes, boils down to the need "to be knowledgeable about the community, but never to make the assumption necessarily that you're a member of the community."

PD2 asserted that part of the archivist's responsibility, and one that is closely tied to cultural literacy, is "to be up on their stuff, as far as LGBTQI sensitivity and understanding, and knowing, learning, and self-educating, not expecting the queer community to do all of it. And learning to be a good ally." Additionally, archivists with strong collections should ensure that "something awesome should be done with them." This helps to increase visibility and educate the public, "as opposed to this hoarding feeling."

Another way that archivists can demonstrate accountability to the community, and a sincere desire to address their concerns, is through education—both education about records management, and education about access and use of archives. Carter indicated that one important role the archivist could play within the LGBT community is emphasizing the importance of saving documents, perhaps by "having a relationship or partnership that would instill [records management] as part of the value of being an LGBT activist," communicating that "you need to keep all this stuff, and why you should, and how you do it." Another responsibility, both to researchers from the LGBT community and to the donors, is creating appropriate cataloging, subject headings, and cross-references to represent the multiplicity of donors' identities, "because a lot of us are not just one thing. We're a little bit more complex."

## Trust

Accountability means, among other things, an institutional investment in LGBT history that transcends simple scholarly trends and the personal affinities of archivists. By trusting an archivist, a member of the LGBT community may choose to donate his or her papers, but by trusting a greater institution or repository and its goals and intentions, a donor may feel a longer-term security in his or her decision.

This commitment to the larger cause of LGBT history challenges the notion of "collecting," and rather focuses on the importance of connecting donors with repositories that meet their needs and desires and in which their collections will be preserved with the most integrity.[51] The archivist collecting LGBT materials must learn to work in concert with others who are invested in the creation of queer histories, who form a network that creates queer history and challenges exclusiveness and exclusion.[52] When activism is "combined with the traditional role of the archivist, the result is a proactive archivist, concerned both with the archives itself and with working toward the promotion of the ideals of the constituents being served... it is an idea far removed from any kind of concept of the archivist's role as that of the passive organizer and gatherer...."[53]

An archivist's involvement in and commitment to the LGBT community, whether as a community member or as an ally, can demonstrate a desire to further the community's needs, to recognize their concerns, and to maintain awareness of current trends and issues. Archivists should become what Pateman calls "passionate advocates" who "need to be angry either through personal experience or by getting involved with excluded people."[54] In a population with high privacy needs and frequent suspicion of those in positions of power, this personal relationship can build faith and allow for collection-building based on personal networks, reflecting the true diversity and true interests of the LGBT community. In combination with a successful track record of documenting LGBT history, personal involvement in community issues can demonstrate necessary investment.

Differences in values and differing political assessments increase the need for establishing solid trust between archives and LGBT donors.[55] Interviewees frequently acknowledged feeling distrust of formal archives, or discussed seeing such distrust among their colleagues. For PD2, this mistrust stems from a history of those in power taking knowledge and materials away from those in marginalized communities. She acknowledged that "there's a lot of fear, and rightfully so, of others, especially the most privileged people, coming and trying to get information about your little niche culture that's been horribly oppressed for generations." This increases the need for trust, and for the archivist to demonstrate that he or she understands the community's needs and values.

But how can one build that trust? As Carter described, a person can have trust in an

---

51    Parris, "Creating, Reconstructing, and Protecting Historical Narratives: Archives and the LBGT Community," 5-25.
52    Marston, "Archivists, Activists, and Scholars: Creating a Queer History," in *Daring to Find our Names: The Search for Lesbigay Library History*, ed. J. V. Carmichael, Jr., (Westport, Conn.: Greenwood Press, 1998), 139.
53    Parris, "Creating, Reconstructing, and Protecting Historical Narratives: Archives and the LBGT Community," 13.
54    Pateman, "Reasons to be Wrathful," 19.
55    Barriault, "Hard to Dismiss: The Archival Value of Gay Male Erotica and Pornography," 219-246.

institution because his or her friends or colleagues have chosen to house their materials there. Not only did she trust the Bingham Center because her friends had their papers there, but she also has seen others follow suit based on her own trust of the repository. PD2 noted that the archivist can build trust through the use of terminology reflecting the community's values and own, internal language. Additionally, "librarians or archivists need to get involved in that community... if you were building this archives, and going into different communities, you would be listening to people's concerns, people would be comfortable to share them with you." Much like Mandy Carter, she mentioned that she is more likely to trust people whom she has seen at community events or with whom she feels some sense of connection. Referring to a librarian who is heavily involved in activist communities, she said, "she has a face, she has a heart, and people know her. And what I think can feel weird about museums and libraries and stuff like that is it's like 'Gimme, gimme, gimme, we're collecting history.'" Investment in the community demonstrates a more reciprocal relationship.

An archivist can demonstrate community investment by acting as a positive ally; this involves asking the community what kinds of involvement are useful and allowing them to draw the line if one oversteps one's bounds. Micham acknowledged this need to be careful about boundaries; she attends events sponsored by organizations whose papers she wants to preserve, but she is always careful to "be very clear about why [I'm] there." When doing activism outside of work or attending events within the LGBT community, she likewise is very clear about her professional role so that no one ever feels like she is overstepping her bounds or like she has misled them. Micham noted that when trust needs to be established with a community with which Duke has a historically shaky or absent relationship, she often depends on people who can act as intermediaries. "You find the person that's associated with Duke and part of the Duke community, and also a part of that community, and that believes in... your archival cause, to go into the community first and sort of fly your flag and see what happens." This resonates with Carter's statement that she implicitly trusted the Bingham Center because members of her community trusted it, as well.

## Conclusion

LGBT community archives, formed in response to the lack of representation of the LGBT population in formal archives, continue to flourish due to their important roles within the LGBT community. By responding to community needs, many of these community archives address common concerns of the LGBT population: visibility, self-determination, accessibility, privacy, accountability, and trust. These same elements can be incorporated into formal archives wishing to better meet the needs of their LGBT donors. Additionally, a careful consideration of the community archives model can lead to productive discussions among archivists wishing to document the LGBT population, leading to improved outreach techniques and donor relations.

After a close examination of many of the elements making up LGBT archives, I will close with one interviewee's reflections on the importance of archives and archivists within the LGBT community. Discussing the concept of the archivist as activist, PD3 said:

For me, growing up and coming out as queer, my parents aren't queer, my siblings aren't queer, no one else in my family is, that I know of, and so if it wasn't for meeting elders in the community... and then reading tons of books and having access to other kinds of history such as archives, I would have thought of myself as totally isolated and broken from history rather than being part of it. And so the archivist, in a way, is sort of a weaver who takes these disparate threads of history and myth and experience and story and helps weave them together into a fabric where we can see ourselves as part of a coherent history. And that weaving process is largely taken for granted for communities that run through families of blood, families of biological relation, whereas for queer folks we don't have that, so we have to find new modes of weaving, and new weavers.

## Interview Notes

Carter, Mandy, interview by Angela L. DiVeglia, April 29, 2010.
Micham, Laura, interview by Angela L. DiVeglia, February 25, 2010.
PD1, interview by Angela L. DiVeglia, March 16, 2010.
PD2, interview by Angela L. DiVeglia, June 14, 2010.
PD3, interview by Angela L. DiVeglia, June 19, 2010.
PD4, interview by Angela L. DiVeglia, June 28, 2010.

# Inventing History:
## The *Watermelon Woman* and Archive Activism

### *Alana Kumbier*

Cheryl Dunye's feature film, *The Watermelon Woman*, looks and acts like a docu-mentary— complete with vintage film footage, photographs, and interviews—but it's a fiction. Taking the hybrid form of an investigation, video-autobiography, and docu-mentary, the film follows Cheryl, a young, African-American lesbian filmmaker, as she investigates and documents the life of Fae Richards, a fictional African-American lesbian actress. Cheryl is motivated by the desire for an historical precedent—for her experience and her creative work—and for something better than the racist repre-sentations of African-American women in Hollywood films from the 1920s through 1940s. *The Watermelon Woman* tells an invented story in order to connect the present with a much needed past, and offers a platform for exploring a set of concerns within the specific context of feminist activism and history: How can individuals produce historical knowledge when they lack material evidence? What happens when research-ers encounter difficulties accessing records in libraries and archives? And how might they displace the archive as the authoritative source for historical documentation? *The Watermelon Woman* leads viewers through libraries and archives, exploring the question of what happens when the records researchers expect to find, the records that would allow them to produce historical knowledge about an individual or group, are not there. The film shows how libraries and archives matter to individuals in intimate and everyday terms, and reminds its audience of the many other places where histories of under-documented communities reside.

*The Watermelon Woman* (1996) follows Cheryl, a young filmmaker played by Dunye. Cheryl begins to study the history of African-American women on film by watching movies from the video store where she works.[1] She becomes fascinated with a black actress from the 1920s, 30s, and 40s, who is credited in old Hollywood films as "the Watermelon Woman." Cheryl learns that "The Watermelon Woman" was Fae Richards, a black, lesbian actress who (like Cheryl) lived in Philadelphia. Cheryl embarks on a quest to learn as much as she can about Richards and documents her search on video.

Cheryl's search dramatizes the challenge of researching under- or un-documented subjects, subjects without proper names, identified in records (if at all) by number or stage name, or by association with another, more prominent figure. Her attempts to locate information in archives and libraries are met with frustrating and disappointing

---

1   Cheryl Dunye, et al. *The Watermelon Woman*. videorecording. First Run/Icarus Films, New York, NY, 1997.

ends. The lack of accessible information about Richards frustrates Cheryl, and she turns to community-based sources, including a local film scholar, Richards' fans and her longtime partner, to fill the gaps in the textual record. Cheryl's research, which starts as a project motivated by intellectual and artistic curiosity, provides a means for her to make sense of her own desires, relationships, and aspirations. It becomes clear that there is more at stake for her than getting the facts right, or providing an authoritative account of Richards' life. The product of Cheryl's search is a short documentary that she incorporates in *The Watermelon Woman*, first as rough footage, later as a short film at the end of the movie. After we see Cheryl's short, before the film's final credits roll, Dunye reveals her historic invention (or, more appropriately, her *intervention*) in two sentences: "Sometimes you have to create your own history. The Watermelon Woman is fiction." In order to manifest a history that is *present* in memory and structures of feeling and *absent* from the archival record, Dunye exceeds the limits of the archive. Using a strategy akin to Saidya Hartman's critical fabulation, she imagines what could have been, and makes her method evident.[2] The possibility of what could have been creates a

> 'space of a different kind of thinking, a space of productive attention to the scene of loss, a thinking with twofold attention that seeks to encompass at once the positive objects and methods of history [...] and the matters absent, entangled and unavailable by its methods.'[3]

By claiming this space and its possibility, Dunye instantiates a new mode of historical knowing, and models a praxis for others grappling with the limits of the archive.

As *The Watermelon Woman* highlights the effects of archival limits, it also critiques the ways libraries and archives mediate access to information, and draws attention to the power relations that undergird research in both spaces. We need to recognize and identify these relations so that they "can be questioned, made accountable, and opened to transparent dialogue and enriched understanding."[4] The specific power relations that Dunye explores in *The Watermelon Woman* involve records; multiple—contradictory—historical narratives; and access to collections in conventional libraries and archives, grassroots archives, and homes.

## Shaping the historic record, shaping social memory

The first of these power relations has to do with records—more precisely, their absence. When archivists make choices about what to collect and preserve and what to destroy, they "fundamentally influence the composition and character of archival

---

2   Saidya Hartman, "Venus in Two Acts." *Small Axe.* 26 (2008): 11.
3   Lisa Lowe quoted in Hartman, "Venus in Two Acts," 11.
4   Joan M. Schwartz and Terry Cook, "Archives, Records, and Power: The Making of Modern Memory." *Archival Science.* 2 (2002): 2.

holdings and, thus, of societal memory."[5] When a record or document becomes part of an archival collection (i.e., gains a new context *as archival*), it is granted a status and importance that other records and documents do not possess. Letters, photographs, diaries, organizational files, and ephemera are deemed worthy of collection and preservation, while most other records are not. When processing collections, archivists make choices about how to describe records, such as what terminology and subject headings to apply to a given collection, which then affects how researchers can access records when they search online catalogs and finding aids. Before getting to this point, however, the records themselves must exist.

The ability to create records depends on a number of social, educational, and economic factors, including access to the materials and means to produce documents, and access to the education and training required to maintain them (especially in the age of electronic and digital document creation).[6] Due to discrepancies in access to materials, means, and education, some individuals and groups are better equipped to produce and maintain records than others, leading to a situation in which "certain voices [...] will be heard loudly and some not at all; certain views and ideas about society will in turn be privileged and others marginalized."[7] In turn, records that make it into the archive have the ability to influence "the shape and direction of historical scholarship, collective memory, and national identity, [... and] how we know ourselves as individuals, groups, and societies."[8] In other words, due to social conditions, not all groups have had the means to create records, and, in turn, archival collections have been shaped by those same social forces. Because histories are articulated using evidence from archival collections, they, too are socially-conditioned. The (socially-contingent) contents of the archive largely determine which—and whose—stories will be told. The archive is shaped by the record *and* shapes the record.

In response to the problem of missing records and limited collections, Dunye invents a lineage for contemporary African-American lesbian cultural production. In her introduction to an interview with Dunye, media studies scholar, film producer, and videographer Alexandra Juhasz (who was also Dunye's partner) notes that Dunye describes her style of film- and videomaking as "the *Dunyementary*, which is a hybrid of narrative, documentary, comedy, and autobiography."[9] The *Dunyementary* form allows its creator to authorize her own work and the work of her central character, Cheryl. Juhasz offers this description of the relationship between Cheryl and Dunye:

> The 'Cheryl' character, played by Dunye, wants to be a filmmaker but feels she needs to know about the lives of her foremothers before she can fully claim this identity

---

5   Schwartz and Cook, "Archives, Records, and Power," 3.
6   Ibid. 13.
7   Ibid. 14.
8   Ibid. 2.
9   Alexandra Juhasz. *Women of Vision: Histories in Feminist Film and Video*. (Visible Evidence. Minneapolis: University of Minnesota Press, 2001) 291.

and voice for herself. Because the lives of black women in film, let alone black lesbians, were never considered worthy of the historical record–so were never documented–the Cheryl character has a hard time finding authorities who will do their job and authorize the existence of black lesbians from the past. This is when Dunye (the filmmaker) decides to entirely fabricate the life of a woman who did not but could have existed, Fae "the Watermelon Woman" Richards […][10]

Instead of accepting the limits of the historical record, Dunye draws our attention to the exclusion of black women in film from dominant accounts of film history. Her depiction of Cheryl and Fae's stories remind us of the significant difference between being visible on film (or involved in movie/video production) and being recognized as a "woman in film." Cheryl works as a wedding-videographer-for-hire, which means that weekend after weekend, she creates records of a highly and commonly documented life event. This work provides her with money and additional experience, but it does not help her articulate an identity or garner recognition as an African American filmmaker. For that, she needs to research and tell Fae's story, meet members of Fae's community, and connect their experiences with hers.

Given that *The Watermelon Woman* was Dunye's first feature film, and had limited theatrical distribution, we might imagine that telling Fae and Cheryl's stories also provided Dunye with a kind of recognition she hadn't received from her short videos and films. In her interview with Juhasz, Dunye theorized that while her work is well-received by "the academy," or "all the feminist and all the queer theorists, and all the performance theorists, and all the theorist theorists", she needed to make a feature film in order to attract black audiences, who would offer a different kind of recognition:

> It takes a lot for somebody of my mother's generation, or from a working-class or middle-class black background, it takes a lot for them to go to see work at some avant-garde house. I want to see how my issues play out in the black context. That's one reason why I'm working on a feature, so I can see how my story affects this black audience.[11]

As an actress in Hollywood and race movies, Fae was cast in movies that are popular enough to wind up on the shelves of the video store where Cheryl works. But the context of her visibility reminds us of the constraints African-American actresses have experienced throughout film history: Fae is on-screen, but only as a maid or servant. Her performances aren't credited to Fae Richards but to "the Watermelon Woman;" in addition to denying her identity, the absence of Fae's name from the credits makes it difficult for Cheryl to find her in books and archives.

The material Cheryl encounters as she investigates the life of Fae Richards, including the records in the lesbian community archive and the souvenirs, programs and snapshots collected by Fae's fans and relations, was created specifically for the film.

---

10   Ibid.
11   Juhasz. *Women of Vision.* 301; 298.

The film's fabricated archival materials include snapshots of (a woman posing as) Fae Richards with friends, snapshots of her with Page, glamorous publicity photographs from her studio, photographs documenting her singing at lesbian clubs in Philadelphia, and photos taken by her longtime partner, June Walker. This archive was created by Zoe Leonard for Dunye's project, but the "Fae Richards Photo Archive" also exists as a stand-alone work, comprised of 78 black and white photographs, four color photographs, and a notebook.

The archival collection created for *The Watermelon Woman* serves an evidential purpose in the film, as it is used to re-construct Richards' past, but its status outside of the film (as fictional documentation) means that it cannot function as evidence in a traditional way. Like the film that provides the context for its creation, the collection documents a past that Dunye and Leonard know *is there*, but for which there is no record. The material that constitutes *The Watermelon Woman* is not intended to tell us exactly what happened. Instead, it authorizes and inspires future projects; its existence creates the precedent Dunye required for her own work.

### Accessing collections, accessing information

As *The Watermelon Woman* directs our attention to the ways in which power relations shape the historic record, it also shows us how archives, themselves, are sites in which archivists, librarians, and researchers negotiate power relations. By representing the difficulties their subjects encounter while trying to access archives and libraries, the film addresses issues of access which manifest in a variety of ways: in material terms (i.e., the characteristics of records and archival spaces), in classificatory practices, and in security protocols.

When Dunye shows Cheryl visiting the archives, she reminds us that archives are spaces in which access is regulated, and researchers are subject to surveillance by archivists and other users. Archives may employ closed-circuit video cameras, and require patrons to check bags, register, and present their materials for a security check before departing. Dunye makes surveillance practices a key feature of Cheryl's archival research. During her visit to the Center for Lesbian Information and Technology (CLIT), Cheryl finds a few publicity photographs of Fae Richards in a box. When she attempts to record the images for her documentary, the archivist scolds and discourages her from doing so. When Cheryl appeals to the archivist, the archivist tells her that she cannot grant her permission to use the images until after the next monthly meeting of the collective, who will come to a consensus-based answer to Cheryl's request. Because her trip required time off from work, and travel to a different city (from Philadelphia to New York City), returning at a later date would require time and resources she does not have. So Cheryl resists the rules of the archive and records the photos for her documentary, out of the archivist's line of sight.

## Classificatory practices

Early in her research process, Cheryl visits an unidentified public library. In order to ensure that she has not missed something in her own library search, Cheryl asks for help from the librarian, and in the process, subjects herself to the epistemological and organizational protocols of the library. When Cheryl approaches the information desk to ask for help, the librarian on duty provides brusque and minimal responses to her query. His advice to Cheryl is confusing; he answers as if she knows both too much and too little at the same time. Assuming that she has not done any preliminary research, he asks her if she has checked the "black section" in the reference library; when she asks if there are non-reference texts on women in film that mention Richards, he stops talking in terms of broadly-defined sections, and references Library of Congress call numbers asking, "have you tried the film section, PN 1993 to PN 1995?"[12] When Cheryl tells him that she has, he begins to take her request seriously, and searches the catalog, noting that the only results he retrieves are for Martha Page. The scene helps us understand the challenges non-academic researchers face when asking questions: if she had not already conducted some research on her own, did not know how to use the Library of Congress system, or did not have the tenacity to keep asking for help, she would not have received confirmation that there were no books on Richards in the collection.

It is important to note that the searches the librarian conducts are only as good as the interface and the collection he has at his disposal. For Cheryl's purposes, the distinction between what the librarian *cannot find*, what the library *does not have*, and what *does not exist* is not important, since the end result—no material—is the same. The scene is nonetheless worth exploring here, because it complicates the clear binary of presence/absence in the historical record. The library scene draws attention to the ways in which indexing and classificatory practices employed by librarians and archivists, who work in accord with Library of Congress standards for cataloging and classification, shape what we know about the past, and about the lives of individuals.

When Cheryl consults reference sources to find information about the "Watermelon Woman," she finds only generic subject headings for "Black Women in Film" and references to Hattie McDaniel and Louise Beavers. In her analysis of the film, Thelma Wills Foote observes that generic or stereotypical terms like "Black Women in Film" or "The Watermelon Woman" do not recognize actresses' unique identities. She asserts that these generic and stereotypical references are instances of "epistemic violence against black female subjectivity [...] black actresses of the past lack the indexical specificity in authoritative sources of historical knowledge that would make it possible for Cheryl to conduct conventional research on an individual actress's life story."[13] In addition to

---

12   The Library of Congress call number system would be familiar to regular patrons of academic libraries, but not to patrons of public libraries, where books are typically organized using the Dewey Decimal scheme.
13   Thelma Wills Foote. "Hoax of the Lost Ancestor: Cheryl Dunye's *The Watermelon Woman.*" *Jump Cut: A Review of Contemporary Media.* 49 (2007) 5. Accessed July 12, 2011. http://www.ejumpcut.org/archive/jc49.2007/

causing trouble for the researcher looking for materials on a specific individual, subject headings do not necessarily help researchers doing projects on lesbian, gay, bisexual, transgender, and queer history, either. The category of "Black Women in Film" can include sources on black lesbians, but without the lesbian label, catalog searches will not match those sources with keyword searches on the term *lesbian*. As Polly Thistlethwaite observes, subject headings applied to gay, lesbian, bisexual, transgender, and queer material "are perpetually clumsy and out-of-date."[14] As a result, "mainstream library catalogs and periodical indexes are plagued with deficiencies in description, foiling computer subject and keyword searches. A world of lesbian, gay, transgendered, and queer-relevant material languishes unidentified and even uncataloged in libraries and archives."[15] The problem here is at the level of the classificatory system: the terms available to catalogers are insufficient to the task of creating specific and nuanced descriptions of materials; these terms are approved for use by the Library of Congress (LoC), and any official change to descriptive terminology must be approved by the LoC before it can be widely applied to materials.

Access to items is also influenced by how subjects represented in collections identified themselves. If record creators were "closeted, or […] did not self-identify as queer, homosexual, lesbian, gay, or transgendered," any queer, transgender, or homosexual content in their files will not show up at the level of the catalog record or the finding aid. In such situations—and sometimes in situations in which it's clear that subjects had homosexual, queer or transgender identifications or relationships—catalogers and archivists are empowered to make decisions about what headings to apply to a given collection. If descriptions do not explicitly point to collections having gay/lesbian or queer-related content (if, for example, a relationship is described as a friendship instead of a partnership, romance, or sexual relationship), that content is not recognizable as such. Thistlethwaite argues that this practice of "coding or softening" archival descriptions is

> at the root of queer invisibility in historical record. It is this tradition of closeting by mainstream archivists that leaves lesbians present, yet incognito in mainstream historical record. When archives fail to name or explicitly identify collections with established or even speculated queer content, they construct a veiled, closeted history – a silent, unannounced inheritance no more apparent in the mainstream public than it was in the pre-Stonewall era.[16]

Subject headings constitute a kind of recognition, one that makes certain subjects legible. In Dunye's film, we see the effects of Richards' not being granted indexical status, and of being denied specificity in a classificatory system: she cannot be found.[17]

---

WatermelonWoman/index.html

14    Polly J. Thistlethwaite. "Building 'a Home of Our Own': The Construction of the Lesbian Herstory Archives," in *Daring to Find Our Names: The Search for Lesbigay Library History,* edited by James V. Carmichael Jr., (Westport, CT: Greenwood Press, 1998),166.

15    Thistlethwaite, "Building 'a Home of Our Own'," 166.

16    Ibid., 166-7.

17    The library scene also draws attention to the non-naming of Richards in the first place, since Cheryl

### In the lesbian archive

After her visit to the library, Cheryl visits a lesbian community archive. The archive, named the Center for Lesbian Information and Technology (CLIT) is clearly Dunye's parodic representation of the actually-existing Lesbian Herstory Archives (LHA). We tend to think of archives like the LHA as the less-powerful, under-funded, grassroots counterparts to institutional and state archives, and we're usually correct in our perception. Dunye's depiction of CLIT reminds us that grassroots archives are not exempt from the repercussions of power relations. CLIT's volunteer archivist, the collection's contents and their organization, and the archives' collective leadership structure are all subject to Dunye's critique. The role of the CLIT archivist is played by novelist, journalist, activist, and ACT UP archivist/oral historian Sarah Schulman; in character, she parodies the Lesbian Herstory Archives' rhetorics around collectivity, privacy, and "safe space."

The CLIT archive is disorganized and, though the contents of its boxes are out on shelves and physically accessible, visitors would be hard-pressed to identify the contents of any of them. Because records in the archive have not been appraised or described, they are effectively inaccessible to researchers. The CLIT archivist recognizes that this is a limitation; she reassures Cheryl and her friend Annie that "someday we're going to have a great system – people are going to donate materials and they're going to be logged, categoried [sic], sorted, and stored. Right now they're just in boxes." But there are limits to the archivist's concerns, as well. When Cheryl asks for material on black lesbians from Philadelphia, the archivist informs that there is, indeed a collection, and "it's very separate" from the rest of the archive. It is not well-taken-care-of, however. In her enthusiasm to show Cheryl the (disorganized) contents of the first (worn-out and taped-together) box she pulls from the shelf, the archivist carelessly dumps contents out onto a table. Cheryl prevents her from treating a box of material on black lesbians from Philadelphia in the same way, and finds photos of Richards at the top of the pile. An inscription on the back of one of the photographs reads: "To June Walker, Special Friend." Cheryl captures the inscription on video, only to be reprimanded by the archivist, who suddenly cares a great deal about the treatment of the material. The archivist takes the box away from Cheryl, after explaining/exclaiming her rationale: "This is confidential! This is a safe space!" Here, Schulman pokes fun at the Lesbian Herstory Archive's "safe space" rhetoric. Viewers of the film who are not familiar with the LHA may not understand the specific valence of this phrase in relation to the Archive, but will likely understand it as a reference to a mode of lesbian-feminist separatist discourse.

The LHA's use of safe space rhetoric was historically part of its effort to provide

---

notes that "It's not like I can go and ask for information about the Watermelon Woman" (especially since this research is happening in a moment before widespread, popular use of online search engines or encyclopedias, i.e. Google and Wikipedia).

"a physical and historical space for women to transform themselves, to come out – first to recognize and understand themselves as lesbians, then to come out into a community – a grass-roots public that stationed itself between isolated private and mainstream public spheres." A woman could be closeted in her everyday life, but donate her papers to the LHA as a lesbian; she would not have to fear that she would be publicly exposed. The Archive is particularly wary about "exposure [that] involves inclusion in the mainstream press or media," exposure of the sort that would occur if records from the LHA were to be featured in *The Watermelon Woman* (though not completely mainstream, it is a feature film intended for release beyond the film festival circuit).[18]

A significant amount of material in grassroots archives like LHA is not legally approved for publication, representation, or display in public venues. Unless a donor is able to provide legal documentation of her status as the copyright holder for donated material, she cannot be recognized as the owner of that material. Instead, ownership and copyright may accrue to "homophobic next-of-kin [... whose] legal reckoning with the collection may threaten its very existence."[19] When donors entrust the LHA with their papers, they sacrifice (or protect against) public visibility and legibility as lesbians, but still contribute to an historic record that attests to their existence.

### Counter-histories and counter-archives

In addition to critiquing existing archival practices and limits, Dunye employs alternative methods and modes of historical knowledge production. She articulates histories that resist closure, that create space for conflicting narratives, and that integrate multiple forms of evidence, not just what can be found in the archives. She looks back, imagines, and fabricates a history to foment social transformation in the present.

The stories and characters Dunye invents for *The Watermelon Woman* push at the limits of the historic record, and challenge its claims to truth. Dunye creates a counter-history through the film, employing the medium to do what the paper record has not or cannot do. Her counter-history, like others, "opposes itself not only to dominant narratives, but also to prevailing modes of historical thought and methods of research."[20] Her exercise of power reminds viewers that they, too, can resist dominant historic narratives. Though her film will not alter the content of history textbooks, Dunye reminds us that "faced with a relationship of power, a whole field of responses, reactions, results, and possible inventions may open up."[21] Though Dunye nods toward the existence of archives focusing on lesbian histories, her parody elides the potential such collections hold for supporting the kinds of historical research Cheryl wants to do.

Alternative or community archives that develop in conversation with—or in

---

18    Thistlethwaite, "Building 'a Home of Our Own'," 157; 158.
19    Ibid., 165.
20    Catherine Gallagher and Stephen Greenblatt. "Counter-History and the Anecdote." In *Practicing New Historicism*. (Chicago: University of Chicago, 2001): 52.
21    Michel Foucault. "The Subject and Power." *Critical Inquiry*. 8, no. 4 (1982): 789.

resistance to—traditional, institutional archives may provide counter-narratives to the dominant historical record. Like the narratives they collect and preserve, counter archives can "focus on issues of concern for disenfranchised and under-represented communities of Native Americans, Chicana/o, Asian American, and African Americans to construct alternative realities to those constructed through social institutions of dominant culture." Counter-archives can also be organized around sexuality and sexual identity, gender identity, and disability. Counter-archives draw attention to the limits of the archival record housed in dominant cultural institutions by collecting materials that represent experiences and populations not documented elsewhere. These archives articulate "alternative realities," in relation to a dominant culture, and by doing so, recognize that "multiple realities or truths [...] share the same social or philosophical space."[22] The multiple realities or truths offered by different archives may contradict each other, but in doing so, they open events, experiences, and histories to interpretation and investigation that would not be possible otherwise.

In their work on lesbian public cultural archives and AIDS video archives, respectively, Ann Cvetkovich and Alexandra Juhasz argue that such counter-archives are instrumental for remembering and preserving gay and lesbian histories and for catalyzing queer activism (in political, documentary, and other forms) in the present. Though they may be unconventional and idiosyncratic, gay and lesbian archives serve a vital function for their constituents, as they "address the traumatic loss of history that has accompanied sexual life and the formation of sexual publics, and they assert the role of memory and affect in compensating for institutional neglect." Cvetkovich terms the public cultural archive that does this work an "archive of feelings," an archive capable of documenting (or at least recognizing and valuing) experiences of "intimacy, sexuality, love, and activism." She argues that traditional archives cannot meet the demands of a lesbian and gay historical record, which needs to recognize the affective dimensions of lesbian and gay life.[23]

The records in the counter-archives Cvetkovich describes are primarily ephemera such as "occasional publications and paper documents, material objects, or items that fall into the miscellaneous category when catalogued [...] pornographic books, short-run journals, and forms of mass culture that are objects of camp reception," and records of personal life such as diaries, letters, and photographs, which have added significance given the under-documentation of gay and lesbian lives in the extant historic record. While traditional archives select materials based on professionally- and/ or institutionally-defined criteria (e.g., uniqueness, ability to document an important function, historical or legal value, or research interest), gay and lesbian archives "propose that affects—associated with nostalgia, personal memory, fantasy, and trauma—make

22    Anthony W. Dunbar. "Introducing Critical Race Theory to Archival Theory: Getting the Conversation Started." *Archival Science* 6 (2006): 114; 115.
23    Ann Cvetkovich. *An Archive of Feelings: Trauma, Sexuality, and Lesbian Public Cultures*. Series Q. (Durham: Duke University Press, 2003) 241.

a document significant." The archive of feelings is "both material and immaterial," documenting affective experience and recognizing that some experiences "[resist] documentation because sex and feelings are too personal or too ephemeral to leave records." The kinds and forms of documentation (or memory) that characterize the archive of feelings do not simply reside in institutional spaces or even in the physical space of grassroots archives, but also in "personal and intimate spaces" and "cultural genres." The concept of the archive of feelings may be difficult to reconcile with more traditional archival practices, but it can help us recognize the myriad sites and forms unconventional archives can take. *The Watermelon Woman* is rich with these alternative archives, depicting a variety of people, places and practices that enrich and often contradict the institutional historical record.[24]

In addition to visiting conventional research sites, Cheryl records interviews with a range of people who have known (or know about) Fae in different contexts. While some of Cheryl's interviewees have recollections of Fae herself, others offer social or historical context. Though most of Cheryl's interview footage does not make it into her documentary about Fae, Dunye incorporates these multiple accounts in the film. As she begins her research, Cheryl visits independent scholar Lee Edwards, who describes himself as a collector, exhibitor, and lecturer in the area of "race films" produced between 1915 and 1950. Edwards' house is decorated with posters advertising black cast films, including *Dark Manhattan* and *The Bull-Dogger*. He cannot tell Cheryl much about the Watermelon Woman or Martha Page, but he loans Cheryl his back issues of *Photo Play* magazine, and fills some gaps in Cheryl's knowledge of local history, telling her about the black-owned and black-operated theatres that showed Hollywood films in Philadelphia: the Royal, the Standard, the Dunbar, and the Lincoln.

Cheryl then conducts an interview with her mother (played by Dunye's mother, Irene Dunye), which does not yield much information, but leads Cheryl to an interview with her mother's former co-worker, Shirley Hamilton, or "Miss Shirley." In a voice-over introducing the interview footage, Cheryl speculates that Hamilton might be a lesbian, a hunch that Hamilton confirms, near the start of the interview. When Cheryl inquires about the Watermelon Woman, Hamilton corrects her, and provides her with Richards' full name. Hamilton knew Richards as a singer in Philadelphia, after she'd ended her career in "those movies." She tells Cheryl "her real name was Fae Richards. When she sang for us she used her real name...she used to sing for all us stone butches." Hamilton does not know much about Richards' connection to Martha Page, but jokes that if she "remembers her gossip correctly...Martha was one mean, ugly woman." Hamilton also shows Cheryl photographs depicting Richards in her non-Watermelon Woman years, photos she purchased at clubs where Richards performed and has saved in a cigar box for decades. Hamilton's collection is a valuable resource for Cheryl, showing her a new aspect of Richards' experience. The scene reminds us of the ephemeral nature

---

24   Cvetkovich. *An Archive of Feelings.* 244.

of collections like Hamilton's: as she pulls the photos from the cigar box, she holds a lit cigarette in her left hand, close to the pile of highly-flammable photos.

While the story Hamilton tells is ultimately affirmed by another character in the film, Dunye complicates Cheryl's research through interviews with characters who challenge local memories of Richards' past, and refuse to criticize her relegation to roles like the "Watermelon Woman." When Cheryl interviews Martha Page's sister, Mrs. Page-Fletcher, she denies Martha was a lesbian, and will not admit that she might have had a relationship with Richards. While it's clear that Page-Fletcher feels she has something to protect, it is unclear if she's trying to protect her sister's memory, her family name, or her own choices. Toward the end of the interview, as Page-Fletcher becomes agitated at Cheryl, who had pressed her to admit that Page and Richards had a relationship, an African-American maid (in a maid's uniform, no less) enters the room to protect and comfort her.

Cultural critic Camille Paglia (played by Paglia) presents the other major challenge to Cheryl's interpretation of Fae's film work. Paglia's commentary is designed to establish context for interpreting Richards' early roles, her "Watermelon Woman" nickname, and African-American women's relegation to playing "Mammy" characters on film. Paglia refutes Dunye's interpretations of each of these aspects of Fae's career, and her analysis of the history of African-American representation in major motion pictures. Paglia asserts that it is a misinterpretation to think that the "Mammy" figure was "de-sexualizing, degrading, and dehumanizing." Instead, she links the figure to her own Italian-American heritage, noting that casting large women as "Mammies" honored their goddess-like nature, their "abundance" and "fertility." She notes that her Italian grandmothers also "never left the kitchen" (and they were not slaves or servants), and that she does not understand why the watermelon might hold a negative connotation for African Americans, since it was a fruit her family ate at the end of big meals (and shares the colors of the Italian flag). Paglia contextualizes African-American women's history in terms of her own cultural, familial, and personal history, completely ignoring the specific experiences, conditions, and power relations that make those histories dramatically different.

Paglia cannot move beyond her own identity issues, making all things relevant to her cultural heritage, in her commentary on stereotypical representations of African-American women on film. Her analysis does little to support Cheryl's investigation of the cultural context in which Richards' body of work emerged, and in which she lived her life. Paglia's dismissal of significant differences between African-American women's and Italian-American women's experiences reframes the discussion in terms of ahistoric, essential symbols—e.g., the fertility goddess. Paglia's refusal to recognize or address difference seems ridiculous, and her interpretation is too far-fetched to be taken seriously. Offscreen, Paglia is an iconoclast, a vociferous critic of numerous feminist activists, and a polarizing cultural critic. Dunye's choice of Paglia as the film's academic "talking head" is troubling, and points to one of the film's key limitations. Paglia parodies the feminist academic, and Sarah Schulman parodies the lesbian community archivist (as the disorganized space she oversees also parodies the lesbian community archive). Both performances trade in stereotypes of these figures, and contribute to the film's comic tone. While less striking, the representation of the librarian is also stereotypical: he is unable to think outside the classificatory system, and unwilling to help locate resources beyond library walls.

These representations may be funny, and Dunye's teasing may be an insider's kind, intended to poke fun rather than barb. The film's humor envelops its critiques, perhaps to make those critiques more palatable. But something gets lost in the process: the kind of nuanced response a feminist academic and film scholar could provide, which would take the particulars of Richards' life, social situation, and historic moment into account in her interpretation. The CLIT archives are funny, but they could be balanced with a visit to a place akin to the Schomburg Center for Research in Black Culture. And the librarian could do more, as many do, providing referrals when they've reached the limit of their collections or expertise. Representing realities like these might compromise the film's message that institutions are unhelpful, even hostile, spaces. But that complication could be a helpful one, especially if Dunye intends to encourage future researchers to use those spaces, or to donate their own papers to archives.

## Counter-archives in *The Watermelon Woman*

CLIT is the most clearly identifiable counter to mainstream archives in the film, because of its status as an archive, with boxes of records and a volunteer archivist. But other, smaller, personal collections prove instrumental to Cheryl's research. These are the personal collections she accesses through her interviews with Miss Shirley and June Walker, Fae's longtime partner. After her visit to CLIT, Cheryl contacts Walker, who agrees to be interviewed. When Cheryl arrives for their meeting, a neighbor informs her that Walker was taken to the hospital with heart pains. Walker leaves a letter for Cheryl, in which she describes her reaction to Cheryl's invocation of Fae's Watermelon Woman years: "[the call] got me to remember some unhappy things about the past. I was so mad you mentioned the name of Martha Page. She should have nothing to do with how the world remembers Fae." Walker would prefer that Cheryl ignore what she knows about Richards' association with Page, and create a representation that 'corrects' for things Richards' might have been ashamed of, or that perpetuate harmful, stereo-typical images. Walker cares deeply about how Richards' story is told, and her appeal to Cheryl reveals her anxieties about how members of her African-American lesbian community will be remembered, and who will create that record. "She paved the way for kids like you to run around making movies about the past and how we lived then," Walker writes, "Please Cheryl, make our history before we are all dead and gone. Our family will always only have each other."

Cheryl introduces her short biographical film with a response to Walker. She explains that the moments Walker had with Richards, as well as the moments Richards and Page had together, were all precious, but that Richards' life means something to Cheryl, as well: "it means hope, it means inspiration, it means possibility, it means history." Richards' life makes Cheryl's work possible. Cheryl tells Richards' story in order to claim the future she wants for herself: "what I understand is that *I'm* going to be the one who says I am a black lesbian filmmaker, who's just beginning, but I'm going to say a lot more, and have a lot more work to do."

Presented with the opposition between the historic record (in books, movies, and archives) and Walker's representation of Richards' life, Cheryl incorporates these conflicting perspectives in her short documentary film. She includes material from the archives, from Walker's collection, from Richards' films (both as the "Watermelon Woman" and in black cast productions), and publicity stills in the film. By juxtaposing sources that depict Richards in distinct ways, she fashions a complex representation of her subject. None of these aspects of Fae's life are privileged over others in Cheryl's film.

## Motivating action in the present

*The Watermelon Woman* shows us how archives and counter-archives offer different kinds of sources, and reminds us that sources from different archives support distinct bodies of knowledge and hold multiple kinds of value (historic, sentimental, evidential) for researchers. Dunye also shows us how and why Cheryl uses documents from multiple sources to articulate an historic narrative. But *The Watermelon Woman* goes beyond *showing how*; the film, itself, creates conditions of possibility for its viewers to act in the present and transform their social worlds. The film motivates viewers' critical reflection on the past (as documented and undocumented in the historic record), which can then inform their perspectives on (and action in) the present.

Dunye's use of video to motivate action exemplifies what Alexandra Juhasz terms "queer archive activism." Through queer archive activism, videos from the AIDS activist movement are mobilized in order to encourage viewers to "remember, feel anew, analyze, and educate."[25] In her experimental documentary *Video Remains*, Juhasz layers interviews with lesbian AIDS activists, which she conducted in 2004, over a 1992 interview with her friend James Robert Lamb. Her intent is to highlight differences between past and present experiences of AIDS, and to draw attention to the loss of an AIDS activist movement. The interviews are designed to "[enliven the] old tape" and lead viewers to re-engage in conversations about "AIDS, its representations, feelings, activism, and history."[26] As old footage is "enlivened" by the activist videographers' reflexive commentary, the archival record gains additional significance and becomes

---

25    Alexandra Juhasz. "Video Remains: Nostalgia, Technology, and Queer Archive Activism." *GLQ*. 12, no. 2 (2006): 326.
26    Juhasz, "Video Remains," 320.

a catalyst for activism.

Though it employs fabricated footage (instead of found or archival footage), *The Watermelon Woman* creates a documentary heritage for black lesbian cultural production to enable future projects. Most importantly, the film puts its documents into public circulation. When June Walker implores Cheryl to "make our history before we are all dead and gone," she is also speaking to the film's audience. Though this audience is not comprised of filmmakers, Walker's plea draws attention to the significance of real-world documentary projects. The film also draws attention to histories of representation of African Americans on screen; Dunye incorporates Leonard's footage and photographs in ways that remind us that racist and stereotypical representations still circulate (literally, as Cheryl gets her tapes from the video rental store where she works). As Robert F. Reid-Pharr suggests, the film "tells us that early images of blacks in film are infinitely available yet somehow always lacking. They are but pale and distorted reflections of the vibrant reality of mid 20th century black American life and culture."[27] *The Watermelon Woman* makes this critique and offers some exemplary correctives, including a scene of Cheryl and her friends in a lesbian club, and of singer-songwriter Toshi Reagon performing on the street. In addition to looking for traces of the past and documenting them, the film encourages its viewers to imagine reasons and strategies for documenting contemporary black lesbian communities.

## Conclusion

*The Watermelon Woman* shows us how libraries and archives that "document primarily mainstream culture and powerful records creators" may fail to provide information about members of historically-marginalized or minority groups. Instead of "[privileging] the official narratives of the state over the private stories of individuals," the film articulates histories through individuals' experiences. Instead of complying with "rules of evidence and authenticity [that] favor textual documents, from which such rules were derived, at the expense of other ways of experiencing the present, and thus of viewing the past," the film recognizes, incorporates, and creates alternative forms of evidence, including photographs, oral histories, videos, and a variety of ephemeral material. By consulting individuals with different knowledges (i.e., women who were Fae Richards' contemporaries and fans, not only scholars or experts), and using multiple forms and sources of evidence, Dunye suggests how archivists might "adopt multiple and ambient ways of seeing and knowing." And while the film critiques both traditional systems for organizing information *and* archives that are disorganized, it draws attention to the fact that organizational systems have the power to enable or hinder user access.[28]

---

27    Robert F. Reid-Pharr. "Makes Me Feel Mighty Real: The Watermelon Woman and the Critique of Black Visuality." In *F Is for Phony: Fake Documentary and Truth's Undoing*, edited by Alexandra Juhasz, (Minneapolis, MN: University of Minnesota Press, 2006), 133.
28    Schwartz and Cook, "Archives, Records, and Power," 18.

Through *The Watermelon Woman*, Dunye and Cheryl become archival activists. They place historic records in the service of collective struggles for social transformation, as well as individual struggles for identification, recognition, and creative production. They model unconventional research practices and reveal how archival records can be juxtaposed with other forms of evidence or documentation, illuminating problems with the past, and imagining something better.

Electronic Records
*The Future of History*

# Perfecting the New Wave of Collecting:
## Documenting Feminist Activism in the Digital Age

*Erin O'Meara*

Collecting feminist activists' papers and documenting related social movements has always had inherent problems. Challenges include the transient nature of activist organizations and their members, comprehensively collecting from dispersed groups that do not have regular record keeping practices, and the privacy concerns of activists who speak out on controversial topics. This chapter is a case study representing the early stages of learning how to approach digital materials.[1] While I was the Electronic Records Archivist at the University of Oregon, I worked with a collection of lesbian activist papers with a significant amount of born-digital materials.[2] Tee Corinne was a notable writer, photographer and lesbian activist. After starting a very successful career as a photographer and lesbian activist in San Francisco, she moved to southern Oregon in the early 1980s to take part in the women's "back to the land" movement with Ruth Mountaingrove, a photographer and early video blogger, alongside other women. Corinne was instrumental in building an intentional community in southern Oregon, while still creating powerful artwork. She died in 2006 and left her papers to the University of Oregon's Special Collections. Alongside the donation of the traditional papers came two computers filled with her email and writings, as well as her photographic work from the last several years of her life, when she began working with digital photography.

One of the unexpected groups of files on the hard drive were from Beverly A. Brown, whose papers had been acquired by the University of Oregon several years prior. She was Tee's longtime partner, but neither of them informed special collections staff that they had shared the laptop. The Manuscripts Librarian received the digital portion of Tee's papers after she passed, so staff were unable to work with her on the selection, arrangement and description of the files. If I had been able to work with her, the material might have been arranged and described with a more faithful interpretation of the original order and intention of the creator.[3]

---

1  "Born-digital information is distinguished from digitized, the latter describing a document created on paper that has been scanned (and possibly transformed into character data using OCR). A document created using a word processor may be described as born digital." Richard Pearce-Moses, A Glossary of Archival and Records Terminology. Society of American Archivists E-Publication. Available at, http://www.archivists.org/glossary/index.asp.

2  This paper will refer to "born-digital materials," as opposed to "born-digital collections" because the majority of collections that repositories collect and will be collecting for the near future are hybrid collections of paper and born-digital materials.

3  It is worth mentioning that even with interaction with living donors, archivists still have problems receiving descriptions about the context of creation and how collections were managed and used.

Prior to this donation, special collections had never acquired computers from a donor. The library previously acquired floppy disks, CD-ROMs and DVDs, but entire hard disks were not part of a transfer. The optical media was traditionally inventoried and shelved in archival boxes with the rest of the collection. The computer donation made library staff start to approach digital content in a more proactive way.[4] This was new territory to the Manuscripts Librarian. I was able to provide some basic procedures and best practices for taking the files off the computers and conducting a basic inventory of the contents for later processing. We made an ISO file (a snapshot) of the computer hard disks on a library server and then looked through a duplicate "use" copy to do some basic processing (e.g. removal of application files and other system files that were not needed).

Tee Corinne and her colleague and neighbor, Ruth Mountaingrove, were alike in their openness regarding use of their collections. This may be unusual compared to donors of other manuscript collections, but in the context of feminism and the women's "back to the land" movement at that time, it is not. They were proud of their accomplishments and wanted their stories to be shared. This story is indicative of collecting feminist activist papers that contain born-digital materials. They are collections rich with content that may have mixed ownership and third party privacy issues, but the donors have strong feelings about the future use and visibility of their collections.

Documenting social and feminist activism has been a topic of discussion in archival literature over the years, but there is little mention in the literature about collecting born-digital materials created by activists and activist groups. This essay will address the challenges of collecting and preserving born-digital material that documents feminist activism and will provide some possible technical and administrative solutions. In some instances throughout this chapter, I may refer to activists' papers in general, or cite related collecting efforts. The goal is to provide guidance on how to collect digital materials documenting feminist activism, but the larger concepts can be translated to other related collecting efforts.

The advent of digital tools and the internet has helped archivists identify and connect with activists by forming online relationships via social media sites and being able to survey records hosted on those sites. Online presences can help archivists understand the mission and vision of an organization, or the level of impact a feminist activist has within a community.[5] But the digital world has reinforced some of the difficulties repositories face when they try to holistically collect in an area like social justice or feminist activism. The location and custody of the digital materials and the ephemeral nature of digital content, especially material maintained on the web, pose challenges for archivists. Digital materials can reside in many different locations and are usually under

---

4   This involved both collecting staff and IT staff, who faced storage and technical requests after this acquisition.
5   Examples of this include promotion of activities, public stances on issues, blog posts and related comments, number of "fans" or "friends" on social networking sites.

little documentary control. Examples of locations of these materials include personal and organizational computers, email servers, and third-party websites like Facebook, Myspace, Twitter, blogs, Yahoo and Google groups, to name a few. Activists are often more concerned with the goal at hand, not legacy-building and recordkeeping. The digital era exacerbates this problem. Pre-Custodial Intervention (PCI) is a good way to pragmatically enable records management and preparation of materials for archival repositories, but it is easier to apply in a traditional organizational environment, not an activist or grass roots setting.[6] Suspicion of outsiders or temporary participants and the very nature of recordkeeping within activist organizations can make this strategy difficult and sometimes impractical, but some of the concepts of PCI, which will be detailed later, can be used to make collecting ultimately more successful.

Feminist activist efforts are usually centered around one or a few core group members. These core members manage email discussion groups, the blogs and the Facebook pages. This can be a double-edged sword for archivists. The core group can make it easier for the archivist to target specific members, but it also puts the digital materials at risk with only a few members serving as the "institutional record keepers" for the group. As Andrew Finn, Mary Stevens, and Elizabeth Shepherd assert in the context of community activist archives,

> ...the organisation's dedication and dynamism often tends to come from a small number of key activists who embody the vision and commitments of the archive. This individual dimension has significant consequences...it appears that one of the most dangerous times for the long-term sustainability of a community archive is in the period after its original driving force moves away or passes on.[7]

This is also true with regards to collecting feminist activist papers. Timing is always a challenge when collecting this material–the maturity of the group or the activist's career can affect what is available to preserve, but it is also important to make contact before the key players leave the group or abandon the effort. There are similar timing issues with acquiring digital materials for long-term preservation. Archivists need to be able to acquire the digital content before digital decay and obsolescence sets in, but must still respect the feelings of donors if it feels like it is too soon to think about the transfer of records into a repository.[8]

Other researchers hypothesize about different challenges. In the context of lesbian oral history Elise Chenier suggests that collection funding and privacy issues are some of the main barriers to preserving this material. At many institutions, funding for

---

6    Kevin Glick, Laura Tatum and Daniel Hartwig. Pre-Custodial Intervention: Let Them Do the Damn Work! Society of American Archivists Annual Meeting, August 30, 2008, available at, http://www.ibiblio.org/saawiki/2008/index.php/Session_502:_Pre-Custodial_Intervention:_Let_Them_Do_the_Damn_Work!
7    Andrew Finn, Mary Stevens and Elizabeth Shepherd. "Whose memories, whose archives? Independent community archives, autonomy and the mainstream." *Archival Science* 9 (2009): 79-80.
8    Archivists may maintain long-term relationships with donors and receive accruals of new content throughout the life of the donor or they can wait until the bulk of records no longer in active use by the donor.

lesbian and gay collections is limited, and the preservation of non-textual documents (including digital records) can test the staffing and budgetary limits of smaller archives. Privacy concerns can affect the willingness of interviewees to sign consent forms or deposit their oral histories:

> women are much more reluctant than men to consent to granting others access to their interviews…in some cases, narrators have reason to be concerned that if placed in the wrong hands, their testimony could compromise their personal safety and security in the present day. [9]

This sensitivity of some individuals could be extended from oral histories to paper and electronic records.

Personal privacy and the contemporary nature of some digital material make it even more important to think about access control in the digital age, especially if the repository where the materials will be stored makes them available publicly on the internet. If archives provide open access to materials on the web that were once password-protected or restricted in private online communities, how can we communicate to our donors that we can provide the same level of security they have been afforded on the web in the digital repositories we are building? Donors might be expecting the same type of access control that they are used to getting from third party services like Yahoo Groups, until the material has reached a level of "historical-ness" that makes it less sensitive to the members of the group. Archives need to develop consistent procedures for reviewing and restricting born-digital content that contains private or sensitive information. Language about access restrictions in the donor agreement can alleviate this issue, but the inclusion of recent and topical digital material may make donors hesitant to donate since they may worry security could be compromised more easily with digital files.[10] A recent software project that is being developed might be able to allow archivists to provide anonymous transfer of materials from activist donors who wish to transfer semi-anonymously. The software is called Tor and is currently being used by numerous groups who want to maintain online anonymity.[11]

### Pre-Custodial Intervention

As mentioned earlier, Pre-Custodial Intervention (PCI) is one strategy for facilitating the collection of born-digital material. PCI includes interacting with collections

---

9   Elise Chenier. "Hidden from Historians: Preserving Lesbian Oral History in Canada." *Archivaria* 68 (2009):256-259.
10   The Paradigm Workbook from the Personal Archives Accessible in Digital Media Project has guidance on what issues to cover in a donor agreement that includes digital material, http://www.paradigm.ac.uk/workbook/record-creators/agreements.html. In addition, the Workbook includes a Model Gift Agreement as an example, http://www.paradigm.ac.uk/workbook/appendices/gift-agreement.html.
11   More information about the Tor Project, https://www.torproject.org/.

before they are submitted to the repository. This strategy can work with feminist groups that are currently active, and it is commonly used when repositories are working with small organizations or non-profits that make regular donations. The author employed a PCI strategy with a local union chapter while at the University of Oregon. She provided onsite records management training in the chapter's office, and also surveyed their filing cabinets, file systems and electronic media to identify records that will make their way to an archive at some point in the future. This strategy is time-intensive, but is ultimately beneficial for both parties involved by helping the donor understand which records are of value and ways to keep them organized. As a result, the repository receives a more holistic and better-organized set of material from the donor and the organization is able to improve efficiencies in the workplace due to improved records management practices.

The idea of PCI is not new. Although not using the term, Paquet describes this concept in an article in 2000, "The consequence of this approach would be the development of a partnership with the donor. This partnership would see the periodic transfer of electronic records, thereby avoiding the problems associated with technical conversion."[12] PCI is advantageous for digital material because more attention would be paid to the material and regular deposits would be made, lowering the risk of file loss or corruption.[13]

Susan Davis points to the need for the role and position of collectors to shift,

> [archivists] are not involved at the records creation stage, nor are they necessarily consulted on the larger policy decisions within their institutions, nor do they have opportunities for early involvement with outside donors. This lament has been echoed within the profession for years.[14]

Collectors attempt to fulfill the role that PCI recommends earlier in the life cycle of the records, but we need new strategies to successfully place ourselves in this context. If collectors negotiate for a seat at the table earlier on, they need to be conversant and confident when surveying and working with creators of born-digital material. When collectors are not comfortable with new technology and forms of media, they will usually tend to avoid them when working with a donor. If the institution as a whole is uncomfortable with electronic media and doesn't have clear policies in place, potential donors might seek to place their materials at another archives that is familiar with preserving and providing access to born-digital materials.

---

12    Lucie Paquet. "Appraisal, Acquisition and Control of Personal Electronic Records: From Myth to Reality." *Archives and Manuscripts 28* 2000: 89.
13    Loss could occur through hard drive crashes, lapses in website hosting, abandonment of social media sites, superseded email addresses and listservs, just to name a few.
14    Susan E. Davis. "Electronic Records Planning in "Collecting" Repositories." *American Archivist 71* (2008): 185.

### Digital Preservation

The literature on electronic records and digital preservation is vast and growing. The archival community is publishing more case studies on how large repositories are addressing the acquisition, processing, preservation of and access to born-digital materials, but there is still a need to hear how smaller institutions can approach born-digital personal papers.[15]

The Blue Ribbon Task Force on Sustainable Digital Preservation and Access succinctly describes their perspective on the goals and activities of digital preservation,

> "Preservation insures against multiple risks to information assets over time. Such assets must be actively managed for sustained periods of time, using best practices for data stewardship across the full lifecycle of creation, description and curation, deposit in secure storage, use, and reuse. Some digital materials require relatively intensive levels of preservation to ensure usability, and others much less. But in all cases, access to information tomorrow depends on preservation actions taken today."[16]

This quote calls attention to the organizational planning necessary for digital preservation. Another resource on this topic that places high value on organizational planning and policies for digital preservation is the Inter-University Consortium for Political and Social Research (ICPSR). Their websites on digital curation present a well-reasoned approach for institutions beginning to address the long-term stewardship of digital materials.[17]

Preservation in the digital era shifts focus away from traditional modes of safeguarding the format towards ensuring the authenticity of the information conveyed. As Luciana Duranti has suggested, "as a result of media fragility and technological obsolescence, the term preservation as applied to electronic records no longer refers to the protection of the medium of the records, but to that of their meaning and trustworthiness as records."[18] Maintaining the trustworthiness of born-digital materials revolves around the environment and activities performed around the materials. Keeping the records safe from alteration (intentional or unintentional) is one of the basic components

---

15   Recent examples include, the Society of American Archivists' *Campus Case Studies* series available at, http://www.archivists.org/publications/epubs/CampusCaseStudies/casestudies.asp and Michael Forstrom's Article in the *American Archivist* titled, "Managing Electronic Records in Manuscript Collections: A Case Study from the Beinecke Rare Book and Manuscript Library." The Internet Archive hosted a conference that brought together numerous stakeholders and practitioners with case studies on personal archives called, "Saving our Present for the Future: Personal Archiving 2010," slides and video of talks are available here, http://www.personalarchiving.com/conference/.
16   Blue Ribbon Task Force on Sustainable Digital Preservation and Access. "Sustainable economics for a digital planet: Ensuring long term access to digital information," February 2010, accessed on July 23, 2010 at http://www.jisc.ac.uk/media/documents/publications/reports/2010/brtffinalreport.pdf.
17   Inter-University Consortium for Political and Social Research website, available at, http://www.icpsr.umich.edu/icpsrweb/ICPSR/curation/preservation/policies/.
18   Luciana Duranti. "The InterPARES Project," p: 10. From *Authentic Records in the Electronic Age: Proceedings from an International Symposium*, Vancouver, February 19, 2000. (Vancouver: University of British Columbia) 10.

of ensuring trust. Keeping the content, context and structure of the materials intact is a more technical way of articulating digital preservation. Repositories need to be consistent in the way they acquire, manage and preserve born-digital materials, which is akin to ensuring the evidentiary value of records that are produced for legal action. Archivists need to be able to ensure with some level of certainty that the digital material is what it purported to be when it was transferred to the repository.

Over the last few years, several good resources for handling born-digital collections have been created. As previously mentioned, the Paradigm Workbook on Digital Private Papers addresses nearly all aspects of collecting digital personal papers.[19] The core message of this reference publication is to develop documentation, including clear procedures and policies based on national or international standards for metadata, file-naming conventions and preservation activities. The Paradigm approach develops the infrastructure, core competencies and documentation that will prepare the repository for the variety of issues and complexity that comes from collecting and preserving born-digital personal archives. The PLATTER Toolkit is another fairly recent publication that focuses on assessment of preservation activities and development of clear preservation planning goals. The toolkit stresses that institutions must review their approach regularly as technology, standards and best practices change.[20]

## Collecting Strategies

Collecting hybrid collections with both born-digital and analog materials can be onerous. Some of the challenges include: multiple digital presences representing an individual or an organization, digital objects stored in various locations (online and on local machines), and messy or non-existent relationships between the digital and the analog records. A large portion of personal electronic records that are currently created falls into two categories: a) material created on a personal computer and saved locally or b) content created in a networked or online environment. Local content would be word processing documents or digital images stored on a computer. The main arena for information sharing and recruitment for activist groups now falls into that second category, primarily through various forms of social media sites. There is now a shift to where content is more frequently created in or hosted in a networked or cloud storage environment, such as Flickr, Picasa or Google Docs. Content created on third-party sites like Yahoo and Google Groups, Wordpress, Facebook and LiveJournal is often protected by licenses and terms of use agreements. Collecting in light of some of these restrictions has forced archivists to develop new clauses in their donation agreements and ask for donors' passwords to active accounts to gain access to material. Archivists

---

19    Oxford University Library. "Paradigm Workbook on Digital Private Papers," http://www.paradigm.ac.uk/workbook/index.html.
20    HATII, "Repository Planning Checklist and Guidance," http://www.digitalpreservationeurope.eu/publications/reports/Repository_Planning_Checklist_and_Guidance.pdf

are now employing content-scraping or harvesting tools at the public web level or collecting from the back end with passwords or assisted access to protected sites.[21]

One of the more complicated areas of collecting is the acquisition of e-mail messages and other modes of mobile communication, such as text messages, instant messages and "tweets."[22] The Library of Congress is now collecting tweets from public Twitter accounts, but some repositories still like to acquire specific accounts or subject areas denoted in hashtags in the tweet. Mobile messaging and mobile video sharing are increasingly prevalent ways to quickly share information, especially during events such as marches, protests and activist planning.[23] Direct messages are very personal, and individuals often form emotional and protective attachments to even their work e-mail accounts, in addition to their private email and mobile messaging accounts used at home. When archivists collect papers regarding an activist organization or movement, donors may only want the repository to collect the emails and other messages pertaining to that area. Due to the ease of search and growth in inbox storage allotments, a large portion of e-mail users use the big "inbox" management approach and do not use folders to organize their messages. In this case, it is very difficult to select portions of an inbox for acquisition, and it might be preferable to acquire the entire inbox and select and appraise during the processing of the collection. There are numerous web tutorials on how to export e-mail messages and an entire inbox from the various e-mail applications in use. Archivists have also developed software to select messages from an inbox and convert those messages into XML format.[24] A repository can determine an acquisition strategy for e-mail that is most appropriate to their collecting scope and existing technological resources.

### Rights and Privacy Issues

When you use a third-party service on the web or use software on a computer to create or publish material, you have explicitly or implicitly agreed to some terms of use from the company that owns the software or service. These rights cover appropriate use and may include terms about the rights to content created or stored by the software or service provider. These terms have long-term implications for archivists when they are

---

21    Sometimes the sharing of passwords can be a violation of the terms of service agreement from a social media site. Archivists and donors need to review these terms of service before deciding how to capture and preserve content from hosted services such as Facebook or Twitter.

22    Tweets are posts or status updates on Twitter (www.twitter.com) a microblogging site. Tweets are limited to 140 characters, but can contain links, references to other Twitter users and images.

23    Uploading video from mobile devices such as pocket cams and smart phones onto YouTube or Facebook has become the core mode of communication for activists. The 2011 "Arab Spring" protests have become a major example of the power of mobile documentation and social media. For more information, see Philip N. Howard, "The Cascading Effects of the Arab Spring." February 23, 2011, Miller McCune, available at http://www.miller-mccune.com/politics/the-cascading-effects-of-the-arab-spring-28575/.

24    The Collaborative Electronic Records Project developed an e-mail parser. Available at, http://siarchives.si.edu/cerp/.

documenting people and groups. Most donors do not know that there might be issues transferring material from these sites to the archives, so there is work to be done by archivists to educate donors about what rights they have and what can be transferred.[25]

Privacy issues should be addressed before transfer. The donation of an entire hard drive or of a complete snapshot of a computer's contents can enable the transfer of potentially sensitive information that the donor may not know about. Sensitive information like social security numbers, passwords, bank account information may be stored on a computer. Data mining techniques used by the digital forensics community are being modified for use in archives to identify this type of material.[26] There may also be information that the donor transfers that they do not want to be part of their official donation like website browser history, online purchase history and deleted files still living on the computer. Discussing these issues with donors might be challenging, but wording in the donor agreement should cover what data the archives is transferring and how they will protect any personally identifiable information that is identified while processing the collection.

### Establishing Good Working Relationships with Donors

As mentioned earlier, it is crucial to identify the member within the group who is their "digital project archivist" – the person managing their digital framework/ presence (e.g. Facebook, blog or website administrator). Building a relationship with this person is essential for collecting digital content. Gaining and building trust is a key logistical component to collecting feminist activist papers, especially if they were recently created in digital form.

A timeline for donation can be different for digital materials then analog materials. Time sensitive issues arise when trying to capture digital content before software and hardware obsolescence or bit or link rot occur.[27] Archivists may need to think about practical timelines for restricting access to the collection if they receive the digital materials soon after they are created. On the other hand, some groups may want a lot of publicity over the donation and want to have a method for nimble access to the newly deposited materials. Once an archivist works with the group's "digital archivist" to obtain the digital material, another issue to arise is authorship. With group sites like Google Docs, it can be very difficult to ascertain who contributed to shared documents and who the contributors were. The group may have authored something collaboratively,

---

25    Some resources to start with include the Terms of Service Tracker website, http://www.tosback.org/ timeline.php, the Data Liberation Front, http://www.dataliberation.org/, and the Electronic Frontier Foundation, http://www.eff.org/.

26    Tools like Bulk Extractor, http://afflib.org/software/bulk_extractor and Forensic Tool Kit, http://accessdata.com/products/computer-forensics/ftk are starting to be used by archivists for this reason.

27    The term "bit rot" is used when referring to the decay of files by the degradation or loss of bits within the file. When bits are "flipped" or missing, files can become corrupt or completely incomprehensible. Link rot refers to the hyperlinks that are "dead" or no longer available over time.

but who were the individuals that contributed the most to each of the documents in the group's workspace? Of course, this isn't a new problem—feminist and other activist collectives also created paper documents with collective or anonymous authorship.

Michael Forstrom encourages more interaction by archivists in the field with personal papers creators: "repository employees are creating and sharing digital preservation guidelines with authors, conducting records surveys, developing new donor and legal agreements and transfer tools, and arranging snapshot accessions of authors' digital archives."[28] General examples of guidelines and templates for collecting organizational and personal papers have been published, but creating one specific to a domain might provide more relevance to the records creators.[29] This could be called a "field approach" to collecting records, which includes:

- Meeting with donors and conducting surveys to gather information about their digital papers and how they created and maintained them
- Using guides to help assess digital media and formats in the field
- Bringing a portable hard drive or flash drive into the field when meeting with donors and surveying their materials.

Archivists may want to take a sample of the collection back to an electronic records specialist in their organization so that they can assess the preservation strategies that need to be applied.

When working in the field, archivists can learn how the donor interacts with technology. More practically, it is helpful to know how creators are actively managing their files on their computer and if they are using any file-naming conventions. This behavior will probably differ between formats (photos vs. word processing documents) and environments (online vs. local hard drive). In addition to asking questions about the material on their computer, archivists may ask about material created and/or published on websites. Identifying where the donor fits in the technological landscape can help inform how to survey and locate valuable material. Archivists should not assume older donors are not conversant with technology; likewise, they need to assess their own comfort level with technology. For example, if an archivist is working with a technologically savvy donor who wants to donate software that she has developed as part of her collection and they are uncomfortable with talking about source code, they should acknowledge that and seek help from a IT colleague in their institution.[30]

---

28    Michael Forstrom. "Managing Electronic Records in Manuscript Collections: A Case Study from the Beinecke Rare Book and Manuscript Library." *American Archivist* 72 (2009): 477.
29    Some examples of guidelines include "Don't Throw It Away: Documenting and Preserving Organizational History" from the University of Illinois at Chicago, www.uic.edu/depts/lib/specialcoll/pdf/DTIA.pdf, "Creator Guidelines: Making and Maintaining Digital Materials: Guidelines for Individuals" from the InterPARES 2 Projects, http://www.interpares.org/ip2/creator_guidelines/creator_guidelines.html, Council for the Preservation of Anthropological Records (COPAR) brochures, http://copar.org/bulletins.htm.
30    Paquet sees current donors falling into two generations, but I see it ten years after her publication as more of a spectrum of computer users. You need to figure out where the donor fits into the spectrum if technology issues arise. "The first generation are 50 years or older who began, late in their careers, to use the first personal computers. The second generation were born in the 1960s and 1970s, and who began, earlier in their

A lot can be learned from experience working with donors who have digital content. One way to systematize acquisition of digital content is to think about building a schema or workflow for acquisitions. The Tufts Accessioning Program for Electronic Records (TAPER) is a good example of creating a tool that enables a workflow, even if the specifics of each acquisition differ. [31] The Submission Agreement Builder Tool is open source software that project staff developed to enable control over submissions. Working with donors and acquiring digital content takes time, but so does planning for the long-term preservation and access of the materials.

## Planning for the Preservation of and Access to Digital Materials

There are many approaches to digital preservation. Choosing a realistic approach that is sustainable and works within your organization is essential to begin building a program that can handle born-digital materials. Archivists should build programs by adding sustainable services functionalities and staff expertise gradually and consistently over time.

*Preservation planning.* Preservation planning is a time-consuming process that many institutions do not allot sufficient resources towards. Planning, even just establishing a strategic path and basic procedures will make it much easier to handle a surprise acquisition that contains digital materials. Using a tool like the aforementioned PLATTER Toolkit is an effective way to see where your organization is, in terms of digital preservation readiness, and it is not extremely time-intensive to fill out the toolkit. Building infrastructure, staffing the program and identifying roles and responsibilities, allotting financial resources, establishing policies and procedures, and building capacity for the future are key components to a digital preservation program. Engaging in a planning process can help establish, plan, track and evaluate a digital preservation program. Beyond planning and assessing, there are numerous approaches to safeguarding digital content.

*Bitstream preservation.* Bitstream preservation is essentially maintaining the bits and bytes as they enter a repository, or keeping digital objects safe from alteration. The idea of persistence at a very basic level sums up bitstream preservation.[32] This is implemented technically by creating redundant copies of material and scheduling regular fixity checks (such as MD5 checksums), to test all the copies for bit rot or other forms of data corruption. This type of approach is the first layer of implementing a digital preservation strategy. The next step beyond bitstream preservation is format normalization and migration. Preservation formats are identified and procedures are

---

careers, using computers with the capacity and technology to allow them to create a greater volume and range of records." Paquet, "Personal Electronic Records," 73.

31    The TAPER project was an NHPRC-funded grant. Deliverables can be found here, http://dca.tufts.edu/?pid=49.

32    The notion that the digital objects can survive, through time without alteration or degradation.

established to migrate newly acquired files into an identified preservation format.[33] Through time these files may need to be migrated to newer versions or more stable formats, which is called format migration or refreshment.

*Ingest shortly after acquisition.* Many repositories currently acquire born-digital material on media and shelve it in acid-free boxes in the stacks, alongside the paper collections. This is called the "disk in a box" strategy or a "transferred via retired media" process and can result in easy media degradation and format obsolescence when the media ages out of sight and out of mind.[34] It is much more difficult to do regular "health checkups," like file integrity checks with checksums and file format validation, when material is not available for automated inspection and validation on a server. A more proactive strategy would be to ingest into a digital repository upon acquisition or soon thereafter. A compromise would be copy files into a secure staging area on a server that is backed-up regularly until the material is ready to be processed.

*Ensuring access through time.* An area that is often overlooked with born-digital content is planning for effective use of the collections for future research. With current archival modes of description and access it can be difficult to provide access to hybrid collections in a way that is clear to the user. Emory University's experience with the Salman Rushdie papers has shown how difficult it can be to provide access to born-digital content when strict access controls are in place.[35] Work at the University of California at Irvine (UC Irvine) with the Rorty papers employed a simple presentation layer for born-digital faculty content and looked at use statistics to inform future modes of access.[36] The Rorty example showed that many users came directly through search engines and not through a finding aid to the collection. There is still much to be done in this area and hopefully archivists' work with donors and engagement in the larger feminist activist community can help inform how archivists design and provide access to digital materials.

### Looking Ahead: New Tools and Opportunities

The Tee Corinne example illustrates how a special collections library might begin to handle groups of born-digital records. I joined the staff of the University of North Carolina at Chapel Hill (UNC) and, from that experience, I will discuss how new tools

---

33    An example would be to maintain the original file and migrate a copy into a "normalized" format such as all GIF image files into the JPEG2000 format.

34    Michael Forstrom discusses this concept in detail in his article, "Managing Electronic Records in Manuscript Collections: A Case Study from the Beinecke Rare Book and Manuscript Library." *American Archivist* 72 (2009): 466.

35    Emory's Manuscript, Archives and Rare Book Library acquired his papers and several of his computers and with negotiations with him, decided to emulate his files on a modern computer to simulate his computer environment on several outdated Macintosh computers, http://marbl.library.emory.edu/innovations/salman-rushdie.

36    The Richard Rorty digital files were placed on UCISpace, the campus institutional repository where the archivists could collect detailed use statistics.

and new perspectives are changing how archivists collect and process born-digital content. The introduction of new tools alongside processes across the entire special collections begin to address the preservation concerns raised earlier in this chapter.

Documenting and using consistent procedures for handling born-digital materials throughout the curatorial process is crucial to handling more digital content over time. At UNC's Wilson Special Collections Library, archivists are developing a field manual for collectors approaching digital materials. The manual will contain identification information about media, formats and types of material in digital form that are commonly acquired. It will also include basic questions to ask the potential donor, like what computers have they used to create the material? Have they moved the material from older computers onto more recent machines? Were they the only ones using the computers at their home or office, or are there unrelated files created by a spouse or co-worker? The hope is that the toolkit will enable curators across collecting units to feel confident when working with born-digital content. We are also building the capability to consistently handle the material once it is accessioned by developing a born-digital processing guide that technical services staff can customize.[37] In addition to new procedures, new technology is needed to allow technical services staff to arrange, describe and preserve the digital materials. A workstation is being developed where new material can be acquired. There will be a computer, as well as a jukebox for media acquisition similar to the Prometheus Jukebox stations at the National Library of Australia, as well as a write blocker.[38]

New archival tools and tools from other disciplines are moving the archival field.[39] These new tools allow institutions, large and small, to devise holistic plans for preserving digital collections. Open-source processing tools like the Curator's Workbench and Archivematica are being developed to enable repositories around the world to implement curation services, rather than cobble together small scripts and tools.[40] There are also new testing environments where archivists can evaluate tools for managing digital collections, such as the Planets Testbed.[41] New practitioner-led research and

---

37    We are using a template approach since UNC processes university records differently than manuscript collections housed in the Southern Historical Collection.

38    The Prometheus Jukebox is a tower that enables acquisition from various media like floppy disks and CD-ROMs. Specifications for how to construct one are listed here, https://sourceforge.net/projects/prometheus-digi/files/Documentation/Prometheus_Component_Installation_Guide_SF-v1.pdf/download. Write blockers are used in the digital forensics community in order to prevent machines from writing over values or damaging files. They allow read commands, but do not allow the machine that is acquiring the media to perform write commands, therefore reducing the chain of custody needed for the files to be used as evidence.

39    Tools from the digital forensics field are now being used to analyze and process digital personal papers in order to ensure their authenticity. See the recent CLIR report by Kirschenbaum, Ovenden and Redwine entitled, "Digital Forensics and Born-Digital Content in Cultural Heritage Collections" available at, http://www.clir.org/pubs/abstract/pub149abst.html.

40    The Curator's Workbench is open-source software developed at UNC. It is a tool that enables accessioning, arrangement and description of digital objects, http://www.lib.unc.edu/blogs/cdr/index.php/2010/12/01/announcing-the-curators-workbench/. Archivematica is an open-source digital preservation system that is currently being built by Artefactual Systems, http://archivematica.org.

41    The dedicated hardware and software environment provided by the Planets Testbed is located here,

development projects have the hope of generating relevant tools for archivists. Projects like AIMS – Born Digital Collections: An Inter-Institutional Model for Stewardship and the aforementioned TAPER: Tufts Accessioning Program for Electronic Records both have deliverables focused on helping digital archivists acquire and manage material.[42]

There is also a rise in the popularity of new tools for capture and management of content in the creators' domain. Curation activities do not start with the intervention of a collecting repository. Creators often want to take part in preserving their digital content while it is still in their custody and now software can help them take control of and preserve their online presence.[43] Self-curation tools, although not a solution to digital preservation, can enable PCI with feminist activists so repositories will be able to more easily take custody of their digital collections.

## Conclusion

Beyond basic technical concerns, one of the most important collecting activities, even in the digital age, is to build good relationships with records creators. Forging relationships with feminist activists is key to building representative and complete collections. The incorporation of the digital preservation strategies within this approach will make a repository's collecting strategy ready for acquiring digital collections. This includes maintaining regular interactions with donors to develop a more consistent accrual process. Regular accruals of digital materials will enhance the ability to preserve it before it is lost or damaged. As donors' hard drives crash or get superseded; as they go through several email addresses and other changes in technology, regular accruals will help to build a more complete collection over time. Archivists are finding that more born-digital content is lost through abandonment of websites and email addresses than bit rot or media obsolescence. This new hypothesis emphasizes the importance of the PCI approach of regular contact with donors and regular deposit of web and email-based material in the digital age.

As we look to the future, I am hopeful. Activists seem to be more aware of the need to manage their digital content more carefully than paper records, whether it is content within an online presence or files on a computer. McGovern and Kenney describe five organizational stages for digital preservation: *acknowledge, act, consolidate, institutionalize, and externalize*.[44] I think we are seeing a disciplinary shift from *act* to *consolidate*, where

---

http://testbed.planets-project.eu/testbed/.

42    AIMS is an inter-institutional grant funded by the Mellon Foundation, http://www2.lib.virginia.edu/aims/. TAPER is a Tufts-led project funded by the National Historic Publications and Records Commission, http://dca.tufts.edu/?pid=49.

43    Software tools like Give Me My Data for Facebook, http://givememydata.com/, Facebook's native application to download your data, http://www.facebook.com/blog.php?post=434691727130, Twapper Keeper for Twitter feeds, http://twapperkeeper.com.

44    Anne R. Kenney and Nancy Y. McGovern. "The Five Organizational Stages of Digital Preservation," in *Digital Libraries: A Vision for the Twenty-first Century*, a festschrift to honor Wendy Lougee, 2003. Available from the University of Michigan Scholarly Monograph Series website:

the archival community is "segueing from projects to programs." More dedicated, long-term funding and staffing are being allocated to digital curation and electronic records activities.[45] With this shift to a programmatic approach, I think even small to medium-sized institutions will be able to start to address issues of collecting born-digital papers, going well beyond the "disk in a box" scenario. This shift will benefit repositories collecting feminist papers, since many of them are independent or smaller archives within large research institutions.

http://quod.lib.umich.edu/cgi/t/text/text-idx?c=spobooks;idno=bbv9812.0001.001;rgn=div1;view=text;cc=spobo oks;node=bbv9812.0001.001%3A11.
45    Over the last five years, there have been several institutions hiring Electronic Records Archivists and Digital Archivists that have had the management of born-digital objects listed as major responsibilities in their job duties.

# No Documents, No History:
## Traditional Genres, New Formats

*Amy Benson and Kathryn Allamong Jacob*

From Schlesinger Library's founding in 1943, documenting women's activism has been central to its mission. What was first known as the Women's Archives began with a gift to Radcliffe College by alumna Maud Wood Park, an ardent suffragist and first president of the League of Women Voters, of 1,156 folders of her own correspondence, the papers of co-workers for suffrage, other material that she had gathered on the movement, and more than three hundred books on women's rights. Park considered her gift to be both a scholarly resource and a memorial to the power of women's efforts to secure the vote.

The Women's Archives opened in a small suite of rooms furnished with Victorian antiques in Longfellow Hall. Almost immediately it began to grow. Historian Mary Ritter Beard, who well knew the power of primary material and famously noted "no documents, no history," donated collections. So did Harvard historian Arthur M. Schlesinger, who noted the paucity of scholarship about women in his 1922 book *New Viewpoints in American History* and deplored most historians' assumption that "one-half of our population have been negligible factors in our country's history." These and other historians saw the Women's Archives as the nucleus of a research library for the study not merely of the suffrage movement, but of all women's activity in America.

That women's activism made up a large part of that activity was reflected in new acquisitions. In the Archives' first two years, the papers of physician Mary Putnam Jacobi, who organized the Association for the Advancement of the Medical Education of Women, and Leonora O'Reilly, an immigrant's daughter who became a fiery labor organizer for the Women's Trade Union League, were added to its suffrage material. By the late 1960s, the Women's Archives had become the Arthur and Elizabeth Schlesinger Library on the History of Women in America, and its collections filled two entire floors of the old Radcliffe College Library. At its twenty-fifth anniversary in 1968, the Library's manuscript holdings included nearly three hundred collections of personal papers and the records of forty-nine women's organizations. These new collections documented the whole spectrum of women's activism. Mid-nineteenth-century causes such as abolition, temperance, peace, and women's rights are represented by the letters of Julia Ward Howe, Susan B. Anthony, and Lucy Stone. Papers from the next genera-tion of activists feature strong-willed political organizers like Helen Brewster Owens, a lieutenant of Carrie Chapman Catt, who described her grassroots campaigning for suffrage in Kansas and New York. The last phase of the suffrage crusade is documented in collections that include the papers of National Woman's Party leaders Doris Stevens and Jane Norman Smith.

Other reform impulses that burgeoned in the 1890s can be traced through collections at the Library: the papers of Ethel Sturges Dummer, a philanthropist and social welfare worker in juvenile courts who was active in the mental hygiene movement; settlement house leader Mary Kingsbury Simkhovitch; and two Boston settlement houses, both founded by women—Denison House in the South End and the North Bennet Street Industrial School in the North End.

The arc of women's activism from the early 1900s through World War II is documented in collections like those of Jessie Donaldson Hodder and Miriam Van Waters, successive superintendents of the Massachusetts State Reformatory for Women at Framingham, Massachusetts; working women's advocate Hilda Worthington Smith; pioneering activists in medicine like Mary Sewall Gardner, founder of the National Organization for Public Housing Nursing, Dr. Alice Hamilton, an expert on industrial poisons, and Dr. Mary Steichen Calderone, a leader in sex education; and Florence Luscomb, whose activism for suffrage, international peace, civil rights, women's rights, and against the war in Vietnam spanned eight decades.

With the surge of the Second Wave of the women's movement in the 1960s, the Library's manuscript and book collections grew rapidly as feminist activists highlighted the importance of women's history, created their own documents and publications, and wrote their own books. As the movement gathered momentum and members and became more organized, a cascade of new collections began to pour into the Library and continues still. These include the papers and records of Betty Friedan, Flo Kennedy, Charlotte Bunch, Pauli Murray, Bernice Resnick Sandler, Alix Dobkin, Andrea Dworkin, Judy Chicago, Shere Hite, Bread and Roses, National Organization for Women, National Abortion Rights Action League, Women's Encampment for a Future of Peace and Justice, *Sojourner*, and Persephone Press.

While a passion for social justice unites all of these collections, from that core gift of suffrage material in 1943 to the collections of post-World War II feminist activists like Susan Brownmiller, they all share something else as well: notwithstanding a few audiotapes and films, these collections, which now number more than three thousand, are all paper-based. Carbon copies of letters on fragile onionskin paper; pink and aqua plastic-covered, rhinestone-studded diaries; thick ledger books with names and numbers of members in fledgling organizations; brittle mimeographed broadsides announcing public protests; cardboard signs from the March for Women's Lives; blurry purple typescript on mass mailings and calls-to-arms run off on spirit duplicators; scrawled letters on pages covered with nearly-indecipherable cross-writing; newsletters on such poor quality paper that splinters seem possible; programs, polemics, and articles on highly acidic newsprint carefully pasted onto even more acidic scrapbook pages with hideously tenacious glue; photographs, once attached with paper corners, flutter out of albums by the dozen; rousing speeches written out in longhand on pages filled with marginalia. Paper, paper, paper, paper, paper.

Despite the wide range of preservation issues presented by these paper-based documents, we know how to store, catalog, and make them available to researchers, thanks to our long association with them. Schlesinger Library and other archives are very, very good at this, having done it for decades. But for almost a generation now, paper documents have been losing ground to born-digital material such as blogs, web sites, and e-mail. Many blogs are akin to online diaries; an organization's web site supplants its print collateral; and e-mail has largely taken the place of letters and paper correspondence. In the past two years, Schlesinger Library has acquired forty-six collections that include some quantity of electronic material in formats such as Microsoft Word documents and Lotus Notes spreadsheets, and on media ranging from 5.25" diskettes to CDs, memory sticks, and even complete hard drives. The Library's resources for studying women's activism in the 19th and 20th century are rich and deep. How will we guarantee the same depth and richness of resources for the scholars of the future who want to study third wave and future feminist movements, whose records and papers are created directly, and sometimes exclusively, in a digital environment? How will we store, catalog, and make these electronic documents accessible?

This is the challenge with which the Library and all archives that collect contemporary material are wrestling. The format of information may be changing, but that doesn't mean we can stop collecting it. We can't, not if we want to continue to meet our core objective of documenting the lives of women in America. At Schlesinger Library, we've begun to tackle this challenge with three specific traditional genres of material that until recently have been paper-based: diaries, print collateral (brochures, promotional material, conference programs, minutes, event calendars, etc.), and correspondence. We're exploring how to select, store, catalog and make accessible their approximate digital equivalents—blogs, web pages, and e-mail.

Blogs share many characteristics with traditional paper-based diaries. Our collections include the diaries of more than three hundred and fifty women that date back to the early 1800s and offer a range of viewpoints from the ordinary to the history-changing. Filling hundreds of bound volumes, they record the personal histories of homemakers, wives, mothers, teachers, activists, abolitionists, suffragists, and feminists across the centuries. The diaries of Harriet Jane Hanson Robinson, a Lowell mill girl, begin in the 1840s and document her passionate work for the abolition of slavery, for women's rights, and all human rights into the early 20th century. The diaries of Evelyn Wallace (1923-1981) detail her daily activities, menus, housekeeping chores, and finances. The hand-illustrated diaries of writer, activist, and feminist Cindy Crabb, author of the influential zine *Doris*, begin in the mid-1980s and are ongoing into the 21st century.

This range of subject matter is found in blogs as well. As diarists have done before them, bloggers record their thoughts, triumphs and frustrations, muse about their lives and the world around them, reveal likes and dislikes, and record their comings and goings. Unlike traditional diaries, however, blogs are generally open to the public, and are, in many cases, used to communicate with, inform, or build a broader community. In some cases, that community is limited to friends and family members with whom people share the stories of their lives, but in other cases a blog is used to relay information, give and gain support, encourage action, call others to arms, or serve as a rallying point for activism around a particular topic such as health, family issues, politics, or personal freedoms.

Clear parallels between diaries and blogs can be seen in three of the blogs that the Library is following: Karma Express (http://karma-express.livejournal.com/); Nykola. com (http://www.nykola.com/); and Blue Bird Escape (http://www.bluebirdescape. com/). Each of these blogs is written by a young woman as she searches for her place in the world. In their blogs they cover topics from body image issues to adjusting to life in a new country to trying to live up to parents' and society's educational expectations. Other types of blogs, like those of feminist activists Barbara Ehrenreich (http://ehrenreich.blogs.com/) and Charlotte Bunch (http://womensmediacenter.com/blog/author/charlotte-bunch/) offer commentary on social and feminist issues of the day. Because many of these blogs contain the type of content that Schlesinger Library has collected in the past, curators recognized the need to be able to acquire this type of born-digital content for its collections.

In addition to blogging, activist women and activist women's organizations have also taken to publishing on the web. Primary source materials such as minutes of board meetings, newsletters, broadsides, membership information, fundraising campaigns and event calendars make up a large portion of Schlesinger Library's physical collections. Maud Wood Park's initial gift included calls to action and announcements of meetings of the National Woman's Party and the League of Women Voters. Dr. Mary Calderone's papers include publications and information on the Sex Information and Education Council of the United States. The records of two activist groups that have disbanded—the Genes and Gender Collective and the Women's Equity Action League (WEAL)—include promotional material, minutes, appeals for funds, and material on conferences and annual meetings. All of this printed material helped an organization explain its *raison d'etre*, communicate with members and garner interest. Scholars study this material to discover how an organization changed or is changing over time, and consider how it reveals the public face it presented to the world. And while many existing activist organizations still publish paper-based newsletters, or print annual reports, for many groups, these paper publications are now either supplemented or replaced entirely by electronic publications, most often provided through a web site.

Web sites not only provide basic information about an organization (or individual) but have the potential to provide supplementary material, links to past publications, and pointers to related resources. Schlesinger Library holds the papers of the International Foundation for Gender Education (http://www.ifge.org/), the National Abortion Rights Action League (http://www.naral.org/), the National Organization for Women (http://www.now.org/), and the Boston Women's Health Book Collective (http://www.ourbodiesourselves.org/), all of which have extensive web sites that document their structure, membership, programs, and efforts at outreach. If Schlesinger Library is to be the repository for these institutions, it must be able to incorporate their web-based material into their collections.

Correspondence is another cornerstone of Schlesinger's collections. We have letters, lots and lots of letters, written on all sorts of stationery—flower-bedecked, black-bordered, and lined. We have letters between Julia Ward Howe and the women with whom she worked on so many causes; twelve- to fifteen-page letters written to Betty Friedan after the *Feminine Mystique* appeared in 1963; and letters from the 1970s begging the Boston Women's Health Book Collective for help with issues about health and sexuality. And then in the 1980s, the first hint of change came to the archives, the camel's nose under the tent, the first evidence of a new way of corresponding called e-mail. Not the electronic files themselves, at first, but page after page of paper print-outs that begin with the oh-so-familiar heading "From: Sent: To: Subject:" There are printed e-mails in the June Jordan papers about her activism on behalf of bisexual, women's, civil, and human rights and in the papers of women's health activist Barbara Seaman from women sharing their medical ordeals. And then, early in this century, the electronic messages themselves began to arrive. The progression in the collection of singer/songwriter and activist Holly Near is striking as it moves from traditional paper-based fan letters and occasional hate mail to folders full of print-outs of her first e-mail messages to the disks and an actual hard drive containing the e-mail files themselves.

It is clear to historians, archivists, researchers and the women who created them that the paper documents already in archives are vital to learning about and understanding the history of feminist activism. As these types of documents go digital, Schlesinger Library—and all repositories, really, no matter whether they document environmental, labor, political or health activism or no activism at all—must begin to select, capture, store, and make available these materials in their new formats. What follows is a description of how Schlesinger Library has begun to grapple with this migration of the documentation of women's lives from paper to bits and bytes by embarking on two major pilot projects supported by Harvard University Libraries and its Office for Information Systems (OIS): WAX (Web Archive Service) and EAS (Electronic Archiving System).

Our efforts to capture blogs and web sites began in earnest in 2006 with Schlesinger Library's participation in Harvard University's Web Archiving Pilot. The pilot project was intended to investigate the feasibility and sustainability of developing a web archiving service at Harvard. For the pilot, OIS worked with two university partners in addition to Schlesinger Library: Reischauer Institute of Japanese Studies and Harvard University Archives. OIS developed the system and tools, while the three partners undertook curatorial functions and provided crucial input regarding collection requirements and user needs.

## Diaries = Blogs

For the pilot, Schlesinger Library chose to focus on women's blogs, creating a collection called, "Blogs: Capturing Women's Voices." Our goal was to take the pulse of women publishing digitally in blog format. The pilot project offered us an opportunity to test our ability to document women's use of a new technology, to capture their voices at the beginning of the 21$^{st}$ century, and to gain first-hand experience with the issues and challenges involved in collecting and archiving born-digital material.

## Choice

One of the first challenges was the selection of the blogs themselves. Collecting diaries on paper differs in many ways from capturing similar content in the form of blogs on the web. With paper records, the Library is often lucky to find one or a few examples of content that has made it through the march of time unscathed. But as anyone who has searched the web knows, there is an abundance of every kind of content—literally, almost endless choice. When so much is available, the challenge becomes deciding what to choose. Many factors went into our decisions about which blogs to collect. Because the content, even though in a new format, becomes a permanent part of the Library's collections, it was necessary that it fit within the Library's collecting policies. Every effort was made to identify blogs that would have lasting research value, a concept that is difficult to define under any circumstances, but perhaps more so with blogs, as their use for research is less well understood. Another factor centered on the notion of "representative" blogs, an idea that one or two blogs of a certain type could serve as models to illustrate the characteristics of that type. After much discussion among the pilot participants, a questionnaire was developed to help assess blog candidates for inclusion in the project. Questions ranged from whether the content was being captured elsewhere by another institution to identifying restrictions on a blog that might block capture or future use of the content; we were essentially trying to determine which blogs were worth the time and expense of capturing, reviewing, and paying long-term storage costs. After much discussion and research, we chose 33 blogs for the pilot. They ranged from *Abortionclinicdays*, by two anonymous abortion providers (http://abortionclinicdays.blogs.com/); to *Babyfruit*, by Aliza Sherman about birth, miscarriage, breast feeding, and postpartum depression (http://babyfruit.typepad.com/baby/); to *Mamita Mala-One Bad Mami*, by Meagan "la Mala" Ortiz, a "radical Nuyorican mami" (http://www.lamamitamala.com).

## Permissions

After identifying the blogs for inclusion in the project, the next issue we wrestled with was copyright. Of course, each blogger holds the copyright to her posts. While the posts are published and are freely available on the web, capturing that content, and then storing and republishing what is essentially a duplicate copy in the archive presented certain legal concerns. Also, some bloggers actively prohibit harvesting of their site by using robot exclusion files. An exclusion file consists of coded instructions to web crawlers, granting or denying permission to capture the site's content. Other bloggers effectively prohibit crawlers from capturing their sites by password protecting them; it is difficult for crawlers to negotiate a login screen. After consultation with Harvard's Office of the General Counsel, the Library decided to obtain explicit permission from the bloggers themselves before including their content in the archive. This task proved to be more challenging and time-consuming than anticipated. Many of the blogs selected for the pilot were written by women who had chosen to blog anonymously. In cases where the bloggers could be identified, letters were sent out requesting permission for inclusion in WAX. Generally, responses were positive, although the Library was turned down by the representative for a female-to-male transgender blog who was uncomfortable with the association of the blog's content with Schlesinger Library, a repository for women's history. In another case, after permission was received from a blogger, the Library was contacted by the angry web master of a site whose content was being captured collaterally because it was linked to by the selected blogger. After explaining the WAX service and the Library's mission, the web master was not only willing to allow the capture but became a champion of the cause to preserve this ephemeral material. A more common and difficult problem was lack of response to the Library's request. Eventually, we built in to our request-for-permission letters a "no-response" clause indicating a date after which, if no response was received, permission would be assumed. With permissions in place, we could move on to the next step in the process: the web capture.

## Technology

WAX is comprised of two interfaces: a curator interface called WAXi that has tools for managing collections and harvests, and a public interface through which end users can search and access the archived web content. In addition, WAX has a crawler system that works behind the scenes to capture snapshots of the curator-selected blogs and web sites at specified intervals. In WAXi, curators enter a URL for each site, or "seed." The URL represents the starting point for the crawler to begin capture. Once the content is captured, curators use the tools in WAXi to assess, describe, and then push the content into Harvard's Digital Repository Service (DRS) for preservation, after which it becomes available to users. As a result of this process, long-term stable access is provided to this otherwise ephemeral material. The steps are straightforward, but not without their challenges. During the course of the pilot, the Library wrestled with decisions about the content itself and had to address issues that resulted from the state of web archiving software.

Even after choosing to include a blog in the pilot and obtaining permission to capture it, the Library's curators and archivists had to make other decisions that had an impact on the relevance, value, usability, and sustainability of the material. One such decision involved *scope*. The scope of a harvest determines how much of a site will be captured. Within WAXi, a curator has three options. The smallest scope limits the capture to a single section, or directory of a web site, which was useful when the blog was just one part of a larger site. Using the second scope option, the curator sets the capture for an entire site, but not beyond. This level of capture includes all sub-directories and pages, including sections of the site such as the blogger's profile and the blog archives. Alternatively, a curator can expand the capture to go one "click" beyond the blog site to capture web content that is linked to from the initial site. This broadest scope option is useful for capturing the context of a blog. For example, a blogger might comment on a news story or a post on another blog. If the other site's news story or post

Tuesday, July 27, 2010
## The Kids Are Alright
So, I ran across this post in Bully Blogger a little late, but it offers an interesting critique of the movie as a finely acted but stereotypical and conservative ordeal characterizing "lesbian desire as a flickering flame always on the verge of extinction and of lesbian-male rivalry as always a mismatch."

> While the film's moral outcome is supposed to favor the women and leave Paul out in the cold, it actually delivers, whether the film means to or not, a scathing critique of gay marriage. If the message here is "see gay marriages are just like straight ones - we all face the same problems," then surely the outcome of the film would be the end of marriage, the desire to find other kinds of arrangements that work? But no, this film, like many a heterosexual drama that turns the family inside out only to return to it at the film's end, shows that marriage is sexless, families turn rotten with familiarity, lesbians over parent and then it asks us to invest hope into this very arrangement.

I knew there was a reason I haven't felt compelled to see this movie.
Posted by KC at 7:11 AM  0 comments
Labels: film, lesbians, movies

*Figure 1. A Link to Content on another Site within a Blog Post*

isn't also captured, the context is incomplete, and quite possibly the relevance of the post is lost. Using this expanded option, "linked-to content" is captured in addition to the content from the original site. In the example opposite, the post is from the blog of independent journalist Kelly Cogswell (http://kellyatlarge.blogspot.com/), which the Library collects. The underlined text "Bully Blogger" in the body of the post links to a post on another blog (http://bullybloggers.wordpress.com) which was also captured.

A curator must decide the scope for each seed and how much external material is needed to provide context for a blogger, her posts, and readers' comments. How much is "noise", and how much of the "noise" might be of interest to future scholars? Curators must strike a balance between capturing too little and too much. Constraining a capture to the blog itself may remove essential context for posts and damage the blog's relevance and value. On the other hand, expanding the scope of all seeds to include linked-to content can result in the capture of great quantities of unvetted web content, some of which, the Library learned, may be pornographic, and much of which is not relevant to the Library's collection goals. The capture of the additional material adds to staff time needed to review harvests, resulting in higher costs, and the retention of larger harvests increases storage fees. Thus the choice of scope for each seed has a significant impact on the relevance and value of the collection as well as on long-term costs.

The *frequency* of harvests also has a similar impact on resources. Every harvest must be reviewed by staff and stored long-term, so that frequent captures add dollars to the bottom line. However, by capturing a blog just once a year, the Library runs a real risk that a blog will "go dark," meaning that a blog's content becomes unavailable, either because a blogger stops blogging and removes the blog content from the web, or decides to restrict access to the blog. In either case, that content is lost to the Library. Over the course of the two and a half years of the pilot, eleven bloggers in our pilot collection, one third of the initial group, stopped blogging or began requiring a password to view their site, underscoring the ephemeral nature of this material and the importance of determining and setting an appropriate frequency for captures.

Even with blogs at little risk of disappearing, determining the best frequency of capture was a challenge. At the start of the pilot, capture frequency was set to once a month for all of the blogs, but it soon became clear that once a month was too frequent. In the typical blog format, posts are organized chronologically, with the most recent content appearing front and center on the site and earlier posts accessible through the site's archives. Each month, all new posts were captured by WAX crawlers, but along with the new came all of the previous posts in the sites' archives dating back to the beginning of the blog. As a result, the Library was capturing a lot of duplicate content with each monthly harvest. As a potential solution, the Library could capture a blog's archives the first time the site was captured, and then exclude the site's archives from future captures. However, in WAX's public interface, each harvest stands alone as a separate, unconnected file so that users can't navigate from one to another. Thus, while viewing a later harvest, if a user clicked on the link to the archives of a blog, she would get a message that the content was not in the archive, even though it had been captured in an earlier harvest. As expert users of the system, Library curators know that all the relevant content has been captured and could be accessed, but there is no easy way to convey that information to the public.

The separate nature of each harvest creates a similar problem when bloggers change the title of their blog or their blogging platform (from Typepad to Blogger, for example) because it results in a changed URL. For example, "Sisters Talk," by Genia Stevens, an African American lesbian mother from Wisconsin, was one of the pilot blogs. At the start, the blog's URL was http://sisterstalk.tblog.com/. After a time, the blogger changed blogging platforms. She continued her blog under the original title, but it now had a different URL (http://sisterstalk.net/blog/). For now, there is no way to combine, or even link the harvests that occurred under the two different URLs. They appear as separate blogs in the public interface, which will likely cause confusion for the researcher, but which we will try to mitigate with information on the help page.

In addition to the impact curatorial decisions described above have on the long-term value of harvested content, web archiving technology has an impact on what can be captured and the degree to which a capture looks like the original site. Web technology is constantly evolving and expanding into new frontiers, and web archiving software cannot keep up. This gap can create at least two kinds of problems. One is with the capture itself: in some cases, it is not possible to actually capture the content displayed on the live web site. For example, at the time this article was written, capturing streaming videos like the ones found on YouTube, is very difficult. Many institutions conducting web archiving such as the Internet Archive and the British Library are working on solutions to this problem and we hope to be able to add the ability to collect video on the web in the future.

The other problem is the way archived content is rendered for display to users. It might be expected that a capture of a web site would look exactly like the original site when viewed in a contemporary browser. However, web sites are complex entities, made up of many separate files that may come from a variety of sources so that the timing of a harvest, or a web master's decision to block images from harvest may result in missed content and the archived site will not be an exact replica of the live site. Additionally, many blog platforms use Java Script to expand and collapse calendar menus for access to previous posts, or to expose and hide reader comments. The Java Scripts do not perform correctly in the archived copy of a web page. In the public interface, a user will see a "content not found" message when trying to expand a menu or view comments, making it appear as if the content is not archived, when, in fact, it was captured, but must be accessed in a different way. If there are several such "missing" elements in a harvest, the archived copy may end up with substantial differences from the original site. The curator must determine how much of the look, feel, and functionality, or "user experience" is necessary to retain the value and usefulness of the blog content.

### Print Collateral = Web Sites

Despite the challenges encountered, the web archiving pilot overall and Schlesinger Library's blog project within it was an overwhelming success. WAX was launched as a production service in February 2009. Schlesinger Library is pleased to have the ability to capture web content that falls within its collecting purview. Buoyed by this success, we have begun developing a second web Archive Collection called "Schlesinger Library Sites" (SL Sites). In this case, the collection focus is on the web content of the people and organizations whose papers are held by the Library. In effect, the Library wants to capture the kind of content about an organization or individual, formerly published in paper format, such as brochures, calendars, policies, by-laws, and the like —the print collateral— but that is increasingly available only in electronic format.

Many of the challenges faced while creating the blog collection were simplified in the building of the SL Sites collection. Due to the nature of the collection, the selection of sites is straightforward. This WAX is simply an extension of the Library's current holdings: if Schlesinger holds an organization's papers and the organization has a website, we capture it. For example, the records of the Gloucester Fisherman's Wives

*Figure 2. Center for New Words Web Site in WAX*

Association were recently processed, and at the same time, their web site was added to WAX and set up for regular captures. WAX allows us to extend our collecting to the born-digital content produced by these organizations that we would otherwise miss.

The Library sees permission to capture a person or organization's web site as an extension of the existing legal agreement it has with each donor, so no new permissions needed to be sought. Having an agreement in place greatly reduced the time and resources spent on permission issues as compared with the blog project. While we didn't seek permission from each donor, we did notify them all of our intention to capture their web content. An additional outcome of this project was a revised donor agreement form that explicitly requests permission to capture a web site.

Because the focus of this collection is on the content produced by the organizations themselves, Schlesinger curators decided to constrain harvest scopes for all the web sites in the collection to the primary site only, rather than the expanded scope chosen for the blog collection. This choice reduces the quantity of material harvested and the issues resulting from the capture of the extra, unvetted content. And, whereas blogs are often hosted on third-party sites that can include unrelated and possibly unwanted advertising and other content, an organization generally controls its own site and all of the content within it, making the review of harvests much simpler. The Schlesinger Sites Collection will continue to grow as the Library's collections grow, adding web sites as new collections are acquired.

The Library's mandate is not complete with the capture and archiving of this electronic content; it must also describe and make the content accessible to users. To increase users' ability to discover the blog content that we have captured, we add a bibliographic record to Harvard University's main catalog, HOLLIS, for each blog. In addition to the author's name and a description of the blog, the HOLLIS record includes relevant subject headings and a link to the archived content through the WAX public interface. We also added a bibliographic record to the catalog for the blog collection as a whole. Where the archived web content is part of an existing collection for a person or organization, we are integrating it with their paper collections through the finding aid and the bibliographic record for the collection, both of which provide links to the archived web site harvests through WAX.

At this point in time, while most web content continues to be available and accessible, it is easy to wonder about the time, effort, and resources spent capturing and archiving this content. However, of the original thirty-three blogs in the pilot, Schlesinger has already seen almost fifty percent of them disappear in the three years since the harvesting began. Even in the very new SL Sites collection, we have harvests of four web sites that have since disappeared from the web, and we know of one web site that disappeared before a successful capture could occur. Once again, "no documents, no history." To continue its collecting mandate, Schlesinger Library must identify, capture and archive the documents that will reveal women's history to future scholars, no matter the format.

### Letters = E-mail

Quite literally bit by bit, electronic mail has replaced the letter as the primary means of correspondence in the world. All archives, regardless of their collecting focus, are experiencing the change, and it is felt keenly and tangibly at Schlesinger as new collections arrive as small boxes of disks instead of cartons of paper-based documents. The ease and rapidity of e-mail correspondence has both promoted its proliferation and obscured its significance as part of the historical record. Even today, few organizations have explicit policies about the types of e-mail employees should retain and which should be deleted. It is the casual attitude toward the preservation of e-mail, rather than spectacular technology failures that more often conspires to thwart the archivist. The importance of collecting and preserving e-mail as part of the historical record is not in doubt, but today's curators must determine how best to handle this growing mass of electronic primary source material.

Where the handwriting is clear and the language known, we humans have no trouble reading letters from hundreds of years ago. With e-mail, however, some kind of technology is required in order to access its content, and the necessity of technological mediation is the crux of the challenge in preserving e-mail for future generations. With each change in technology, new hardware and software are employed for the writing, sending, and reading of e-mail, often introducing incompatibilities with past content. It may be that messages can be read in only one specific program, or they may become corrupt and completely unreadable when migrated to a new system. Unfortunately, we have no time machine in which to travel back and mandate a single system for all users, so we are left to deal with the situation as we find it. But fortunately, there are tools that make it possible to convert older mail formats to newer ones, and much work has been done to create standard mail formats suitable for long-term preservation. Harvard University drew upon these tools and efforts when developing a system to assist its libraries with archiving the e-mail making up an increasing portion of their collections.

Schlesinger Library is home to hundreds of feet of paper-based correspondence among women, many of them activists, going back to the early 1800s. In the last two years, the Library has acquired four significant collections of e-mail in electronic format. All of Harvard's libraries are in the same boat: the amount of electronic content will only continue to increase. Recognizing the need to be able to process and preserve e-mail, in 2008 Harvard University Libraries began a pilot project designed to develop and test a system for the archiving and preservation of e-mail. Three Harvard units are participating in the pilot: Schlesinger Library, the Harvard University Archives, and the Center for the History of Medicine at Harvard's Francis A. Countway Library of Medicine. Archivists, curators, records managers, and librarians from all three institutions, together with the staff at Harvard's Office for Information Services (OIS), determined the functional requirements for an e-mail archiving system that would meet the diverse needs of such a large organization. At the end of the pilot, Harvard curators and archivists will have a system to ingest, process, and preserve e-mail. It is anticipated that the system will become a permanent, centralized service at the University, and will continue to be maintained and developed after the pilot.

The first version of the web-based e-mail archiving tool for curators called EASi (Electronic Archiving System interface) was released early in September 2010, just at the time this article was being written. Over the course of the coming year, pilot participants will test the system and provide feedback about major functional areas such as workflow, metadata, and interface design. Schlesinger chose the e-mail of singer/songwriter and activist Holly Near as its test collection. Near's e-mail archive will complement the hundreds of her paper correspondence already at Schlesinger Library, and Near agreed to review and sort the e-mail herself before sending it to us to remove items that were not intended for the collection because of their sensitive nature.

### Workflow

As a first step in processing an e-mail collection, curators deposit e-mail files in a central storage location maintained by OIS. The deposit triggers a process that imports the files into the EASi system and converts the e-mail to a normalized format. The ability to import e-mail created by a variety of clients is a key feature of EASi because of the great variety of e-mail clients in use: Microsoft Outlook; Entourage; Eudora; Gmail; Thunderbird; and Yahoo, to name just a few. E-mail messages are actually complex communications packages made up of multiple parts (headers, message bodies, attachments) and each e-mail client handles these components in different ways. The normalization process makes it possible to view e-mail from many different clients within the EASi system.

After normalization, the content is automatically virus-checked, scanned for spam and for two types of high-risk data: credit card and social security numbers. Other processes for automatic recognition of data that represent potential security risks may be implemented in the future. Once the e-mail files are imported, normalized, and scanned, curators determine the appropriate level of processing for the collection. If resources aren't available for full-level processing, a curator can minimally process a collection within EASi, and then push the collection to the DRS for preservation. Moving e-mail collections to the DRS, even with minimal processing, reduces the risk of losing the files if they were to remain on less than optimal storage media such as CDs, DVDs, hard drives, or flash drives for long periods of time. Curators will be able to return to collections to complete more in-depth processing should resources become available later.

Even though the EAS interface is still in development, it is possible to outline its basic features. In addition to searching, browsing, and reading e-mail messages and their attachments, curators and archivists will be able to use system tools to organize the e-mail into collections, add rights and access restriction metadata, associate e-mail addresses with people and organizations, and delete e-mail messages and/or attachments. They will be able to work on single e-mail messages, on groups of messages, or on a collection as a whole, assigning tags to categorize messages and setting dates as reminders of actions to be taken in the future. These tags and flags will allow curators to manage their processing workflow more easily.

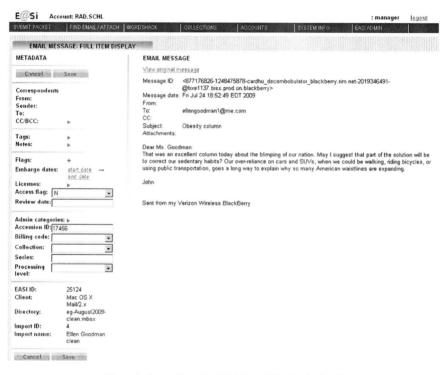

*Figure 3. Screen Shot of a Brief Record Display in EASi*

In addition to the content of the message itself, e-mail messages have headers that contain information about the sender, recipients, dates and size of a message. These data points can be used to sort and organize the e-mail messages in ways that are not possible with paper files. At the touch of a button, messages can be put in date order, sorted by sender, recipient, or subject line. The content of all messages will also be searchable by keyword, allowing a user to locate every reference to a name or term of interest such as RU-486 or mifepristone, an abortion inducing drug which was approved for use in the U.S. in 2000, no matter how large the collection.

EASi will also provide curators with authority control tools, allowing them to manage variations in names, e-mail addresses, and institutional affiliations of senders and recipients. In cases where an e-mail address obscures a person's real name, or when the same person uses more than one e-mail address, use of the authority control file will support robust searching within and across collections.

These tools will assist curators in assessing e-mail content for relevance, and for privacy and security issues beyond the limited automated processing that occurs on import. Issues of privacy restrictions and copyright are difficult enough to deal with in paper records. Considering the vast number of e-mail messages that archives will receive, the review process will present a serious challenge. Ideally, archives would not receive sensitive material, but, as is the case with paper collections, donors are not always able or willing to weed their material before it comes to us. How will we identify and remove or restrict content that poses a security or privacy risk? The sheer quantity of e-mail messages makes the idea of reading or even scanning each message for privacy concerns impossible. We can rely upon embargoes on the content for set periods of time, as we do with many paper collections, but all archivists and curators are hoping that additional automated tools will be developed to assist with this time-consuming but important task.

Another area of concern with electronic files stems from the fact that most digital files can be copied again and again without variation or loss. Many types of electronic files are editable and it is rarely evident when such changes are made. Paper letters can, of course, be manipulated or even forged, but the ease and relative undetectability of changes in electronic documents places a burden on the curator, the archives, and e-mail archiving systems to deliver to the end user collection materials as they were received, or with clear statements about changes made and why. Both for legal reasons and for the scholarly record, archives must be able to guarantee that the electronic files they deliver to an end user are identical to those they received from the donor. To that end, EASi tracks actions taken in the processing of a collection, such as when messages are deleted, creating an audit trail from import to deposit.

## Going Forward

The very nature of electronic documents makes possible interactions with the source material that could significantly impact how researchers work and open exciting new paths of inquiry. Current users of the system, and eventually scholars, will be able to use search tools to narrow their focus to e-mail from specific time periods, to specific recipients, or both. Each instance of a word, or phrase in even a vast collection of correspondence can be identified and viewed, eliminating the need to read through message after message as one must with letters. Other tools such as simple text analysis programs could be used to count word occurrences within a collection and use them to create tag clouds, or other visual aids as windows on a collection. With large e-mail collections, it may no longer be possible to read every message one by one as is often done with letters on paper, but rather research may require the assistance of a machine to compute or commute the content into manageable portions. It is an open question whether electronic collections would even require the creation of a traditional finding aid. As Harvard's pilot progresses, we may gain additional insight into these and other questions.

In light of the enormous quantity of e-mail that will become part of archives everywhere, and the resources that will be required to process it, curators and archivists must begin to explore new methods of processing. Working with donors early in the process, whenever possible, to encourage them to weed and organize their electronic correspondence, could produce enormous benefits. Curators must look for ways of reaching out to donors and potential donors to educate them about good e-mail management practices that will facilitate the eventual processing and archiving of their e-mail. However, as most curators know, donor review of their own material is difficult to enforce. Even for the owner of the material, the quantity may be too much to review. And, while additional automated tools may become available in the future, we may need to consider alternative processing methods that will balance our need to safeguard the privacy and security of our donors and our mandate to support scholarship through access to these valuable primary source materials.

While the e-mail archiving pilot project began as a means to handle material already in archives at Harvard, it soon became clear that e-mail was just one type of electronic record that curators would need to collect, process, store and preserve. Early in the process, staff at OIS realized that the system architecture should be designed to handle other types of born-digital content in addition to e-mail, such as spreadsheets, data sets, and file groups made up of more than one file type. EASi has changed its name from E-mail Archiving System interface to Harvard's Electronic Archiving System interface, making clear the expanded nature of its mission.

In September 2011, when the EASi pilot is complete, Schlesinger Library staff anticipate having a tool for the processing and preservation of the e-mail within its existing collections and within collections to come. Although the pilot will end when EASi goes from a test system to a production environment, development of the system will continue. The next major step will be the provision of access to end users. Providing access to end users was not a requirement for the pilot project, but the necessity of developing a public interface was kept constantly in mind and significantly influenced the development of the existing system. Data and features that will be needed to support user access have already been built into the system and should facilitate its eventual development. In the meantime, curators will be able to offer mediated access to e-mail content through EASi when appropriate.

When contemplating a future in which even more and more of our communication and interactions will be via some sort of electronic media or by methods we can't begin to fathom today, it is easy to get lost in what can often look like a maze of minutia. But while grappling with the details of these challenges, we can't lose sight of the bigger picture, the reason for saving and making accessible the documents of women's lives and women's activism. These documents can open windows onto not only women's lives but onto all lives and all of American history. This is powerful stuff. These primary sources, no matter what their format, have the potential to fuel innovative interpretations of our shared past and offer lessons for the future. Whether paper-based diaries, print collateral, or letters stored in acid-neutral boxes on shelves or blogs, web pages, e-mail or formats we can't anticipate today stored in bits and bytes in a digital repository or who knows where and how, we must identify, capture and archive the documents that will reveal women's lives to future scholars. We are all feeling our way; there is much to learn and to share. But we can hear Mary Beard whispering at our shoulder, "No documents, no history."

# Second Wave

*Our History Is Not Yet Past*

# The Juggling Act: Cooperative Collecting and Archival Allies in the Collection Development of Second Wave Feminist Materials

*Elizabeth A. Myers*

## Introduction

Archivists engaged in the process of actively developing their collections—the focused practice of outreach, networking, and relationship building to increase subject holdings or expand into new areas—tread complex and challenging terrain.[1] For lone arrangers or a solo collection development staff member, the task is even more daunting due to the large amount of resources required in the development process. Such resources, including time, energy, knowledge, and enthusiasm, are the bedrocks archivists use in building connections to new donors and maintaining ties with existing ones. Each of these components increases exponentially when cultural, racial, ethnic, sexual, religious, age, geographic, or economic barriers exist to slow or hamper the establishment of those relationships. Even if potential donors are generally accessible and amenable to starting the conversation about donation, the process is not necessarily easy. Relationships, built through the establishment of fundamental trust between the donor and the institution as embodied in the archivist, can take weeks, months, and even years. And the legal and physical transfer of materials requires at a minimum the need for space, staff, and supplies to honor even the most basic deed of gift. Finally, since the relationship with the donor rarely ends with the donation itself, there must be a commitment on the part of the archivist to maintain the relationship in the future—whether in the form of periodic communications or something more substantial. Ultimately, this framework for thinking about the collection development process assumes that most, if not all, of the thornier issues have already been addressed, including the existence of a clearly defined collection development policy, an understanding of the public(s) served by the archives, a thorough analysis of existing facility/institutional resources, and fully articulated rationales for expanding into new collection areas.[2]

Though much of what archivists do can be considered essential work, the formulation of a documentation strategy and active engagement in collection development is at the very heart of the archival enterprise. From the earliest stages of the profession, archivists were given a blueprint, refined over decades, on rethinking what collec-

---

1    This chapter was originally delivered in part as "The Juggling Act: Negotiating Third Party Collaboration in the Collection Development of Second Wave Feminist Materials," by Kelly Wooten on behalf of the author at the Society of American Archivists Conference, Washington, DC, 2010.
2    For a comprehensive, contemporary, and essential examination of collection development see Frank Boles, *Selecting and Appraising Archives and Manuscripts* (Chicago: Society of American Archivists, 2005).

tions we have, why we have them, and how we are complicit in their gathering as well as long term care. All archivists, at all levels of institutional size, must grapple with collection growth. This is equally true for archives with space to grow and for those archives already straining under inconsistently guided expansion. At the same time, there are larger systemic and contemporary issues complicating matters for archivists working to collect materials. The short, over-generalized list includes the question of relevancy of physical archives in the face of widespread and generally incorrect public perceptions of digitization/digital assets. Another problem is the challenge posed by sustained periods of economic uncertainty. Lastly, the slow but certain weakening of the value of humanities-based education in the United States potentially points to an uncertain future for archival audiences.[3] In this challenging climate, how does one create the structures and relationships, internally and externally, that make active collection development successful?

For archivists looking to collect materials most at risk—by un- or under-documented populations and subcultures—a sense of urgency is added to the work. In particular, for archivists or archival allies interested in women's records there is an increased burden placed on the responsibility to justify the need for separate women's collections and women's archives. Even now in the linguistics of popular culture terms like "feminism," "feminist," "radicalism," and "Women's Movement" remain at best heavily contested.[4] Thus, one may argue that archivists interested in documenting women face a double burden of relevancy along with the other obstacles encountered by any archivist in the collection development process. The essentialism so central to the second wave women's movement, born of the larger Civil Rights Movement that in turn yielded the demand for unique archives and archival collections to women, is hardly a universally valued concept among academics, archivists, and the public. Do women's collections need to be in women's archives? Are women's collections undervalued in mixed-gender archives? Is it necessary for women to collect women's records? These are just a few of the questions that persistently shadow women's archives. No doubt, the study of women and women's history was the impetus behind the founding of women's research centers and women's archives from the 1970s through the 1990s. Yet, as the research projects and methodological frameworks of women's history and women's studies are altered

---

3   For a starting point on these complex issues, see Kate Hafner, "History, Digitized (and Abridged)" *New York Times* (March 11, 2001); Fernando Cervantes, et.al., "The Future of Humanities" *Times Literary Supplement* (5/12/2010 and ongoing); Katheleen Woodward, "The Future of Humanities—in the Present and in Public," *Daedalus* 138 (Winter 2009): 110-123; Peter Hirle, "The Impact of Digitization on Special Collections in Libraries," *Libraries and Culture* 37 (Winter 2002): 42-52; and Max Evans, "Archives of the People, by the People, for the People," *The American Archivist* 70 (Fall-Winter 2007): 387-400.

4   Even in archival literature, there is a paucity of secondary resources related to the specific context of women's archives. An exciting new edition, not yet available at the writing of this chapter, is the edited work *Women's Archives Reader* edited by Tanya Zanish-Belcher and published by the Society of American Archivists. Another recent option is Nupur Chaundhuri, Sherry J. Katz, and Mary Elizabeth Perry, *Contesting Archives: Finding Women in the Sources* (Urbana: University of Illinois Press, 2010) but the focus is generally how historians and other scholars relate to women's sources globally, with an equal concentration on methodology and women's archival collections.

with the inclusion of gender and sexuality studies, how do archivists make the case for women's collection's uniqueness? A more radical question may be, should they? These more theoretical questions have real implications for archivists conversing with potential donors and can be easily overwhelming to an archivist trying to build women's collections. The more isolated the archivist, the more daunting the prospect of collection development. Yet there are powerful and effective models for archivists in the search for new women's collections.

The most essential and perhaps obvious model is to share the load with partners. Collaboration is not new to archivists, librarians, museum specialists or other participants engaged in public history and knowledge sharing.[5] Cross-professional collaborative projects, especially within institutions such as universities and colleges with libraries and archives, are common. Indeed, with the blending of access points between archives and libraries through MARC, EAD, or Contentdm with OCLC features, basic collaboration is getting to be more commonplace.[6] But in the specific work of collection development, the conversation around third party collaborations—those outside or wholly unrelated to the parent institution—and archives is just beginning to gather steam. What follows is a case study of a third party collaborative process specific to women's archives, women's organizations and partnerships, and women donors. However, it is also a model for the general collaborative process whenever a third party or archival ally may be involved. As will be demonstrated by the case study, success of third party collaborations may well be dependent upon recognizing and even embracing the increasing fluidity of the respective roles between donors, archivists, and allies in the process.

---

5    Examples of such partnerships include a call to action by Liz Bishoff, "The Collaboration Imperative: If Librarians Want to Lead in Creating the Digital Future, They Need to Learn How to Work with their Colleagues in Museums and Archives," *Library Journal* 129 (January 2010): 34-35 and case studies such as LJ Pijeaux, "The Birmingham Civil Rights Institute: A Case Study in Library, Archives, and Museum Collaboration," *RBM* 8 (2007): 56-60 and Nancy Chaffin Hunter, Kathleen Legg, and Beth Oeherts, "Two Librarians, an Archivist, and 13,000 Images: Collaborating to Build a Digital Collection," *Library Quarterly* 80 (January 2010): 81-103.

6    The comprehensive history and application of common library cataloging and its relationship to archives and manuscript collections can be found in Kathleen D. Roe's *Arranging and Describing Archives and Manuscripts* (Chicago: Society of American Archivists, 2005). The adoption of librarian cataloging formats such as MARC (Machine Readable Cataloging) help archivists better control, organize and standardize how archival collections are described. This is intended to create better access points to the collections by researchers using usual library search engines, such as their local library catalog , or union catalog systems such as offered by the nonprofit OCLC (Online Computer Library Center). More recently, EAD (Encoded Archival Description) has been instrumental in adopting similar cataloging principles to finding aids to offer better access via the web but without the intermediary of a licensed—and therefore often restrictive—library catalog. As has been pointed out, EAD offers both stability and uniformity in the format of the online finding aid but without the rigid limits of MARC. Similarly, with regards to digitization, materials born digital or migrated to digital form can be cataloged using existing catalog systems or new systems. For example, with the popularity of some for-profit digital content management systems, such as ContentDM, the creation of a catalog record using the same standards of MARC has become an integrated part of the process of asset management, control, and access.

## Reaching Out, Getting Started

Collaboration has always been at the heart of the Women and Leadership Archives at Loyola University Chicago. As a small institution founded in 1994, the Women and Leadership Archives (WLA) has, by necessity as much by desire and design, sought to expand beyond the borders of the university. The foundation collections at the WLA consist largely of Mundelein College and prominent Mundelein College Alumnae. Mundelein was the last four-year women's college in Illinois and founded by the Sisters of Charity of the Blessed Virgin Mary, or BVMs. As such, the WLA collection strength skews largely Catholic toward both lay women and women religious. The solid foundation of the Mundelein records allowed for the WLA to grow quickly in the areas of Catholic women, Catholic women activists, women in social justice movements, women as community builders, feminist theology and criticism, and feminist theologians. Given the size and strengths of these collecting areas, they remain a main pillar of the WLA written collection development strategy. At the same time the mission of the WLA is much broader in scope—indeed the very design of the mission, "to collect, preserve, organize, describe, and make available materials of enduring value to researchers studying women's leadership activities" is extraordinarily inclusive.[7] Though every former director of the WLA left an imprint on the collection development of the archives, each shared the common belief that "leadership activities" should be interpreted as broadly as possible. Thus the fundamental questions are: How does the current collecting scope best honor the mission? What can be done to expand the collections? How does one maintain the current base of donors while reaching out to new communities of women, women's subcultures, and individual women?

These questions are ultimately framed by the institutional structure and limits of the WLA. As of early 2011, the staff consists of one full time person, several paid graduate assistants, several unpaid graduate and undergraduate interns, and volunteers. The WLA is currently over 90% processed with an estimated backlog of only six to nine months. In a similar vein, onsite storage sits at only 60% capacity. Thanks to fiscal support from the University Libraries and the Ann Ida Gannon, BVM, Center for Women and Leadership of Loyola University Chicago, there is a complement of resources available in the form of a general operating budget as well as a growing gift fund enabled by donors and friends of the archives. Though the WLA has no onsite preservation lab, resources are available to handle any special case of preservation, digitization, or complex storage problem should the need arise.

Within this framework, time management and appropriate resource allocation remain key in creating and executing a sustainable collection development plan. Utilizing the unique strengths and overcoming the shortcomings of the WLA in collection development remain contingent upon being able to (1) tap into a donor community,

---

7  Women and Leadership Archives website: www.luc.edu/wla

(2) arrange an education, outreach, or sponsorship event, (3) make meaningful connections or conversations with donors, and if successful (4) facilitate the transfer of materials to the archives. Between 2003 and 2007, a certain level of administrative fluctuation hampered these basic goals. During that same time period, the WLA moved from one building to another on Loyola's lakeshore campus. Despite the new beautiful location, increased space, and institutional support, scant new material came in. The new material that did arrive came mostly from previous commitments, not new donors. In 2005, for example, the WLA received less than seventy linear feet of material, sixty-four of which came from prior commitments. Even with a newly formed advisory board created the same year, there was little promotion or awareness of the archives even among Loyola's faculty and staff. Another major roadblock was a lack of focus in future collection development. The WLA was known as a place for Catholic women's papers, but again, how could the archives live up to and maintain its broader mission?

Combined, these issues meant that though there were legacy collections/donors to consider and wonderfully detailed existing case files on potential donors, there still was a sense of starting from scratch. However, to engage in collection development from the ground up required a level of time that as director of the Women's Leadership Archives I was hard pressed to find while also running the day to day operations of the archives including teaching, outreach, collection management, maintaining the WLA web presence, general reference, inner-and-extra university committee work, and supervision of staff. Understanding both the need for new collections and the limitations of my resources meant that I simply could not do everything myself. I had to seek outside partnerships if I was going to build the collections, especially around non-Catholic women and non-Catholic women's organizations. I did not have to cast my net far before I found the Chicago Area Women's History Council or, rather, they found me.

Only a few months into my new job in 2007, the Director of the Chicago Area Women's History Council, Mary Ann Johnson, approached me. The Chicago Area Women's History Council (CAWHC) is a non-profit organization whose mission is to, "promote the study, interpretation, and preservation of women's history."[8] Founded in 1971, the CAWHC serves as a network for "historians, archivists, teachers, museum professionals, oral historians, preservationists, activists, and others interested in the study of Chicago women past and present."[9] Originally envisioned as a network for scholars engaged in women's history, the organization has since branched out with a more inclusive, public history focus. This change is evident in the organization's own name change from Chicago Area Women's History *Conference* to Chicago Area Women's History *Council* in 2003. Over the past forty years, the CAWHC sponsored meetings at the prestigious Newberry Library, supported conferences, workshops, tours, teacher training, discussion groups, and "other education programs designed to share women's

8   Chicago Area Women's History Council website: www.cawhc.org "About Us," accessed 3/3/2011
9   Ibid.

history with a broad audience."[10] I knew of the organization through their last project, the immense and incomparable *Women Building Chicago, 1790-1990: A Biographical Dictionary*. Published in 2001, the book was the final product of ten years of labor involving dozens and dozens of volunteers, contributors, and scholars.[11]

In the course of our early discussions, Johnson explained that the Council was embarking on a new project that was designed to have a substantial archival component. Then titled, "Documenting the Women's Movement in Chicago, 1960s-1980s," the project was said to have three discernable phases: first, a survey of existing archives for women's movement records and the creation of a public, searchable database of the results; second, conducting and collecting oral histories with women of the movement and the placement of those oral histories in an archives; and third, the discovery of at-risk collections which ultimately could be directed to and/or placed in an appropriate archives. My level of participation in the project would be to serve as an archival advisor to the Council, to be the principle repository of the oral histories, and to serve on the Council board for a term of not less than two years. I readily agreed.

Ultimately two archivists principally advised the initial phases of the project, University Archivist of DePaul University, Kathryn DeGraff and me. DeGraff's wisdom was clearly needed and keenly heeded during her shorter term as advisor. She perceived immediately that there should be a wider approach to the archival component. She suggested that the project include other Chicago area archives/archivists interested in continuing to collect women's movement records and/or begin new collections. In other words, Loyola and DePaul should not be the only beneficiaries of materials nor receive substantive favoritism within the project. To my thinking, this insight is reflective of a gradual shift among archivists, to view collecting through an intra-collaborative prism and with greater transparency. Both of these concepts are basically, but not exclusively, feminist principles of sharing information, resources, and access to and with donors. Innate to this structure, as opposed to the purchase of materials or the treatment of collecting as a high-stakes competition, is the recognition that no single archives can or should accept everything that it is offered even if there is a desire to do so. Instead, by collaborating, all archives potentially benefit and archivists are able to operate ethically and responsibly. Essentially, by recognizing that some collections are better served at another archives, archivists are able to unveil and admit an ugly truth—many archives have reached full capacity, are understaffed, or are suffering from other, sometimes severe, resource limitations.

With a more open archival framework decided upon by the CAWHC, we began to reach out. After sending out feelers for interest on local listserves and simply by calling around, a core of ten archives, with varied missions, locations, and collections, voiced a

---

10   Ibid.
11   Lunin Shultz, Rima and Adele Hast, eds. *Women Building Chicago 1790-1990: A Biographical Dictionary* (Bloomington: Indiana University Press, 2001).

strong interest in participating in the project.[12] After a few meetings and many, many emails, a booklet was created to share with prospective donors that listed the following information about each repository:

- the general collecting scope;
- future areas of collecting interest;
- format, size, or other limitations;
- hours of operation;
- and contact information.

Plain by design, the booklet listed all archives alphabetically, thus giving advertent preference to none. Council members utilized the booklet to promote the archival component equitably. In addition, at the official public launch of the project held at the Chicago History Museum in March 2008, CAWHC volunteers collected information from attendees via a short survey form. This resulted in three quantifiable pools of information: (1) volunteers willing to work on the project; (2) activists with knowledge about the movement for potential oral histories; and (3) potential donors with archival material in their possession. Often, the lines between these categories were blurry, as some women identified as all three. Nevertheless the forms were helpful to the CAWHC as a starting point to gauge public and community interest as well as the potential type and volume of archival material in donor's hands.

After some deliberation at the board meetings, we decided that a Council member who was not an archivist but had unique knowledge of the Chicago archival community would play matchmaker between those women who had archival materials and the participating archives interested in collecting the materials. In the interest of maintaining an ethical distance, I in no way participated in the matchmaking or discussions about its progress. The pairing of potential donors and archives was based on the collecting scopes of the respective archives—as self-defined by the archives in the booklet—and the presence of existing collections. For example, the initiative paired newly discovered Chicago NOW records with the repository that already possessed some Chicago NOW records. This approach recognized that local merging of existing collections was ideal not only for the archives, but for the researchers who would have to travel less between archives in order to visit related materials. Despite the fairness of the matchmaking, newer archives such as the WLA were at a disadvantage in that we had few existing collections to pair with newly discovered additions. Nevertheless, the disadvantage proved less so when entirely new collections of either individuals or

---

12    The final ten included: Art Institute of Chicago Ryerson and Burnham Archives, Chicago Public Library Special Collections and Preservation Division, Chicago Public Library Woodson Regional Library—The Vivian G. Harsch Research Collection of Afro-American History and Literature, DePaul University Special Collections and Archives, Women and Leadership Archives of Loyola University Chicago, Newberry Library Roger and Julie Baskes Department of Special Collections, Northern Illinois University Regional History Center, Northwestern University McCormick Library of Special Collections, University of Chicago Special Collections Research Center, and University of Illinois at Chicago Special Collections and University Archives.

organizations emerged, such as was the case with a group of feminist artists—which will be discussed in greater detail below. With the booklet in hand, donors make their own informed choice, with some degree of advice, about where to put their materials—a process that continues today.

It is worth noting that at several large public events held to publicize the project, including the project launch, the Council strove to include as diverse a group as possible in terms of speakers, audience, and archivists. Very often, esteemed women's history scholars such as Sara Evans and Stephanie Gilmore gave heft and purpose to the project by framing their own research in terms of what they could or could not find in an archives. In addition, the Council tried with great effort to find and encourage women of the movement to bring them into a welcoming environment within which to discuss their histories, stories, and collections. However, reaching a broad base of the women's movement proved consistently difficult in that, like the movement itself, racial and ethnic diversity was found wanting. Finding women of the movement using traditional research methods such as biographical dictionaries and membership lists coupled with assistance from web based resources still meant that many women were unintentionally excluded. Reaching the most diverse audience, with special respect to race/ethnicity and sexual orientation, continues to be a goal rather than a reality.

Ultimately, the successful pairing of donors and archives concluded the first part of the project. The CAWHC did not participate further in the discussions between donors and archives, but focused its contribution on the act of pairing. After the initial push, however, the limits of the matchmaking role and the observation that we did not reach as many diverse women as hoped became clear. After some lively debate, the CAWHC understood that the project timeline needed to be expanded to include the immediate post-World War II time period and extend as far as 2000 if we truly sought to capture the width and breadth of the women's movement. In addition, the Council had to rethink basic concepts of locality, regionalism, activism, and even the phrase "second wave," if we were to reach the largest segment of women and women's organizations. More specifically, we all had to think beyond national names and groups and beyond national issues and legal fights that often encompassed the better-known aspects of women's liberation in the mid-to-late twentieth century. When we extended the very definition of activist, a whole new horizon opened up to include women who did not think of themselves as agents of change but who, nonetheless, challenged the very local gender- and sex-based inequalities they confronted. By expanding the definition of activist, we were also able to think more inclusively about different areas of activist expression: political, public protest, quiet resistance, art, music, theater, health, neighborhood organizing, cooperatives, local markets/marketing, and so forth. To underscore the idea, by enlarging the traditional definitions of activism and participation the Council succeeded in embracing the truly 1960s mantra: the personal was political and, in our case, local. Thus, potential donors were able to self-define their own historical identities, choosing roles like activist, mother, wife, lover, daughter, friend, student, radical, moderate, conservative, lesbian, bisexual, feminist, traditionalist, progressive, liberal, volunteer, employee, Socialist, Democrat, or Republican. Within this new framework, the project gained a sharper definition and moved forward broadly to include entirely new groups of women. As a group, the CAWHC succeeded in constructive self-reflection by rethinking its own role, definitions, and understanding of women's contributions which resulted in a deeper and more complex venture overall. Ultimately this resulted in the rechristening of the project as "Documenting Women's Activism and Leadership in Chicago, 1945-2000."

Because of the new and exciting change to the project's breadth and scope, it is possible to draw some conclusions about the beginning and initial launch, particularly couched within the archival perspective. The results of three full years of participation clearly resulted in some major successes. First, by participating in the project, being present at Council events, and encouraging multiple archives to participate, I was able to build stronger working relationships with other local archives. By extension, the partnerships between archives morphed into professional networks between archivists. Through those networks, I learned a great deal about other archives and developed a deeper appreciation of their institutional goals, structures, and limits. I ultimately came to understand the value of group collecting strategies—or cooperative collecting, as I have come to think of it—as a way to foster collegiality and decrease potential, even if unintentional, exclusions. In other words, collecting did not have to be hyper-competitive even when it came to very exciting collections. Ultimately, no archives could accommodate all of the materials unearthed as a result of the Council's project. Working together, via an unbiased "yenta," meant that important at-risk collections were salvaged and made safe. At a minimum, those collections were brought to the attention of professional archivists who could advise and guide donors at every stage of the donation process. Even for donors not yet willing to part with their materials, there were memorable instances of archivists helping to answer preservation questions as a form of community outreach or professional volunteerism.

As a second point of success, through the number of public events associated with the project, the publicity through the CAWHC and WLA websites, a spot on National Public Radio, local press coverage, and the professional cooperation shared among archives, the WLA's profile has risen both within and outside of Loyola University Chicago. In this particular time of fiscal uncertainty, underscoring archival relevance and connectivity to the community is a win-win, especially with administrators who often require such tangibles as markers of progress or success. As an experienced orga-nization, the CAWHC kept tally of how many people attended events, used surveys to follow up with individuals, wrote successful grants for project funding, and partnered with local universities and colleges to work toward building the database for women's collections. To be able to claim membership in such an organization and demonstrate concrete, material gains (new users, new donors, new collections) again pushes back against the relevancy issue. This was especially true for the WLA. If there was ever a question of the need for a women's archives, even in a place as diverse and archives rich as Chicago, the success of this project to date is a resounding answer: *yes*.

The third point of success is clearly related to the second: The WLA received a total of 22 new collections of varying sizes as a result of the project. The majority of these new collections came from a specific group of donors, Chicago area women artists. In fact, the real success of third party collaborative collecting between the CAWHC and WLA can be explored in greater detail through the project's outgrowth in the Artemisia Artists Archives Project. Through this unique collaboration, donors, archivists, scholars, and archival allies worked toward the mutual goal of connecting, collecting, and celebrating women's history.

### The Artists of Artemisia Project

As fortune would have it, local artist and feminist Barbara Ciurej decided to attend the 2008 launch of the CAWHC project. As she recalled to me later, hearing the speakers and listening to the stories of other attendees inspired her to think about women's history writ large and her own history as two intertwined ideas. Through the event, in her words, she realized that "this might have something to do with me." Ciurej, like many attendees that day, filled out the survey form and turned it in to CAWHC volunteers. As detailed in that form, Ciurej was a former member and former president of the Chicago feminist art gallery, Artemisia. Founded in 1973, Artemisia served as a cooperative space and organization to support women artists who faced very real discrimination in the larger, more institutionalized art world. Named after the 17th-century Italian Baroque artist Artemisia Gentileschi, the gallery, "rejected the hierarchical structure of patriarchal governance and distributed authority among all members, implemented a rotating leadership, made all decisions a participatory process, conceptualized power as empowerment, rather than domination, and argued that the process was as valuable as the outcome."[13] The gallery operated for just over three decades and for many complex reasons closed in 2005.

The important and extensive records of Artemisia, after intervention by former co-president Ellie Wallace and art historian Joanna Garder-Huggett, went to the Art Institute of Chicago. A few years later when the CAWHC launched the documenting project, however, the Art Institute was not actively seeking the records of individual Artemisia artists though they remained interested in building the Artemisia Gallery collection. This allowed for a great opportunity to collaborate between archives, to keep related materials local even if at two different repositories, and to enjoy the fact that no one archives bore the responsibility of saving these materials alone. Ultimately, neither repository was solely responsible for all of the material related to Chicago women

---

13   Gardner-Huggett, Joanna. "The Women Artists' Cooperative Space as a Site for Social Change: Artemisia Gallery, Chicago (1973-1979), *Social Justice* 34 (2007), p. 30.

artists—an impossible task—but rather to work in tandem in the collecting effort.

The impetus behind reaching out to the artists did not come from the archivists, however. Because of Ciurej's personal interest, she and I were able to start a series of conversations that started in the more typical realm of archivist-donor discussions but quickly went into new and very exciting territory. As a former president of Artemisia, Ciurej maintained many of her contacts with former Artemisia members. She believed that those former members, many of whom were still members of the Chicago art community or continued to claim those roots despite relocation, would be interested in archiving their own materials. Though she has been proven right since, at the time I remained only cautiously optimistic. From the perspective of the WLA, bringing in the artists' papers to start a new collection area strength would go a long way toward meeting the true intent of the WLA mission. The artists are themselves extraordinarily diverse. Some joined the ranks of university faculty, while others remained unaffiliated. All enjoyed public exhibitions of their work whether locally, regionally, nationally, or internationally. As could be expected, the art forms and mediums were as varied as the artists themselves. This last point posed the only drawback from an archival point of view: what to do with the art itself? Because the WLA collecting policy already spelled out that the WLA could not accept any large, three-dimensional objects I was able to rely on precedent. Further, through conversations with Ciurej, I was able to understand that there were other ways for artists to represent their work, especially by proxy. For example, an artist could not donate a large, multidimensional installation piece, but they could donate photographs of it, show/exhibition cards, two-dimensional materials (slides, proofs, negatives, photographs) used in pieces, video(s) of the show or used in the show, newspaper notices, reviews, gallery booklets, and other ephemera.

Inspired by Ciurej's enthusiasm and through her connections, we planned an outreach event on June 30, 2010. The speakers included Ciurej, myself, Mary Ann Johnson, Mary Woolever (Archivist, Ryerson and Burnham Libraries at Art Institute of Chicago), and Mary Ellen Croteau (Artist, Director of Art on Armitage, the Illinois Representative of the Feminist Art Project, and a former President of Artemisia Gallery). More than 30 former Artemisia members attended. The main purpose of the event was to explain that the Art Institute was still interested in taking Artemisia Gallery records but that the Women and Leadership Archives was interested in the papers of individual artists. Given their reaction afterward, I may infer that most had not considered that their own papers were of value or interest to researchers or archivists. Further, most of the women were not intimately familiar with archives as a concept or place. Therefore, my presentation was more in the vein of introducing the larger framework of archives, terms, and details specific only to the WLA. From that initial event, four women became donors, the first of whom were Barbara Ciurej and her business/creative partner Lindsay Lochman.

Had those women been the only donors to start collections at the WLA, the event itself would still be considered successful by any measurement. But again, largely due to Ciurej's deep conviction about the need for Chicago women artists to be documented in an archives and my desire to build a collection around the strength of women artists at the WLA, we were not done. Most recently in March 2011, Ciurej and I again hosted the artists of Artemisia at a second event. Rechristened by Barbara the "Artemisia Artists Archives Project," we sought to bring the same (or more) women back to Piper Hall to (1) offer that they bring materials with them to start a collection, (2) have the opportunity to tour the archives including the reading room and secure storage area, (3) hear from Joanna Gardner-Huggett, PhD, who produced scholarly work on Artemisia and used available archival material extensively, and (4) be offered practical information on building a collection at the Women and Leadership Archives. The event resulted in eighteen new collections begun *that night*. Of those collections, many have already been added to by additional deposits of material. In addition, five more donors no longer residing locally have promised to send materials.

While I was at first uncertain of the practicality of potential donors bringing materials en masse, with decent organization and preparation, all of the boxes of materials were properly received, identified, accessioned, and donor agreements completed in due order. All attendees, but especially those women who brought collections the night of the event, were offered sample deeds of gift. Thus, by the time their own deeds arrived, they were already well informed on the legal issues and in almost all cases, ready to sign. Hence, the normal sequence of receiving materials was unchanged, even if the arrival of materials was unorthodox.

Outside of the obvious commitment of individual artists to donate materials, these events also offered an opportunity for the women to network, reminisce, and otherwise reconnect. The spirit at both events was lively and collegial; women shared stories of the past activities but also caught up on current goings-on. Not surprisingly, through those conversations, it was revealed that two former Artemisia members started their own oral history project entirely independent of any scholar or archivist. Called the "Seventy Plus Project," the goal is to interview as many seventy-year old and older Chicago artists, male and female, as possible and donate those interviews to local archives. The next level of that project is to begin to interview art dealers and gallery owners of a similar age. Several artists present were added to the Seventy Plus roster that night who might otherwise have been unaware of the project. This last point deserves some further reflection, especially from the point of view of archival professionals and in the larger context of collection development.

A consequence of these convergent agents—third party, donor, archivist, and scholar—is nothing less than the emergence of a different model of collection development. Not a replacement of older, tried and true methods, but another option. Within this feminist model is a blurring of authority, specifically, the right to generate the historical records, the right to collect the history, the right to generate the history, the right to contribute to the history, and the right to maintain that history. From this model emerges a persistent truth: the creation of the historical narrative is not dependent on all parties agreeing to share resources, information, and access but rather the conviction that the historical record is all the more rich and complex as a result of cooperation not competition. Further and no less important, no one ally in the effort carries the resource burden alone. In AAAP work, for example, a scholar helped to find an archival home for materials and gave weight to the need for archives to exist so she could do her research. In turn, the donors were active participants in the creation and formation of their own history. They did not need nor require the assistance of public history professionals to tell them that oral histories are a great way to supplement the manuscript records, making for more complex collections overall. As a result, the role of the archivist was not just to be the passive recipient of materials or even the active collector, but to participate in an active and ongoing conversation about these women's history. Perhaps that it took the form of suggestion or advice but it was also to listen and respect the forms in which they chose to express themselves, such as non-institutional oral histories. In other words, the archivist and the scholar were not the authoritative sieves through which all information and access had to flow. Admittedly, this is a model that works best for modern manuscripts when donors are one and the same as creators of the manuscript collections. At the same time the cooperative model may generally be more attractive under other circumstances in which archivists are confronted with limited resources and still a desire to responsibly and strategically expand.

## Challenges and Conclusions

No project is ever instituted without the impulse to look back at what has happened and what might have been done differently. In the case of working with a third party, there are plenty of opportunities to reflect on what worked well and what did not. Obstacles during the early phases of the project largely centered on individual's issues of control or lack thereof. The increased number of collaborators and being subject to the scheduling of several third parties demanded a lot of patience with the process itself, especially when it came to the pacing and execution of the early phases of the CAWHC project. Similarly, though ethical and just, the matchmaking process proved to be challenging for me both personally and professionally. Rather than just agreeing in theory with the ethical framework—sharing new discoveries and balancing my insider knowledge as a Council board member—was a constant test. I knew first among my archives colleagues when a great new find was made which often chafed against my own desire to expand the collections of the WLA. Though I was outwardly successful and not yelling, "I'll take it!" when new, interesting material was found, internally it was more of a struggle. As well, I had to be very clear to others at the CAWHC when I offered general advice as an archives professional and when I represented the needs and concerns of the WLA as director. The line of demarcation between the two roles was not always clear and, admittedly, remains to this day difficult to negotiate. In contrast to these more personal struggles, I can offer some general suggestions on how to form similar fruitful partnerships. There are four basic issues to consider when thinking about this type of collaboration and coalition building in collection development. This is not intended to be an exhaustive list.

(1) **Establish clear lines of reporting / authority within the project.** In other words, who has the right, if anyone, to speak for you or the archives that you represent? For example, can project partners or volunteers meeting with potential oral history candidates also suggest to them making a collections donation? How much can such project agents speak for the collecting needs or limitations of your archives, if at all? The pros and cons to this issue are fairly obvious in that the more people promoting the archives the better. The negative is that there is a higher risk of misrepresentation of the facility, its capabilities and shortcomings.

(2) **Work with a clear if flexible project timeline.** Although I knew a project of this nature would be open ended, I did not entertain the idea that it could go on indefinitely. Similarly, I could have better assessed my own level of time commitment. For example, the CAWHC board meets every other month on a Saturday and then more often as necessary and for events. A reasonable time commitment, to be sure, but as my personal and professional obligations shift over the years, is the same time commitment sustainable? At what point should the terms of my commitment be renegotiated? Having a fully articulated timeline, as detailed as possible, helps all parties plan for the future but at the same time should be written in pencil to evolve as the project also changes.

(3) **Establish fully articulated resource needs.** If time commitment is an issue, what about other forms of commitment such as event space, monetary support, printing, travel, or other related costs? Not to be confused with the expense of taking in new collections, these intangible resource needs should be part of the initial conversations (and considerations) with other collaborators and often revisited as the needs of the project evolve. Knowing the level of commitment from other partners or full extent of existing project resources AND plans for getting additional resources such as grants should be explicit from the beginning. This was very true for the CAWHC, which not only planned to write grants in the abstract, but had already identified appropriate grant funders from whom to apply.

(4) **Lastly, know when to bring the project relationship to a close.** Ending active collaborations is not necessarily a negative testament of the project itself. Instead, ending active engagement can signal (as it often does) a shift to a more passive role in the project or even a just a temporary break. Knowing an approximate exit time frame and communicating that effectively goes a long way in continued trust between partners. Abrupt absences by contrast breed distrust and frustration.

As the project has evolved, so has my role in it. The expansion of the general scope of the Council's project is not only encouraging, it is revitalizing after several years of hard work. Ultimately, as women of the women's liberation movement continue to retire from public or professional life, as they relocate or pass away, the necessity of this documenting project is only underscored. Indeed, the very enormity of the movement with its many facets, participants, and vicissitudes also highlights the need for collaborations to make documenting and collecting on this large scale feasible. It is also another way to rethink and practice collection development concentrated on all local resources and resource sharing. Whether such enterprises fall under the slightly controversial banner of a coalition between citizen archivists and professional archivists remains a subject worth exploring. For now I choose the less problematic terms of collaborative collecting and archival allies to describe those incredible partners I had in this development process. I am not only grateful for the expansion of the collections of the WLA, but I have been lucky enough to witness a truly noncompetitive, alliance can be and the positive results thereof. At present, such collaborations remain a simple and clear necessity if we are to truly engage in the endeavor of saving important, localized women's history. In addition, going forward, this model can also serve other communities and other social movements of the same generation as the second wave feminists, but also of future generations. This connection is especially important as the generations naturally supplant one another. The immediacy and context of much of the rights revolution and the essentialism of personal identity born from the mid-twentieth century will be carried on by those who do not remember the struggles personally but enjoy the fruits of that labor nonetheless. In other words, making those connections between the past, present, and future relate not only to researchers' work with the archival materials but just as importantly, with the archivists charged with the stewardship of those collections as well.

# She Who Owns the Press
## The Physical World of Early Feminist Publishing

*Barbara Sjoholm*

Round tins of greasy black ink, long-spouted cans of lubricating oil to squirt into the hot cogs of printing presses, rough blue rags soaked in turpentine; blackened fingers, aching backs, the eye-searing flash of a carbon arc lamp burning words onto metal plates—none of these are probably what first come to mind for most librarians and scholars of the women's movement when they imagine the early days of feminist publishing in the 1970s. The books themselves are often amateurishly designed, printed on any-old paper, lacking ISBNs, without marketing hype or blurbs. My old copy of *Edward the Dyke and other poems* from 1971 doesn't even have its author's name—Judy Grahn— on the front cover. It's stapled at the spine, blue with a cup-sized ring-splash of coffee complementing the line drawing of a woman in a cap. The hand-stamped price in a corner is $1.75. On the back is the address of the Women's Press Collective in Oakland and a list of other titles and posters produced by the collective of seven women.

The Women in Print Movement, the bedrock of Second Wave feminism, has not yet received all the scholarly attention it should in terms of how crucial books and periodicals were in forming feminist and lesbian identity. Printed matter by women— journals, newspapers, and books, particularly poetry, novels, and anthologies—created a constantly evolving and deeply engaging world of reading for feminists, who were the main audience. The voices that emerged from the Women in Print Movement are still studied as a clue to the ideology and history of the feminist movement and of course many of the books themselves are still preserved, as artifacts and documents. Yet something is missing from archival and historical work if the conditions in which the books were produced—the intense physical labor of their production and distribution—isn't also part of the story. Publishing in the 1970s was highly physical, tactile, and mechanical, in a way difficult to comprehend now, when the shift to digital media has completely changed what we think of as a book and when most production is done at the computer, while sitting in a comfortable chair or even lolling on a sofa.

I had been drawn to bookmaking and printing long before Rachel da Silva and I started Seal Press in Seattle in 1976. I colored and stapled my own stories together when I was eight, the same year I decided to become a writer. After a year of college, I dropped out to live in Europe for three years. At some point during that time I took a bookbinding course. I read about the women who had small presses in Paris, Nancy Cunard, Adrienne Monnier, Sylvia Beach, and Anaïs Nin—as well as Virginia Woolf, who set type and sewed bindings for the Hogarth Press in England. A year after I moved to Seattle in 1974 I joined the collective alternative newspaper, *The Northwest Passage,* where we did all the production except the printing ourselves; I learned how to type columns on an IBM Selectric, to paste up the text using a hand-built light table, to affix headlines with Letraset or "press-on" display type and, hardest of all, to measure and cut (and try not to get wrapped around my fingers) the thinnest of border lines to frame articles and photos. As a collective we ranged along the spectrum of current leftist politics and followed an Americanized Maoist practice of criticism/self-criticism (I was praised for my book reviews but criticized for my levity). I learned to spot typos, to eyeball layouts for straightness, and to edit other people's work—all crucial skills for my work to come as an editor and publisher at Seal.

In 1976 I began a part-time course of study at Seattle Community College in commercial printing (to go along with my Intensive Russian studies at the university). I learned how to strip in photographs and make plates and to run a Multilith press—the basics. That June, at a street fair, I ran into someone who told me about Rachel da Silva. She'd had just bought a letterpress, they said, and was starting to print poetry. I got myself invited to a party she was also attending. By the next day she was teaching me how to set type on the old-fashioned Chandler and Price printing press she'd purchased from a downtown business converting to offset. She'd had the two-ton iron press moved into the old wooden garage of her mother's Victorian house in the Eastlake neighborhood. She also bought several complete fonts—Times Roman, Palatino, Garamond— of new metal type from the McKenzie and Harris foundry to put in the type cabinet and into the wooden California cases she also scored for next-to-nothing and that sat on a marble-topped worktable. A small-paned window looked out on her mother Marjorie's lush garden of grape vines and delphinium.

That summer we printed our first poetry chapbook, *Private Gallery* by Melinda Mueller. It took a long time. I set the type, holding the composing stick in my left hand, picking up metal characters one by one and putting them in lines, upside down and backwards, with slugs between the words and leads between the lines. The type was placed into a metal chase like a picture frame and the empty space filled with wooden blocks or "furniture," the whole thing tightened with a metal wedge called a quoin and its key. The chase was then lifted into the press, the rollers cleaned, the platen inked, and the press switched on—it ran noisily on electricity. There was a single switch, but several speeds. You had to be quick to put a sheet from the pile next to you into the correct position (marked by gauge pins on the tympan paper) before the clamshell-closing action of the press made a mess of everything. After all the copies of that single page were printed, the platen had to be cleaned and the type washed, the whole chase unlocked and the type re-distributed. We did not have enough type to do more than one or two pages of poems at a time.

The press was serviceable but by no means new and we were novices (I remained an amateur, a printer's devil). Rachel did a huge amount of fiddling to get the type to imprint darkly enough, but not too inkily, on the page. Letter by letter, page by page, we printed that chapbook from late June through August. We smoked cigarettes, proofread aloud sitting outside on the steps of the garage, and went swimming in Lake Union. Marjorie brought in tuna sandwiches from time to time or persuaded us to go strawberry picking.

We didn't call ourselves a feminist press; we were hardly even a press with one small chapbook, and that fall Rachel moved north to Bellingham to study visual arts and to work part-time at a print shop, making further projects somewhat uncertain. It wasn't until the following summer, when I traveled cross-country to a women writers' workshop in upstate New York and I met June Arnold, an author and the publisher of Daughters, Inc. (known for its success with *Rubyfruit Jungle* by Rita Mae Brown), that it occurred to me that Rachel and I could do more with Seal Press than just print poetry chapbooks and broadsides. We were avid readers of early feminist literature and I was attempting to write fiction about women's lives—the way we lived now. I returned from the writers' workshop consumed by the vision of publishing not only my own short stories ("Why wait to be validated by the patriarchal publishing world?" Arnold challenged me.), but those of other women. We decided to do a letterpress anthology of Northwest women's poetry, *Backbone*, as well as a small collection of my stories using an offset press.

We had no money at all, so Rachel's considerable abilities as a designer and printer, not to mention her connections with different print shops and printers, was key. I had graphic and writing skills but wasn't very mechanically minded. Together we were a good team and over the next few years we began to see what we were capable of as editors, printers, and publishers. We didn't only have an interest in working with women writers, we had the means of production and, increasingly, we had the skills to perform all stages of the printing process. As the slogan of the day had it, "the power of the press belongs to she who owns the press." Those hands-on skills and contacts substituted for capital and for experience in mainstream publishing, which we initially disdained.

By 1978 we were producing poetry books using the letterpress and printing books on offset presses at the Bellingham print shop where Rachel worked after school. We had a friend who was a typesetter in Seattle. She volunteered to set some of our books and I pasted them up, using a home made light table in my one-bedroom apartment. I'd then take the Greyhound bus up to Bellingham and Rachel and I would start printing on Friday evening and work all the way through the weekend. I burned most of the plates and Rachel ran the press. The paper and plates were purchased at a discount from her generous employer. Rachel would print the cover herself and then drive down to Seattle with all of our boxes of paper; then we'd hand collate the pages with the help of friends. Finally we'd take everything to Bayless Bindery in Seattle and a week or two later we'd have a few hundred books.

In these days, when anyone can typeset, design, and produce a bound copy of a nice-looking book almost instantaneously, it's not easy to describe what it was like to work with metal and film and big cans of ink, with clunky noises and photochemical smells, with papers and glues and waxes. Only the books and pamphlets remain from the small press movement of the 1960s and 70s, with their under or over-exposed half-tone photographs, their wobbly too-dark or too-light lines of type, often with typos or the corrections glued on crookedly, bound in stapled and sewn covers—books printed on acidic paper, destined to be read by a handful of people. Rachel and I cared more than many small publishers about the quality of our printing—we had started out doing letterpress poetry chapbooks, after all, and both of us were interested in art and design. We tried to carry the same level of quality into our offset books as well, but we had to contend with the technology of the times. To produce a beautiful book in those days was not only a labor of love, it was labor.

It's difficult to convey the sheer butch glamour of printing. This black-fingered, muscle-building blue-collar work was just the sort of thing that many women found we really liked doing in the 1970s and early 80s. The Second Wave had more than its fair share of car mechanics, plumbers, carpenters, and electricians. Some women went into the trades because the paychecks were much better, and some forced their way up from apprentice to master because they were tough rabble-rousers. Others founded carpentry collectives or car garages so that we women didn't have to depend on know-it-all men to build our fences or repair our cars.

Some women went into the printing trades for some of the same reasons as women fought to join the United Brotherhood of Carpenters—better paychecks and the love of loud noise. The majority, I suspect, were more like me—strong enough to haul boxes, determined enough to learn how a press worked and to stand on my feet for hours, but not *really* all that interested in trouble-shooting printing problems and dismantling and reassembling machinery. Like me, they were in printing for the thrill of it, lured by the vision of a process that created words on paper that could be turned into pages, bound into books, placed on shelves, bought and sold, held in hands, and taken into the heart and mind. That could transform the world.

There was often an obstacle between the woman writer and her public. That obstacle was a printing press. In the 1970s, that changed.

The early annals of feminist publishing are full of stories about women who learned all or some aspects of the printing trades and then additionally took on the job of publishing and sometimes distribution. The Women's Press Collective in Oakland was joined by Diana Press, a lesbian-feminist and socialist print shop with a bindery that published its own titles as well as those of other feminist presses. The Iowa City Women's Press, a collective print shop, also published two iconic works, *The Greasy Thumb Automechanics Manual for Women* and *Against the Grain,* a carpentry manual. Megaera Press, of Northhampton, was the third member of a group called Women's Image Takeover, which included Greasy Gordons, a car service shop. Like some other print shops, Megaera (meaning "Grudge"), took on printing jobs for the community while restricting their publishing projects to lesbian titles (*They Will Know Me by My Teeth,* by Elana Dykewoman). Jackrabbit Press in Eugene, Oregon, was another printing collective that dabbled in publishing (*What Lesbians Do). Press Gang began as a full-service print shop in Vancouver, British Columbia, but moved into publishing with books of poetry and then fiction and nonfiction. New Victoria Printers, in Lebanon, New Hampshire, named itself after Victoria Printers, a women's print shop in nineteenth century England.

Victoria Printers wasn't the only women's printing endeavor of the past. Second Wave feminism was in part about the rediscovery of women's history, and researchers found that women actually had worked as typesetters and printers, from the Renaissance onward, and some even owned their own print shops. In England, Emily Faithfull ran a shop that employed only women printers; she eventually started a publishing company. San Francisco boasted the Women's Union Job Printing Company (WCPU) and the Woman's Publishing Company. The WCPU announced in its publicity, "Women set type! Women run presses!" We didn't have to reinvent the wheel completely. For inspiration we could call on our foremothers, especially those feisty women of the First Wave.

Even women who didn't have their own presses, paper cutters, and bindery machinery still availed themselves of new technologies. Those who were a bit older than Rachel and me had often been anti-war activists or involved in one of the many progressive movements of the sixties. They learned to run mimeograph machines and to typeset using an IBM Selectric with its carbon ribbons and interchangeable typeballs in different fonts; they became adept at pasting up newspaper or book pages and learning the language of printers. In the 1970s, women took classes to learn the basics of graphic newspaper and book design. The many women who worked on community women's newspapers and small literary journals learned that it wasn't that difficult to put together something readable and some went on to become book publishers. The new skills spread right through the feminist community as women taught each other. It's no coincidence that many of the print shops and publishers styled themselves as collectives; one of the aims of such groups was to share knowledge and empower each other.

In 1978, the 300-page volume *A Guide to Women's Publishing* came out from Dustbooks. In addition to listing dozens of women's literary journals, newspapers, publishing companies and print shops, it included annotations often supplied by the women involved, many of which outlined their submission policies—lesbians or Canadians only, for instance—and their strengths and hopes. A number, touchingly, announced that they couldn't afford to pay authors or that they were trying to raise money. *A Guide,* by Polly Joan and Andrea Chesman, also contained a stirring foreword or "Forward," which set forth certain principles and a context for the detailed guide. How familiarly their words still echo with their bold, firm view of the world:

> ...feminist publishing is also feminist politics. It is not an alternative to male
> publishing. It is a political act as creative and diverse as the Women's Movement itself....
> More than any other movement in history, Feminism has been identified with publishing. Taking hold of the American doctrine that freedom of the press is the single most important access route to equality, Feminism has confronted the male heirs of the American Revolution with their own beliefs and strategies turned inside out for the sake

of a *woman's free press.*[1]

Seal Press wasn't listed in the *Guide*—we were still new and under the radar in not-yet-trendy Seattle—nor were several other presses that would propel feminist publishing forward in the 1980s, such as Firebrand, Cleis, and Spinsters, when printing skills became less important than managing cash-flow and finding titles that sold well. The non-profit Feminist Press, Crossing Press, and Naiad were among a handful mentioned in the guide that survived and flourished for many years, along with a number of newspapers. Many other journals and presses, with their wonderful names, Out & Out Books, Motherroot, Shameless Hussy, Karmic Revenge Laundry Shop Press, and (one of my favorites) Lady-Unique-Inclination-of-the-Night, vanished.

I found *A Guide to Women's Publishing* in Seattle's women's bookstore It's About Time and it served as a useful handbook and political beacon for us in the next few years. We began to think about distribution, for instance, and reviews—how not just to print books, but to get them into the hands of readers, including those outside Seattle. We connected with the large network of women's bookstores as well as many independent stores. Originally we thought of ourselves as a Northwest women's press, then an American feminist press and, sooner than one would have thought possible, by 1984, an international publishing company, connected to women authors and other women's publishers around the world.

Rachel and I continued to print letterpress poetry for about five years, but increasingly our books were printed on offset presses. Rachel joined a leftist co-ed printing collective, Workshop Printers, and in 1980, Seal Press and Workshop rented a large workspace in the Kaplan Building in Pioneer Square. We had our books typeset nearby at Franklin Press by John Berry. Rachel and I cut up the galleys and pasted up the pages, using a hot wax roller. Rachel shot the pages with Workshop's massive camera, developed them in the dark room, stripped in the film negatives, burned the plates. Then she and Dan Zucker printed interiors and the covers, most of which were designed by Rachel or Deb Brown, another member of Workshop Printers. Bayless Bindery turned them into books and we picked up the boxes and stored them in increasingly high stacks in the murky depths of the workspace.

In our office space we had an old couch, one desk, and some file cabinets. We had a telephone and a Royal typewriter. We wheeled boxes and packages to the Pioneer Square post office in a folding shopping cart. If we found some used furniture on the street on the way back we carted it back to our office. We had parties in the warmer months and in the colder months we carried on our editorial meetings at Elliott Bay Bookstore's new downstairs café.

Although Rachel and I were initially isolated from publishing circles other than other small local presses (such as Copper Canyon and Graywolf in Port Townsend), we

---

1   Polly Joan and Andrea Chesman. *Guide to Women's Publishing.* (Paradise, CA: Dustbooks, 1978) 2-3.

gradually made contact with other feminist presses, beginning in the summer of 1981, when we traveled to the second Women in Print conference in Washington D.C., a major event in feminist publishing that brought together almost every women's press and bookstore in the nation. The stern lesbian-separatism of some of the speakers was mildly intimidating to us, I recall—not just because of the impractical ideology but because of the vehement eloquence with which certain speakers laid down the line. Should we deal with male typesetters and printers? Absolutely not. (Pragmatism would come to co-exist with separatism in a few years; meanwhile Seal did shift to working with a women's typesetting business, Scarlet Letters, and everything short of book printing was done as much as possible by us or women vendors.) Yet much of the talk was exhilarating. For the first time we had others besides ourselves to talk about printing and distribution. The friendship we forged with the independent-minded women of Cleis Press, Felice Newman and Frederique Delacoste, turned out to be particularly sustaining. We met bookstore owners and reviewers. When we returned to Seattle, Rachel and Deb Brown organized the first (and only) Northwest Women in Print Conference, and many women from Vancouver came down from Press Gang.

In late 1980 Rachel and I advertised for volunteers to help us produce *Getting Free,* the first handbook for women getting out of abusive relationships, and Faith Conlon answered the call. She'd moved to Seattle from New York where she worked for a year or two at Anchor Books as an editorial assistant. With the arrival of Faith, who knew wonderful and mysterious secrets about the business (Pre-pub galleys! Advance reviews! A Fall and Spring catalog!) and with the publication of *Getting Free,* our first big seller (3,000 in just the first two months), Seal moved into a new phase in its history. Our books sold better and we increased our number of titles. We began to pay ourselves and took on a part-time employee.

We were lucky along the way. With a substantial grant from the Norwegian government to publish an anthology of Norwegian women's fiction, we bought our first photocopier. When the city decided to build a bus tunnel under the historic Kaplan Building, they paid for us to move elsewhere and we found spacious new digs in Lower Queen Anne, that offered us separate offices, meeting spaces and a proper warehouse. We took on a full-time book designer, a marketing director, someone to answer the phone, a warehouse manager. We began to see our books regularly reviewed in *Publishers Weekly* and to attend the large trade fairs, putting up a booth in an aisle with other feminist and gay and lesbian publishers. Eventually we chose to work with first Consortium Distribution and then Publishers Group West; we learned the ways of sales reps and sales catalogs. We published more books, sold foreign rights and paperback rights.

Rachel left Seal Press in 1985 (though she remained an owner and Seal author) to take up mountain-climbing in Nepal and attend law school. With her departure and with the demise of Workshop Printers, Seal lost its strong connection to the printing trades. Rachel sold the Chandler and Price press to a local artist, along with all the letterpress paraphernalia we hadn't used in years. All our books were, by 1986, printed at modern commercial printing factories in the Midwest, and that was true of most of the other feminist publishers as well. Although the Women in Print Movement was, from around 1985 to the mid-90s— in that period before the mega-bookstores and Amazon, before the Internet and digital publishing—more influential and more robust than ever, the Golden Age of women's print shops and printer-publishers had passed. With that passing went the memory of the hard physical labor and tactile pleasure of the printing press, paper, and black ink.

In 1982 I published *Ambitious Women* with another feminist press, Spinsters, Ink; it was a novel about two women who ran a print shop in Seattle. The book was also published in England with the Women's Press a year later. The American edition had a black-and-white photograph on the cover of the women printers of New-York based Tower Press; the British version, far more colorful, showed two women in what was meant to be the office of a print shop (much tidier than any such office I'd ever seen). In 1984 I published *Murder in the Collective,* a mystery set in Seattle at a collective print shop, and this was followed by two more mysteries with the same characters. The cover of the mystery showed an anonymous person developing a film of text in an acid bath in a darkroom. The blurb on the back of *Murder in the Collective* read: "The members of Best Printing, a collectively-managed printshop in Seattle, thought they had enough to worry about just trying to stay solvent. Then one night came the proposal to merge with lesbian-owned B. Violet Typesetting..."

To my pleased surprise, the mystery hit a chord (who knew so many people had wanted to murder their collective members?) and became an underground bestseller in the U.S. as well as in England and Germany. Not only did it give Seal Press a big financial boost, but it enabled me to finally quit my part-time clerical job to focus on writing and publishing.

*Ambitious Women* and the three mysteries were all highly political, steeped in feminist and leftist issues of the time. My choice of setting was deliberate and loving: it was the world I knew—that of Seattle collectives and print shops, political rallies, and ideological struggles, a world of machinery and blue-collar work performed by earnest young lefties, many of them women.

I had some sense of history, even before I met Rachel, of the times I was living through. Women's lives and their writings had been forgotten in the past; part of the important work of the Second Wave was recovering all those lost stories and histories, reprinting them, teaching them, studying them. It may have been with that in mind—describing our times as we lived through them— that I wrote novels about our daily lives and the work we did. It was certainly part of why I began to keep scrapbooks of Seal's early years and to add to them for a number of years until the sheer amount of ephemera and press cuttings spilled into files and boxes.

I couldn't have known that saving many of the physical artifacts connected with that era of printing would be as important as the documents themselves. Who envisioned in the 1970s the whole digital universe? Still I saved wooden and metal type, cover mechanicals with color separated film, some metal plates, pages of letterpress printing and catalogs. I saved original manuscripts, scribbled with corrections, photographs, and hundreds of files of correspondence. My archival (packrat?) tendencies were a passion at first, then a habit, finally an informal rule at Seal—*don't throw anything away, Barbara wants it.* Starting sometime in the mid-eighties, when we still had our office in Pioneer Square, I suggested we get an off-site storage unit, and that we put the manuscripts, cover art work, editing correspondence, and ten copies of every book there. I devised filing systems for the office. Although we were completely computerized by the late eighties, Faith and I required that the staff print out letters and file them in cabinets dedicated to publicity, production, and editorial. Every new staff member was instructed in the system and it only began to founder at the very end of the 1990s, when the newest publicists and editors, doing back and forth e-mail all day, found it impossible and a waste of paper and time to print everything out. Still, thanks to Faith, even after I left Seal at the end of 1994 to pursue my literary career, the system continued. Certain books vanished off the shelves and for a while a new warehouse manager didn't realize she was supposed to save copies of each book; still year by year, the off-site storage unit filled up, until boxes climbed eight feet high and no one dared to get into it.

As a result, when we sold Seal Press in 2001 to Avalon, a division of our long-time distributors, Publishers Group West, we had an overwhelming mass of stuff to deal with—or a precious archive of one of the earliest and longest-existing feminist presses. Faith tended to the former view, but I glimpsed the possibility, perhaps I imagined it from the beginning, of making sure the papers of Seal Press went to a library or other institution. Fortunately Ed Vermue, the Special Collections Librarian at Oberlin College, was among several librarians who saw the value of keeping intact and for posterity not only Seal's history as a feminist press, but its publishing history, a unique history that went all the way from letterpress to digital production with intact examples from every period and thorough documentation of every stage of our editorial and business growth.

The Seal Press archives arrived at Oberlin's library in 2002, where they are now catalogued and are available to students and scholars. Seal Press, happily enough, continues to publish women's work in 2010, as an imprint of Perseus (which purchased Avalon) and under the able leadership of publisher Krista Lyons. They've published several of my recent books, so my history with Seal continues, thirty-five years on. Seal may not own any printing presses or even own itself, but its mission to make the voices of women heard is firmly in place.

Recently in a bookstore I picked up a book about women of the Congo, *A Thousand Sisters,* and saw the familiar logo of two seals forming an S shape on the spine. In spite of the painful subject—or perhaps because of it—I felt joyful and very moved in that moment, remembering how two young women, long ago in the summer of 1976, began something that still continued. Without knowing it, we were about to join the river of history and to help create a movement of women writers, publishers, and readers that would help transform the world we lived in.

On the Oberlin College Library site you can see a photograph of me and Rachel as we appeared around 1979. We were thinner then and younger, but that's not the point. Take a look at the type cases behind us, imagine the Chandler and Price press just out of sight to the right. Imagine the bite of metal type into paper, the good smell of ink and turpentine, imagine the sound of a well-oiled press humming.

*Barbara Sjoholm (Wilson), left, and Rachel da Silva, co-founders of Seal Press, 1979[2]*

# Contributor Biographies

Amy Benson is the Librarian/Archivist for Digital Projects at the Schlesinger Library. In this position, she oversees the full life-cycle of digital materials at the Library including identification and selection, appraisal and acquisition, description, database management, storage, delivery, and preservation. Previously, Amy worked as the Program Director for NELINET Digital Services. Amy is an information enthusiast and has a strong interest in the interaction of data and technology. Amy has prepared and presented professional development workshops and seminars on topics ranging from data standards to social networking and Web technologies. Prior to joining the NELINET staff she worked at Harvard's Widener and Houghton libraries. She holds a B.A. in French and Modern Languages from Beloit College, an M.S.L.S. from Simmons College, and an Ed.M. from Harvard University.

Lyz Bly earned her doctorate in American History from Case Western Reserve University in 2010. A historian of contemporary (post 1950) history, her areas of expertise include gender, race, and sexuality studies, subcultures, and popular culture. She is currently revising her dissertation, *Generation X and the Invention of a Third Feminist Wave*, for publication, rewriting the late Raymond F. Betts' monograph, *A History of Popular Culture: more of everything, faster and brighter* (Routledge 2012), and is writing a memoir, *You Think You Know: An Archeology of GenX Grrrlhood*. She teaches gender studies and history at Case Western Reserve and Cleveland State Universities. She lives in Cleveland.

Jenna Brager produces the zines *Sassyfrass Circus* and *Femme à Barbe*, in addition to co-producing *Archiving the Underground* with Jami Sailor. Jenna received a B.A. in American Studies from the University of Maryland, College Park, where she wrote an honors thesis on zine practice. Jenna posts comics and writing at sassyfrasscircus.com.

Angela L. DiVeglia is an artist, activist, and free-range librarian currently living in Vermont. Her chapter is based on research done while she was a graduate student at the School of Information and Library Science at UNC-Chapel Hill. Her website is: http://aldiveglia.weebly.com

Sarah Dyer's zine experience includes a stint as co-publisher of the well-known punk zine *No Idea* as well as years as the creator and publisher of her own titles: *Mad Planet, Kikizine*, and the *Action Girl Newsletter*. The *Action Girl Newsletter* was a networking publication that listed and reviews comics and zines by female creators, which was published between 1992 and 1995. She then created and edited *Action Girl Comics*, an all-female independent comics anthology which continued to run listings and reviews of zines and other comics. Her writing work over the past decade includes English-language adaptations of several popular manga (including *Kodocha* and *DNAngel*), co-writing comics for DC, Dark Horse, Bongo and more, and co-writing for television series including *Yo Gabba Gabba!*, *Space Ghost Coast to Coast* and the *Superman Adventures* animated series.

Kate Eichhorn is an Assistant Professor of Culture and Media Studies at The New School University. Her research investigates the relationship between alternative print cultures and contemporary social movements. She is currently completing a book-length study on feminist archives, *The Order of Resistance: Feminist Archives in the Present.*

Jenna Freedman is a zine librarian and librarian zinester. She is the Director of Reference & Instruction Services at Barnard College in NYC and a member of Radical Reference, a collective of library workers that meets the research needs of activists and independent journalists. She has published articles on zine librarianship and presented around the United States and in France on that topic as well as on other themes of library activism. She is the 2007 winner of the Elizabeth Futas Catalyst for Change Award, a *Library Journal* Mover & Shaker, and edits a zine reviews column for *Library Journal*. Her website is: http://lowereastsidelibrarian.info

Alexis Pauline Gumbs is a queer black trouble maker, a black feminist love evangelist and a survivor of sexual assault. As co-founder of UBUNTU a women of color survivor-led coalition to end gendered violence and create sustainable transformative love and the instigator of the Eternal Summer of the Black Feminist Mind multimedia community school, Alexis creates and participates in rituals for healing, survival and transformation. Alexis has a Ph.D. in English, Africana Studies and Women's Studies from Duke University and is proud to have been named one of the 50 people transforming the world by UTNE reader in 2009, a Reproductive Health Reality Check Shero and a nominee for a Black Women Rising Award in 2010 and the recipient of a Too Sexy for 501c3 Trophy in 2011! To stay updated or communicate with Alexis go to blackfeminismlives.tumblr.com.

Kathryn Allamong Jacob is the Johanna-Maria Frænkel Curator of Manuscripts at the Schlesinger Library at the Radcliffe Institute at Harvard University. She holds a B.A. from Goucher College, an M.A. from Georgetown University, and a Ph.D. from Johns Hopkins University. Prior to joining the Schlesinger staff, Jacob was the archivist at the Johns Hopkins University, assistant historian of the United States Senate, an archivist at the National Archives, a program director at the National Historical Publications and Records Commission, and deputy director of the American Jewish Historical Society. Jacob was co-editor of the *Biographical Directory of the American Congress, Bicentennial Edition,* and she is the author of three books: *Capital Elites: High Society in Washington, D.C. After the Civil War*; *Testament to Union: Civil War Monuments in Washington, D.C.,* and *King of the Lobby: The Life and Times of Sam Ward.*

Alana Kumbier is a Research and Instruction Librarian at Wellesley College. She is co-editor of *Critical Library Instruction: Theories and Methods*, and is working on a book about queer archival practices called *Ephemeral Material: Queering the Archive* (forthcoming from Litwin Books). In her free time, she is a zine-maker, queer variety arts performer, Boston Radical Reference Collective co-organizer, and letterpress printer.

Elizabeth Myers, Ph.D., is the director of the Women and Leadership Archives at Loyola University Chicago, a position she's held since 2006. She has a total of eleven years of experience in archives and special collections with principle interests in education, outreach, and collection development. She teaches regularly at Loyola, she has also given dozens of lectures and workshops concerning archives and women's collections to archival, academic, and public audiences. She was recently published in *Public Relations and Marketing for Archivists* (2011) and is pursuing an active research agenda related to identity-based archives and special collections.

Erin O'Meara is currently an archivist at the Gates Archive. Before joining the Gates Archive in 2012, she was the Electronic Records Archivist at the University of North Carolina at Chapel Hill. She has also served as the Electronic Records Archivist at the University of Oregon. She received her Master of Archival Studies in 2004 from the University of British Columbia. While at UBC, Erin conducted research for the InterPARES 2 Project pertaining to the preservation of archaeological records.

Alison Piepmeier is author of *Girl Zines: Making Media, Doing Feminism* (New York University Press, 2009), the first academic study of zines by girls and women. She is also co-editor of *Catching a Wave: Reclaiming Feminism for the 21st Century* (Northeastern University Press, 2003), a collection that is widely taught in Women's Studies classes, and author of *Out in Public: Configurations of Women's Bodies in Nineteenth-Century America* (University of North Carolina Press, 2004). She directs the Women's and Gender Studies Program at the College of Charleston, where she is also associate professor of English, and she is a member of the Governing Council of the National Women's Studies Association.

Jami Sailor currently produces the zines *Your Secretary*, *Hex Key*, and co-produces *Archiving the Underground* with Jenna Brager. Her long running zine *No Better Voice* was featured in Alison Piepmeier's *Girl Zines: Making Media, Doing Feminism*. Jami Sailor received her M.L.I.S. from Dominican University where she specialized in archives and community informatics. She blogs at yoursecretaryisout.wordpress.com.

Barbara Sjoholm is the author of the travel books *The Palace of the Snow Queen: Winter Travels in Lapland*, *Incognito Street*, and *The Pirate Queen*. Before changing her name in 2001, she published a number of works of fiction, mystery, and non-fiction as Barbara

Wilson, including the award-winning *Gaudi Afternoon* and the memoir *Blue Windows: A Christian Science Childhood.* Her books have been translated into five languages. Her essays have appeared in *The New York Times, Slate, Smithsonian,* and *The American Scholar,* among other publications. She is also a translator from Norwegian and Danish. Sjoholm cofounded Seal Press in 1976 and was a publisher and editor for many years. She was also the editorial director of Women in Translation, devoted to publishing fiction by women around the world. www.barbarasjoholm.com

Kelly Wooten is the Research Services and Collection Development Librarian for the Sallie Bingham Center for Women's History and Culture at Duke University's David M. Rubenstein Rare Book & Manuscript Library, and Librarian for Sexuality Studies for Perkins Library. She provides reference and instruction for women's studies, sexuality studies, and many other interdisciplinary areas, as well as planning a wide variety of public programming to highlight the women's history collections at the Bingham Center. Her special interests include book arts, girls' literature and girls' studies, contemporary feminist movements, and zines. Before joining the staff at Duke in 2006, she was the Public Relations and Annual Giving Coordinator for UNC's Health Science Library. She received both her B.A. in Women's Studies and English Literature and her M.S.L.S. from the University of North Carolina at Chapel Hill.

# Index

CPSIA information can be obtained at www.ICGtesting.com
Printed in the USA
BVOW012022150413

318242BV00009B/353/P